THE BOOK OF SETTLEMENTS

Landnámabók

University of Manitoba Icelandic Studies
Vol. I

THE BOOK OF SETTLEMENTS

Landnámabók

Translated
with Introduction and Notes

by

HERMANN PÁLSSON

and

PAUL EDWARDS

University of Manitoba Press
Winnipeg, Manitoba
Canada R3T 2M5
uofmpress.ca

Printed in Canada
Text printed on chlorine-free, 100% post-consumer recycled paper

Reprinted 2012

Library and Archives Canada Cataloguing in Publication

Landnámabók. English
The book of settlements = Landnámabók/ Hermann Pálsson and Paul
Edwards, translators.

Reprint of the ed. published 1972 as v. 1 in the University of Manitoba
Icelandic studies.
Includes bibliographical references and index.
ISBN 978-0-88755-698-2 (pbk.)

1. Iceland. 2. Old Norse prose literature—Translations into English.
I. Edwards, Paul, 1926– II. Pálsson, Hermann, 1921– III. Title.
IV. Series: University of Manitoba Icelandic studies v. 1

PT7267.E5P3 2006   839.68'08   C2006-906621-3

The University of Manitoba Press gratefully acknowledges the financial
support for its publication program provided by the Government of Canada
through the Canada Book Fund, the Canada Council for the Arts, the Manitoba
Department of Culture, Heritage, Tourism, the Manitoba Arts Council,
and the Manitoba Book Publishing Tax Credit.

Publication of this book has been made possible through the financial support
of the Icelandic Language and Literature Fund, Icelandic Department at the
University of Manitoba. Support for the original publication was also provided
by the Social Sciences and Humanities Research Council of Canada
and the Canada-Iceland Foundation.

FSC
www.fsc.org
MIX
Paper from
responsible sources
FSC® C016245

Acknowledgements

This book has been published with the help of a grant from the Humanities Research Council of Canada, using funds provided by the Canada Council, and a grant from the Canada–Iceland Foundation. The following organizations also provided strong encouragement and support during the planning of this volume:

> The Icelandic Festival of Manitoba
> The Icelandic National League
> The North American Publishing Company Limited
> The Betel Home Foundation

Thanks are due to Dr. Jóhannes Nordal, Chairman of *Hið íslenzka fornritafélag* and Ágúst Böðvarsson for their kind permission to use the maps of the original editions from which this translation was made. The place names have been adapted to the translation.

The illustrations in this edition are from photographs by Páll Jónsson and Gunnar Hannesson.

The drawing on cover and dust-jacket is reproduced with the kind permission of Haraldur J. Hamar and Heimir Hannesson, editors of *Atlantica & Iceland Review*.

Table of Contents

List of Illustrations

Editors' Foreword

Up until the present time the Old Icelandic *Landnámabók* has been practically unknown beyond the relatively limited circle of those who possessed the ability to read Old Icelandic—scholars with special philological training and Icelanders whose native language is still essentially that of their ancient forebears. It will be a source of satisfaction and pleasure to those who value this work that it is now being made available in a new translation to a wider reading public. It is hoped that this will be a public comprising not only students and scholars with a professional interest in Scandinavian antiquities, but all those whose interests encompass more than the modern world.

The world of *Landnámabók* still lives vibrantly in the poetry and sagas of mediaeval Iceland, a great deal of which has already been made available to the English speaking public in translation, not least of all by the admirable work of the present translators. It is most fitting, therefore, that they should now put their pen to a text about which a nineteenth century Icelandic scholar once said that the loss of this work alone would in some respects have weighed more heavily for the history of his country than of all the other sagas together.

It is the hope and intention of the editors of this volume that it should be the first and founding work in a series of publications in the field of Icelandic studies. The series will derive its homogeneity from its devotion to themes from Icelandic literature, history and culture. It is intended to present monographs and translations in both the mediaeval and modern periods and to emphasize, as far as possible, the international contexts of the subject matter.

We hereby extend our most grateful thanks to Hermann Pálsson and Paul Edwards for so kindly offering the present volume to serve this purpose.

HARALDUR BESSASON ROBERT J. GLENDINNING

UNIVERSITY OF MANITOBA

The Book of Settlements

Introduction

I

Iceland was the last country in Europe to become inhabited, and we know more about the beginnings and early history of Icelandic society than we do of any other in the Old World. The *Book of Settlements* is our chief source, tracing the discovery of Iceland by the Scandinavians and the emergence of the Icelandic nation during the Viking Period. While Scandinavian raiders were plundering in England, Scotland and Ireland, a number of farmers and peasants set sail from Norway and the Western Isles for this new land, to build a new society for themselves and their children. As late as c. 860 AD, Iceland was still an empty land, except for a few Irish anchorites driven there by viking attacks and settlements on their homeland. These Irishmen were said to have been in Iceland as far back as 795, just after the beginning of the Viking Age,[1] and for the next three quarters of a century they had the country to themselves. Then, around 860, the peace was shattered by Scandinavian seafarers who seem to have gone to Iceland unintentionally, having been blown off course; and soon afterwards, perhaps about 870, the first settlers established permanent homes there. To begin with, there seems to have been a mere trickle of immigrants, but during the period c. 890-910 there was a steady stream, claiming possession of all the best farm lands. This "Age of Settlements" was over in 930 when the settlers and their sons adopted a common law for the entire country,

---

[1]Writing about 825 in France, the Irish monk Dicuil mentions three Irish anchorites who had sailed to 'Thule' thirty years earlier. The latitude he assigns to 'Thule' makes it certain that this must have been Iceland. (*Liber de mensura orbis terrae*, Berlin, 1870, 42-44). The first Norwegian settlers in Iceland called these anchorites *Papar*, see p. 15 below.

instituted the legislative and judicial Althing, and organized their society on a new basis, by which political power was shared out between 39 chieftain-priests (*goðar*) representing every part of the country. This was a peaceful farmers' union, based on the equality of all free men. It had no monarch, no army, no royal court. Above all, what gave it cohesion was the common law. The chieftains had judicial and legislative powers, and also priestly duties, but they depended on the support of other farmers. The highest official in the land, the Lawspeaker of the Althing, was elected by the chieftains, his period of office lasting three years, after which he could be re-elected for another term. The Althing met annually for a fortnight at Thingvellir to consider and change the laws and settle disputes. At the same time thirteen local assemblies were set up, one for every three chieftains. Soon after the middle of the tenth century, the country was divided into four Quarters—a division reflected in the structure of the *Book of Settlements*—and each of these had a court dealing with legal disputes between litigants of different local assemblies within the same Quarter. This political organization lasted without major changes until Iceland came under Norwegian rule in 1262-4.

We have already mentioned that the chieftains had certain priestly duties, but these came to an end with the adoption of Christianity by the Althing in AD 999 or 1000, and soon the Church became the most important organization in the country. The first native bishop of Iceland, Isleif Gizurarson (1056-80) laid much stress on the education of the clergy and during his term of office a number of schools were founded. His son and successor, Gizur, (1082-1118) was responsible for two important innovations: in 1097 a tithe system was set up for the whole country, and it has been suggested that this may have contributed to the first compilation of the *Book of Settlements*, as we shall see later. Secondly, Gizur divided the country into two bishoprics, of Holar for the North Quarter, and of Skalholt for the rest of the country. This happened in 1106, and it strengthened not only the church, but learning too. Not long afterwards, Benedictines founded the first monastery at Thingeyrar (probably about 1113), and several others, as well as Augustinian houses, were founded during the course of the twelfth century. The codification of the Icelandic laws began in 1117, and in 1127 a new church law was adopted.

During the eleventh and twelfth centuries there was an insatiable eagerness for foreign learning. The first two native bishops of Iceland, Isleif and Gizur, were educated in Germany at Herford in Westphalia, and two twelfth century bishops are known to have studied in England, one of them at Lincoln. Others, including the first bishop at Holar,

Jon Ogmundsson (1106-21), and Iceland's first historian Sæmund Sigfusson (1056-1133) went to France. Sæmund wrote in Latin and his works are now lost, but several references to him show that he wrote about the history of Norway and early Iceland. It could be argued that Icelandic historical writing began about the year 1077, after Sæmund returned from France.

The earliest native historian to write in the vernacular, Ari Thorgilsson the Learned, (1068-1148) was educated in the school at Haukadale where he received his clerical training, one of his tutors being the Priest Teit, son of Bishop Isleif. He was closely connected with the See of Skalholt, and it was Bishops Thorlak Runolfsson of Skalholt (1118-33) and Ketil Thorsteinsson of Holar (1122-45) who gave him the task of writing his most famous book *Íslendingabók*, or the *Book of Icelanders*. He tells us that he submitted the MS to the two bishops and also to the historian Sæmund Sigfusson. Ari wrote two versions of *Íslendingabók*, but only the second, shorter version survives. This book gives a brief description of the settlement of Iceland, naming only five settlers, one outstanding settler for each Quarter and also the first Scandinavian settler, Ingolf. Ari is more interested in institutions than personalities and he traces the evolution of the Althing, noting important changes in the constitution and listing the lawspeakers to establish a skeletal chronology for the history of Iceland, and describing the emergence and growth of the church. His record comes to an end in the year 1118 with the death of Bishop Gizur. Ari also appears to have written at least part of the original version of the *Book of Settlements*. This original version is now lost, but its existence is vouched for by Hauk Erlendsson who compiled his own version of it shortly after 1300.

II

There are five extant versions of the *Book of Settlements*, one of them only a fragment. The earliest one, *Sturlubók*, which we have translated here, was compiled by Sturla Thordarson (1214-84). A vellum MS of it existed down to the eighteenth century, when it was destroyed in the fire of Copenhagen in 1728. But before it left Iceland, it had been copied by the Rev. Jón Erlendsson of Villingaholt, and it is his copy (AM 107 fol.) which is our chief source for *Sturlubók*. *Sturlubók* seems to have been completed c. 1275-80.

Next comes the so-called *Hauksbók*, compiled by Hauk Erlendsson (d. 1331). Parts of it (fourteen leaves) survive in his own handwriting. Hauk seems to have written the codex about 1306-1308. In the seventeenth century when the MS was more complete than now and only two leaves were missing it was copied by Jón Erlendsson, whose MS (AM 105 fol) thus fills the gaps in the earlier MS of *Hauksbók* (AM 371, 4to).

The third medieval version of the *Book of Settlements, Melabók*, survives only on two vellum leaves, dating from the early fifteenth century, (AM 445 b, 4to). However, it was in a much better state in the seventeenth century when it was used for the compilation of *Thórdarbók* (see below). The name of the compiler is not known, but the codex was evidently written by someone closely associated with the Melar family, as can be seen from the fact that many genealogies are traced down to that family, ending c. 1300. The most likely author of *Melabók* is Snorri Markússon (Lawman, 1302-07), who died in 1313. Genealogies are traced down to his father and his wife.

In addition to these three early versions there are two dating from the seventeenth century. *Björn Jónsson of Skardsá* put together a composite version (*Skardsárbók*), using *Sturlubók* and *Hauksbók* and completing it not later than autumn 1636. For this purpose he used the same MS of *Hauksbók* as Jón Erlendsson had, with the same two leaves missing. However, Björn managed to read certain difficult passages more correctly than Jón, whose copy can thus be emended by *Skardsárbók*.

Finally there is *Thórdarbók*, compiled by the Rev. Thórd Jónsson of Hitardale (d. 1670). He used *Skardsárbók* but added variant and alternative readings from *Melabók* which was then in a much better state than it is now.

III

These five versions, however, had their antecedents. The most explicit medieval evidence for this is to be found in Hauk Erlendsson's epilogue to his version of the *Book of Settlements* which was written c. 1306-8:

> Now the account of the settlements of Iceland is completed, according to what wise men have written, the first of these being the Priest Ari Thorgilsson the Learned, and Kolskegg the Wise. But I, Hauk Erlendsson, wrote this book, following the one written by Sturla the Lawman, a most learned man, and also that other book, written by Styrmir the Learned. ...

Thus apart from Sturla's there were two earlier versions: one compiled by Ari the Learned and Kolskegg the Wise, the original *Book of Settlements*; and the other by Styrmir Kárason (d. 1245). In his masterly analysis of the complex problems arising from these different versions of the *Book of Settlements*, Professor Jón Jóhannesson[2] arrived at the following stemma, which has been universally accepted by scholars and is unlikely to be challenged:

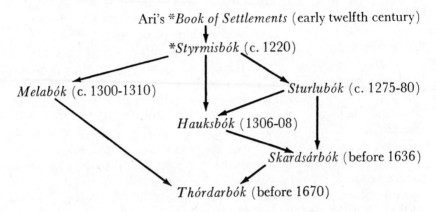

Ari's **Book of Settlements* (early twelfth century)

*Styrmisbók (c. 1220)

Melabók (c. 1300-1310)

Sturlubók (c. 1275-80)

Hauksbók (1306-08)

Skardsárbók (before 1636)

Thórdarbók (before 1670)

Jón Jóhannesson has also shown that *Styrmisbók* is best reflected in *Melabók*, since both Sturla and Hauk added a good deal of material from other sources, particularly the sagas; though since *Melabók* no longer exists apart from the two leaves, we must depend on *Thórdarbók* for detailed evidence of its nature. It is harder to reconstruct a hypothetical text of Ari and Kolskegg, because Styrmir evidently added a good deal to this, his source.

Extant versions indicate that Kolskegg was responsible for the record of settlements from Husavik in the north-east to Jokuls River in Solheimasand. The rest of the original *Book of Settlements* was evidently Ari's work, though he must have depended on the help of many informants. The date of composition is uncertain, but the most likely period would be between c. 1097, when the tithe system was adopted, and c. 1125, when Ari wrote his *Book of Icelanders*. Kolskegg seems to have been somewhat older than Ari, and it is not known how long after 1100 he lived.

When Kolskegg and Ari set to work, only six to seven generations of settlers had lived in Iceland, so it was not too difficult to gather information even about the earliest period of Iceland's history. In many cases the direct descendants of the original settlers were still living on the farms where their ancestors had made their first homes in Iceland, and this helped the compilers to create a reasonably clear picture of the

---

[2]*Gerðir Landnámabókar*, 1941.

settlements. Boundaries between farms, and memories of boundary disputes also provided the Icelanders with knowledge about the original land-claims. In any case, the boundaries often co-incided with natural features, particularly rivers and mountains which helped to fix the details more firmly. When we look at the dependability and accessibility of early information about the past, we must bear in mind that some of Ari's and Kolskegg's informants had been born in the tenth century, less than two generations after the 'Age of Settlements' had come to an end with the institution of the Althing in 930. Ari's fosterfather was born in 997 and must have told him a great deal before he died in 1087, at the age of 90. One of Ari's informants, Thurid Snorri's-daughter, was born in 1023, and died in 1112, at the age of 88. Ari quotes her in his *Íslendingabók*. Her father Snorri the Priest (967-1031) was the son of a woman who had emigrated from Norway with her father in 958, and according to *Eyrbyggja Saga*, Snorri's paternal great-grandfather had come to Iceland in 884. What seems to emerge is this: that the genealogies of people after the Settlement seem to be trustworthy; that statements on land-claims and topographical details are on the whole reliable; that references to serious disputes and other significant events are also on the whole to be taken seriously; and that descriptions of pagan customs, beliefs and so on may be coloured by antiquarianism, but evidently contain a good deal of sound tradition.

IV

In the *Thórdarbók* version of the *Book of Settlements* the following apology is made for the study of the settlements and genealogies:

> People often say that writing about the Settlements is irrelevant learning, but we think we can better meet the criticism of foreigners when they accuse us of being descended from slaves or scoundrels, if we know for certain the truth about our ancestry. And for those who want to know ancient lore and how to trace genealogies, it's better to start at the beginning than to come in at the middle. Anyway, all civilized nations want to know about the origins of their own society and the beginnings of their own race.

This passage is obviously taken from a medieval source, apparently *Styrmisbók*, and there is reason to believe that it may have been taken from the original version of the *Book of Settlements* and so reflect the early twelfth century attitudes of Ari Thorgilsson. What is particularly interesting about this is the underlying suggestion that the study of

Iceland's beginnings was stimulated by foreign misconceptions. It must have been well-known in Western Europe that Iceland (insofar as it was known at all) was inhabited by Scandinavians, who were frowned upon because of the viking raids. The *Book of Settlements* shows us that there were relatively few vikings among the settlers, most of whom were peaceable farmers, possibly in some cases with good family connections in Scandinavia or the British Isles. But these royal ancestries are not to be trusted, though it would be difficult to say whether the genealogies were actually invented by Ari and other learned men in the eleventh and twelfth centuries. It should be noted, however, that some ancestors styled as kings in Hauk Erlendsson's version are not so styled in the earlier version of Sturla and probably not in Ari's or Styrmir's.

Throughout the twelfth century, genealogical lore seems to have been highly regarded and assiduously cultivated. Thus the so-called First Icelandic Grammarian, writing about or just before the middle of the twelfth century, mentions approvingly "the writing of law, genealogies, sacred exegeses, and those works of learning which Ari Thorgilsson with his keen wisdom has put into books." Later, about 1170, Thorlak Thorhallsson who had spent six years studying in Paris and Lincoln, was back in Iceland learning about genealogies from his mother. Then just after 1200, the author of *Hungrvaka*, states in his Preface that one of the reasons why he wrote his book (on the first five bishops of Skalholt) was to encourage young people to read works written in the vernacular, such as those on law, history and genealogy. Finally, it seems certain that at least some of the genealogies in the existing versions of the *Book of Settlements* were not taken from Ari's version but were incorporated from separate works on genealogy, such as *Breiðfirðinga Kynslóð* of the Prior Brand and *Ölfusingakyn* (The Genealogies of the People of Breidafjord, and of the People of Olfus).

V

Sturla Thordarson, the author of the version we translate here, belonged to one of the most powerful and influential families in thirteenth century Iceland. His uncle was Snorri Sturluson (1179-1241), who is best known for his *History of the Kings of Norway* (now usually called *Heimskringla*) and the *Edda*. Sturla was born July 29th 1214, and died July 30th 1284. We know perhaps more about him than about any other medieval Icelandic author, and he is accredited with more works than any of them. Sturla was a leading politician who fought against Norwegian intervention in Icelandic affairs, and was Lawspeaker of the Althing for one year in 1251. He was a poet, and poems he wrote in honour of Kings Hakon and Magnus of Norway still survive. His major prose works are: *Íslendinga Saga*, or the *History of the Icelanders* (1200-62), *King Hakon's Saga*, and *King Magnus' Saga* (the last now only left in fragments). Sturla is also supposed to have written about Grettir the Strong, though the *Grettir's Saga* we have is considerably later (c. 1330).

Sturla is thought to have completed his version of the *Book of Settlements* around 1275-1280, as we have seen already. His main source was *Styrmisbók*, but he also added a lot of material from various sagas,[3] some of which are now lost or only surviving in later redactions. The precise relationship between *Sturlubók* and the *Sagas of Icelanders* has not been definitively explained; while a good many of them must be older than *Sturlubók*, others are later and depend upon it.

VI

The genealogies of the *Book of Settlements* show the continuity of Icelandic life from the beginning of Icelandic society down to the author's own times. In this situation, the immigrants were more than merely settlers, they were the very progenitors of the Icelandic people, so that genealogies took on a particular significance for this society. Many of the settlers were rebels against the domination of the new, increasingly centralized power of the kings of Norway; and even those who were not specifically rebels, were nevertheless people who had chosen to venture from their original homes, and had founded settlements in the British Isles. Thus the early settlers of Iceland were people who, by breaking away from their original societies, had shown themselves to be more than averagely independent. The individual was in fact important to them, and this is reflected in the emphasis which the *Book of Settlements* gives to common events in the lives of ordinary people. As a historical document, it appears at first sight rather monotonous, and indeed, is bound to appear so, as must any genealogical work. But a surprising amount of human detail shines through the lists of names of settlers and their descendants and the places settled. Even the names themselves go beyond arid documentation; by the time this work was written, the old names would already have acquired an exotic and often grotesque flavour, and are often strongly suggestive of personal characteristics: thus we find the world of the *Book of Settlements* popu-

---

[3]One of the characteristic features of Sturla's version is that genealogies are frequently traced down to his grandfather and grandmother (Sturla and Gudny, of Hvamm). Hauk Erlendsson and Snorri Markússon (?) of Melar show a similar preoccupation with their own families in their versions.

lated by such men as Thorolf Twist-Foot, Bolverk Blind-Snout, Hergils Knob-Buttocks and Eystein Foul-Fart. There is an Olvir the Child-Sparer, a generous viking who, we are told, didn't approve of throwing children onto the points of spears. One man is killed in battle because his belt breaks and his trousers fall down. Two men make an exchange:

> Finally Illugi lived at Outer-Holm on Akraness, because he and Holm-Starri exchanged their property, farm, wives, live-stock and all. Then Illugi married Jorunn, daughter of Thormod Thjostarsson of Alftaness, but Sigrid hanged herself in the temple because she couldn't bear the change of husbands. (41)

In another episode, we are told that Herjolf, son of Sigurd Hog's-Head, avenged his father's killing when only twelve years old. But the only detail given is about how he took vengeance for a goat:

> (He) was only eight years old when he killed a brown bear which had bitten one of his goats. This verse was written about it:
>
> > The bear with a burnt arse
> > bit Herjolf's goat.
> > Herjolf with the bent arse
> > paid the bear back. (80)

Minor domestic details appear regularly. A cow, Brynja, roams at a certain spot and the place is named Brynjudale after her. Pigs are released on an island and we are told how many there were of them two years later. A man settles land because his mare lies down there. There is this item about a minor Greenland settler, Thorkel Farserk, which simultaneously humanises him and hints at the remoter world in which he lived:

> He was a man of unusual powers. Once when he wanted to welcome his cousin Eirik but had no seaworthy boat at home, he swam out to Hvals Isle for an old sheep and carried it on his back to the mainland, a distance of well over a mile. Thorkel was buried in the enclosure at Hvalseyjarfjord, and has been there, round about the house, ever since. (93)

Indeed, characteristic of the *Book of Settlements* is the shift between Christian and pagan conventions. On one hand, we hear how, though some settlers brought Christianity with them to Iceland, their descendants slipped away from the faith and returned to pagan practices until Christianity was properly established after 1000 AD:

(Aud) used to say prayers at Cross Hills; she had crosses
erected there, for she'd been baptized and was a devout Christian. Her kinsmen later worshipped these hills, and then when
sacrifices began a pagan temple was built there. They believed
they would go into the hills when they died. (97)

So at times one finds a pro-Christian bias, while at others, one gets a
sympathetic view of the pagans, though it is never anti-Christian. Thus
there is a strong implication of the power of the Almighty against the
heathen in this:

Hildir wanted to move house to Kirkby after Ketil died, not
seeing why a heathen shouldn't farm there. But as he was
coming up to the fence of the home meadow, he dropped
down dead. (323)

A similar implication is found in another episode:

Sturla had a son called Bjarni, who quarrelled with Hrolf
the Younger and his sons over Lesser-Tongue. Then Bjarni
promised to become a Christian, and afterwards Hvit River
changed its course and made a new channel where it flows
now, so Bjarni gained possession of Lesser Tongue down to
Grind and Solmundarhofdi. (42)

On the other hand, we find virtuous and distinguished pagans:

Thorstein was the father of Thorkel Moon who, as far as
anyone can tell, was one of the noblest heathens ever.
When he was lying on his death bed, Thorkel Moon had himself carried out to a shaft of sunlight, and gave himself to the
god who created the sun. He had led a life as blameless as the
best of Christians. (9)

The ritual practices for the taking of land can be either Christian or
pagan. So when Orlyg Hrappsson takes land, he asks the advice of the
Holy Bishop Patrick of the Hebrides:

The bishop provided him with church timber, an iron bell, a
plenarium, and consecrated earth which Orlyg was to place
beneath the corner posts of his church. The bishop told him
to settle at a place where from the sea he could keep two
mountains in view, each with its valley. (15)

On the other hand, Thor was considered by many settlers a safer guide
and protector:

(Thorolf) was a great sacrificer and worshipped Thor. He fled to Iceland because of the oppression of King Harald Fine-Hair, and made landfall in the South, and when he'd come west as far as Breidafjord, he threw his high-seat pillars overboard; they had an image of Thor carved on them. Thorolf declared that Thor would come ashore where he wanted Thorolf to make his home and he promised to dedicate his entire land-claim to Thor and call it after him. (85)

As soon as Ingolf caught his first glimpse of Iceland, he threw his high-seat pillars overboard, hoping for a good omen, and declared he'd settle wherever the pillars happened to be washed ashore. (8)

At other times, a coffin provides the clue:

When the crossing was pretty well completed, Kveld-Ulf fell ill. He asked his men to make a coffin for him, should he die, and to tell his son Skalla-Grim to build his home in Iceland near the spot where the coffin would come ashore, if that were possible. Then Kveld-Ulf died and his coffin was thrown overboard. (29)

And at another, even a captive merman is pressed into service;

In the autumn Grim went fishing with his farm hands, and the boy Thorir lay in the prow tucked into a sealskin bag, which was tied at the neck. Grim caught a merman, and when he got him to the surface, Grim asked, "What can you tell us about our futures? Where in Iceland ought we to settle?" The merman said, "There's no point in my making prophecies about you, but that boy in the sealskin bag there, he'll settle and claim land where your mare Skalm lies down under her load." (68)

Some of these fragments of humanising detail are expanded almost into short stories, or summaries of sagas. At times these may be barely coherent, as the author skims over the surface of what was, no doubt, already a well known narrative—such is the case in the story of Kjallak and Hrafsi in Chapter 111, where we have in indistinct outline a complete lost saga. But at times the author's imagination is captured so much by his material that the tale emerges with remarkable sharpness of outline, as in the episode of Tjorfi's privy in Chapter 284:

Hroar's nephews were Tjorfi the Mocker and Gunnar. Tjorfi

wanted to marry Astrid Wisdom-Slope, daughter of Modolf, but her brothers Ketil and Hrolf wouldn't let her become his wife and married her off to Thorir Ketilsson. Then Tjorfi carved the images of Astrid and Thorir on the privy wall, and every evening when he and Hroar went to the privy he used to spit in the face of Thorir's image and kiss hers, until Hroar scraped them off the wall. Then Tjorvi carved them on the handle of his knife and made this verse:

> Once in cruel spite
> I carved an image
> of the young bride
> with Thorir beside her;
> on my knife-handle
> I've now carved the lady,
> I used to have plenty
> of pleasure with her.

That's why Hroar and his nephews were killed. (284)

It is this quality which prevents the *Book of Settlements* from becoming no more than a catalogue of curious, forgotten names. In fact, it is this preoccupation with the details of common life, including those of minute family relationships, that make the *Sagas of Icelanders* so remarkable. Whether these anecdotes about the early Icelanders are true or not—and indeed several of them seem like extremely tall stories told tongue in cheek—matters less than the pleasure taken by the author in recording the event, its psychological interest, its antiquarian strangeness, its revelation of a past that we continue to share.

Note on the Translation

The present translation of the Book of Settlements *is based on the standard edition of the* Sturlubók *text by Jakob Benediktsson, Íslenzk fornrit, vol. I, 1969. Our original intention was to include selected passages from other versions, and in particular from* Hauksbók, *but we decided against it since it would have swelled the size of the volume considerably. Those who wish to examine variant readings in different texts should consult Dr. Benediktsson's edition. In our interpretation of the text we have relied heavily on his scholarship, and parts of our Introduction are based on his brilliant essay on the* Book.

A brief remark must be made on our treatment of proper names. We have translated most of the nicknames, wherever we thought that a rendering into English was called for. We have also translated the second element in compound place names when this seemed necessary to indicate the topographical detail, as in the names of rivers, islands, creeks and so on.

The Book of Settlements *has been translated twice before*; *by Gudbrand Vigfusson and F. York Powell in their* Origines Islandicæ, *1905, and by T. Ellwood,* The Book of the Settlement of Iceland, *1908. Neither of the two has been consulted for the present translation. We are indebted to Vilhjálmur Bjarnar for his careful scrutiny of the text, and Edward J. Cowan for helping us with the proofs.*

Hermann Pálsson
Paul Edwards

Edinburgh, May 1972

1. *Early references to Iceland*

In his book *On Times*[1] the Venerable Priest Bede mentions an island called *Thule*,[2] said in other books to lie six days' sailing to the north of Britain. He says there's neither daylight there in winter, nor darkness when the day is at its longest in summer. This is why the learned reckon that Thule must really be Iceland, for in many places the sun shines at night there during the long days, and isn't to be seen during the day, when nights are longest. According to written sources, Bede the Priest died 735 years after the Incarnation of our Lord, and more than 120 years before Iceland was settled by the Norwegians. But before Iceland was settled from Norway there were other people there, called *Papar* by the Norwegians. They were Christians and were thought to have come overseas from the west, because people found Irish books, bells, croziers, and lots of other things, so it was clear they must have been Irish.[3] Besides, English sources tell us that sailings were made between these countries at the time.[4]

---

[1]*Aldarfarsbók*. It is not certain whether this refers to Bede's *De temporibus* or his *De temporum ratione*. There are references to Thule in both books.

[2]*Thule* (MSS Thyle, Tyle, etc.)

[3]This reference to *Papar* agrees with Ari Thorgilsson (*Book of the Icelanders*, Ch. I). The word *papi* (pl. *papar*) is borrowed from Irish *papa* (itself a Latin loanword) which occurs in early texts in the sense 'an Irish anchorite'. Place names compounded with the word *papi* as the first element are known in the Isle of Man, Cumberland, the Hebrides, Caithness, Shetland, Orkney, The Faroes, and Iceland.

[4]This could be an allusion to Bede's *On the Books of the Kings*, where he mentions people from Thule having visited Britain in his lifetime, but there are other references in early English writings.

2. Time and Place

At the time Iceland was discovered and settled by Norwegians, Pope Adrian, and after him, Pope John the Fifth, occupied the Apostolic Seat in Rome. Louis, son of Louis, was Emperor over Germany, and Leo and his son Alexander ruled in Byzantium. Harald Fine-Hair was King of Norway, Eirik Eymundsson and his son ruled over Sweden, and Gorm the Old over Denmark. Alfred the Great and his son Edward ruled in England, King Kjarval in Dublin and Earl Sigurd the Mighty over the Orkneys.[5]

According to learned men it takes seven days to sail from Stad in Norway westwards to Horn on the east coast of Iceland, and from Snæfellsness four days west across the ocean to Greenland by the shortest route. People say if you sail from Bergen due west to Cape Farewell in Greenland, you pass twelve leagues south of Iceland. From Reykjaness in South Iceland it takes five days to Slyne Head[6] in Ireland, four days from Langaness in North Iceland northwards to Spitzbergen[7] in the Arctic Sea, and a day north from Kolbein's Isle to the wild regions of Greenland.

3. Snowland

The story goes that some people wanted to sail from Norway to the Faroes—a viking called Naddodd, to name one of them. They were driven out to sea westwards, and came to a vast country. They went ashore in the Eastfjords, climbed a high mountain, and scanned the country in all directions looking for smoke or any other sign that the land was inhabited, but they saw nothing. In the summer they went back to the Faroes, and as they were sailing away from the coast a lot of snow fell on the mountains, so they called the country *Snowland*.

---

[5]Adrian II was Pope 867-72, succeeded by John VIII, 872-82. Louis (the German), son of Louis, was king of Germany 843-76. Leo VI was Emperor 886-912, and his brother (*not* son) Alexander 912-913. King Eirik of Sweden died, according to *The Icelandic Annals*, in 871. King Alfred of England ruled from 871-899 and his son Edward (the Elder) 899-924. King Kjarval has been identified with King Cerball of Ossory who died in 888, but he never ruled over Dublin. For Earl Sigurd (the Mighty) of Orkney, see *History of the Earls of Orkney* (or *Orkneyinga Saga*). King Harald Fine-Hair of Norway is supposed to have ruled for a period of seventy years and died in 931. Gorm the Old ruled Denmark c. 900-935.

[6]*Jölduhlaup*. The identification with Slyne Head in Connemara was made by Eamonn O Tuathail, in *Eigse* VI, 155-56.

[7]*Svalbarði* (Discovered, according to *The Icelandic Annals*, in 1194). There is some doubt as to the identification of this place name. Jan Mayen has been suggested, but considering the distance from Iceland given here, Spitzbergen seems more likely.

They were full of praise for it. According to Sæmund the Learned[8] the place in the Eastfjords where they landed is the one now called Reydarfell.

4. *Gardar's Isle*

A man called Gardar Svafarsson, of Swedish stock, went out in search of Snowland guided by his mother, who had second sight. He made land east of Eastern Horn where at that time ships could put in. Gardar sailed right round the country and proved it to be an island. He built himself a house at Husavik on Skjalfandi in the north and stayed there over winter. In the spring, after he'd put out to sea, a boat drifted away from his ship with a man called Nattfari aboard, and a slave and a bondwoman. Nattfari settled down there at a place called Nattfaravik. Gardar sailed back to Norway, full of praise for the new land. He was the father of Uni, father of Hroar Tongue-Priest. Afterwards the land was called *Gardar's Isle*. In those days it was wooded all the way from the mountains right down to the sea.

5. *Raven-Floki*

There was a man called Floki Vilgerdarson, a great viking. He set off in search of *Gardar's Isle*, putting out from a place called Floki's Cairn on the border between Hordaland and Rogaland. First he sailed over to Shetland, and lay at anchor in Floka Creek. His daughter, Geirhild, was drowned in Geirhildarwater in Shetland. On board Floki's ship was a man called Thorolf, and another called Herjolf, and also a Hebridean called Faxi.

Floki took three ravens with him on the voyage. When he set the first one free it flew back from the stern, but the second raven flew straight up into the air, and then back down to the ship, while the third flew straight ahead from the prow, and it was in that direction that they found land.[9]

They came west to Horn, and sailed west along the south coast. As they sailed round Reykjaness and the bay opened up wide so they could see westwards to Snæfellsness, Faxi had this to say: "It must be a big country we've found; the rivers are big enough". After this the bay was called Faxi's Estuary.[10]

---

[8]Sæmund Sigfusson "the Learned" (1056-1133) was Iceland's first historian, but all his works, including the one referred to here, are now lost.

[9]The story of Floki's ravens has been compared with the account of Noah's raven and dove, *Genesis* VIII.

[10]Now *Faxaflói* (Faxa Bay).

Floki and his crew sailed west across Breidafjord and made land at Vatnsfjord in Bardastrand. At that time the fjord was teeming with fish, and they got so caught up with the fishing they forgot to make hay, so their livestock starved to death the following winter.

The spring was an extremely cold one. Floki climbed a certain high mountain, and north across the mountain range he could see a fjord full of drift ice. That's why they called the country *Iceland*, and so it's been called ever since.

In the summer, Floki and his men planned to sail away, but they were only ready just before winter. They tried unsuccessfully to tack round Reykjaness, and then their towboat with Herjolf on board broke loose from the ship. He managed to scramble ashore at a place called Herjolfshaven. Floki stayed the winter in Borgarfjord. They found Herjolf and sailed over to Norway the following summer. When they were asked about the new country Floki had nothing good to say of it, but Herjolf described its merits as well as its faults. Thorolf said that in the land they'd found, butter was dripping from every blade of grass. That's why people called him Thorolf Butter.

6. *The Blood-Brothers*

There was a man called Bjornolf, and another called Hroald, sons of Hromund Gripsson.[11] They left Telemark because of some killings and settled down at Dalsfjord in Fjalar Province. Bjornolf had a son called Orn who was the father of Ingolf and Helga. Hroald had a son called Hrodmar, father of Leif.

Ingolf and Leif were blood-brothers, and they went on a viking expedition with Hastein, Herstein, and Holmstein, the sons of Earl Atli the Slender of Gaular. They all got on well together, and when they came back home they agreed to join forces the following summer. Next winter the blood-brothers gave a feast for the earl's sons, and at that feast Holmstein swore a solemn oath to marry Helga Orn's-daughter, or else not to marry at all. People didn't like this vow. Leif flushed red, and he and Holmstein parted on cool terms when the feast was over.

In the spring the blood-brothers got themselves ready for a viking expedition, planning to set out in search of Atli. They met up with them at Hisargafl. Holmstein and his brothers were the first to attack, but after they'd been fighting for a while, Olmod the Old, son of Horda-Kari and Leif's kinsman, turned up with support for Leif and

---

[11]A legendary hero. The original (12th century?) *Hromund's Saga* is no longer extant, but a 14th century metrical version of it survives, on which a still later prose saga was based.

Ingolf. Holmstein was killed in this battle and Herstein had to run for it. After that the blood-brothers set out on their viking expedition.

Next winter, Herstein led an attack on Leif and Ingolf, hoping to kill them, but they were put on their guard and made a counter-move against him. There was a fierce battle and Herstein was killed. After that a number of their friends from Fjord Province rallied round the blood-brothers. Then messengers were sent to Earl Atli and Hastein to offer compensation, and a settlement was reached on these terms that Leif and Ingolf were to give the earl and his son everything they possessed.

After that the blood-brothers got ready a large ship of theirs and set out in search of the land Raven-Floki had discovered, by that time called Iceland. They found the land, and stayed the first winter at South-Alftafjord in the Eastfjords. It seemed to them the south part of the country was better than the north. After spending a winter in Iceland, they went back to Norway. Later, Ingolf laid out all his money to go to Iceland, but Leif went on a viking expedition to the west and plundered in Ireland. Once he found a large underground chamber there and went inside. It was dark until light started coming from a sword someone was holding. Leif killed the man and took the sword and a good deal of money besides. After this he was known as Hjorleif.[12] He plundered all over Ireland and took a great deal of loot, including ten slaves called Dufthak, Geirraud, Skjaldbjorn, Halldor, Drafdrit, —the rest of them aren't mentioned by name. After that Hjorleif went back to Norway and joined his blood-brother Ingolf. Earlier Leif had married Helga Orn's-daughter, Ingolf's sister.

7. Sacrifice

That winter Ingolf held a great sacrifice to discover what the future had in store for him, but Hjorleif would never sacrifice to the gods. The oracle told Ingolf to go to Iceland. After that he and his brother-in-law got their ships ready separately for the voyage. Hjorleif loaded his ship with the loot he'd won, and in his Ingolf carried what they held in common. As soon as they were ready they put out to sea.

8. In Iceland

The summer Ingolf and Hjorleif went to settle in Iceland, Harald Fine-Hair had been King of Norway for twelve years; that was 6073

---

[12]The first element in the name (*hjor-*) means a sword.

years from the Beginning of the World, and 874 years from the Incarnation of our Lord.[13]

They sailed close to one another until they made landfall, and
then they got separated. As soon as Ingolf caught his first glimpse of
Iceland he threw his highseat pillars overboard, hoping for a good
omen, and declared he'd settle wherever the pillars happened to be
washed ashore. Nowadays the place where he landed is called Ingolfshofdi. Hjorleif drifted west along the coast. He ran short of drinking water, and what the Irish slaves did was to knead together flour
and butter, saying it was good for thirst. They called the mixture
minthak,[14] but by the time the mixture was ready it started raining
heavily, so they were able to collect rainwater from the sails. When the
minthak grew musty they threw it overboard and it was washed ashore
at a place now called Minthakseyr. Hjorleif put in at Hjorleifshofdi,
where in those days there was a fjord stretching right up to the headland. Hjorleif had two houses built there; the ruins of one of them
measures eighteen fathoms across, and the other nineteen. Hjorleif
spent the winter there. In the spring he wanted to sow. He had only
one ox and told his slaves to pull the plough. One day when Hjorleif
and his men were at the houses, Dufthak put it to his fellow-slaves
that they should slaughter the ox and say a brown bear had killed it,
then they could attack Hjorleif and his men, should they go looking for
the bear. So they went along and told Hjorleif, and when he and his
men spread out in the woods looking for the bear, the slaves set on
them, and murdered them all, one after another, just as many men as
there were slaves. Then the slaves ran away with the dead men's boat
and their wives and goods. They rowed over to the islands they'd seen
to the south-west and prepared themselves for a longish stay.

Ingolf had two slaves called Vifil and Karli, and he sent them west
along the shore to look for his highseat pillars. When they came to
Hjorleifshofdi, they found Hjorleif dead there, so they turned back to
tell Ingolf what had happened. He took the death of Hjorleif and his
men badly. He set out west to Hjorleifshofdi, and when he saw Hjorleif
he said, "It's a sad end for a warrior, to be killed by slaves; but in
my experience, this is what always happens to people who won't hold
sacrifices."

Ingolf had Hjorleif and his men buried, and took over his ship and

---

[13]In his *Íslendingabók* (c. 1125) Ari Thorgilsson says that Ingolf went to
Iceland about the time St. Edmund of East Anglia was killed by the vikings,
in 870.

[14]A loan-word from the Irish, *menadach* meaning "gruel made of meal and
water, or of meal and butter".

various other things of his. Then he climbed to the top of the headland and saw some islands lying to the southwest, and it occurred to him that since the boat was missing, the slaves might have fled there. They set out in search of the slaves and found them in the islands at a place called Eid. They were eating a meal when Ingolf and his men surprised them, and the slaves were so frightened they scattered in all directions. Ingolf killed every one of them. The place where Dufthak met his death is called Dufthaksskor. Many of the slaves jumped over a cliff that's been called after them ever since, as have the islands where the slaves were killed, which were named Westmanna Islands since the men came from the west. Ingolf and his men took the widows of the murdered men back with them to Hjorleifshofdi, and there he spent the following winter. Next spring he sailed along the coast westwards, and stayed the third winter at Ingolfsfell, west of Olfus River. In that year, Vifil and Karli found his highseat pillars at Arnarhill, west of the moor.

9. *Ingolf's settlement*

In the spring Ingolf travelled west across the moor. He made his home at the spot where his highseat pillars had been washed ashore, and lived at Reykjavik. The highseat pillars can still be seen in the hall there. Ingolf claimed possession of the whole region between Olfus River and Hvalfjord south of Brynjudale and Oxar Rivers, including all the Nesses.

Then Karli said "It's not much use our travelling across good country, just so that we can live on this out-of-the-way headland." After that he disappeared, taking a slave girl with him.

Ingolf gave Vifil his freedom, and he settled down at Vifilstoft; Vifilsfell also takes its name from him. He lived there for a long time and became a man of some importance. Ingolf had a house built at Skalafell. From there he noticed some smoke at Olfuswater, and that's where he found Karli.

Ingolf was the most famous of all the settlers, because he came to this country when it was still uninhabited and he was the first man to settle here permanently. After that, other settlers came and followed his example.

Ingolf married Hallveig Frodi's-daughter, sister of Loft the Old, and their son was Thorstein who founded the Kjalarness Assembly before the Althing was established.[15] Thorstein was the father of Thorkel

---

[15]The Althing was instituted in 930.

Moon the Lawspeaker,[16] who as far as anyone can tell was one of the noblest heathen that ever lived.

When he was lying on his death-bed, Thorkel Moon had himself carried out to a shaft of sunlight, and gave himself to the god who created the sun. He had led a life as blameless as the best of Christians. His son was Thormod, who held the principal chieftaincy at the time when Christianity came to Iceland.[17] Thormod was the father of Hamal, father of Mar, Thormod, and Torfi.

10. *Bjorn Buna's descendants*
There was a leading chieftain in Norway called Bjorn Buna, son of the chieftain Wether-Grim of Sogn. Grim's mother was Hervor, daughter of Thorgerd, daughter of chieftain Eylaug of Sogn. Almost all the prominent Icelanders are descended from Bjorn Buna. He married a woman call Velaug, and they had three sons: one was Ketil Flat-Nose, the next was Hrapp, and the third Helgi. They were all remarkable men, and a great deal will be said about their descendants in this book.

11. *Thord Skeggi*
There was a man called Thord Skeggi, son of Hrapp, Bjorn Buna's son. Thord married Vilborg Osvald's-daughter. They had a daughter called Helga who was married to Ketilbjorn the Old. Thord went to Iceland, and with Ingolf's approval settled upon land claimed by Ingolf between Ulfars River and Leiru Creek. He made his home at Skeggjastead, and many important Icelanders trace their descent from him.

12. *Hall the Godless*
There was a man called Hall the Godless, son of Helgi the Godless. Father and son believed in their own strength and refused to hold sacrifices. Hall went to Iceland and with Ingolf's approval took possession of the area between Leiru Creek and Mogils River, making his home at Muli. Hall was the father of Helgi who married Thurid Ketilbjorn's-daughter. Their son was Thord of Alftaness, who married Gudny Hrafnkel's-daughter.

13. *Ketil Flat-Nose in the Hebrides*
Harald Fine-Hair went on a viking expedition west across the sea, as

---

[16]Thorkel Moon was Lawspeaker of the Althing 970-984.
[17]According to early Icelandic reckoning this was in A.D. 1000, but it may in fact have been in 999.

written in his saga.[18] He conquered the entire Hebrides, so far west
that since then no one has ever conquered further, but as soon as
he'd gone back to Norway, vikings, Scots and Irishmen invaded the
islands, plundering and killing everywhere. When King Harald heard
about this, he sent Ketil Flat-Nose, the son of Bjorn Buna, to reconquer
the islands.

Ketil was married to Yngvild, daughter of Ketil Wether of Ringerike Province. Their sons were Bjorn the Easterner, and Helgi Bjolan,
and their daughters Aud the Deep-Minded and Thorunn Hyrna. When
Ketil went west, he left his son Bjorn in charge. Ketil conquered the
entire Hebrides and became chieftain over them, but paid none of the
tribute to King Harald that had been agreed upon, so the king confiscated all his possessions and banished Ketil's son Bjorn.

14. *Helgi Bjolan*

Helgi Bjolan, son of Ketil Flat-Nose went over to Iceland from the
Hebrides. He stayed the first winter with Ingolf and with his approval
took possession of Kjalarness, between Mogils and Mydale Rivers. Helgi
made his home at Hof. He was the father of Killer-Hrapp and Kollsvein, father of Eyvind Hjalti, father of Thorgerd, mother of Thora,
mother of Ogmund, father of Bishop Jon the Holy.[19]

15. *Orlyg Hrappsson*

Hrapp, Bjorn Buna's son, had a son called Orlyg whom he gave in
fosterage to the Holy Bishop Patrick of the Hebrides.[20] He had a great
desire to go to Iceland, and asked the Bishop for guidance. The bishop
provided him with church timber, an iron bell, a plenarium, and
consecrated earth which Orlyg was to place beneath the corner posts
of his church. The bishop told him to settle at a place where from the
sea he could keep two mountains in view, each with its valley. He was
to make his home below the southern mountain where he was to build
a house and a church dedicated to Saint Columba.[21] On board Orlyg's
ship were his blood-brother Koll, Thorbjorn Sparrow and Thorbjorn's
brother Thorbjorn Skuma, the sons of Bodvar Bladder-Bald.

Orlyg and his men put out to sea, and had such a rough passage

---

[18]King Harald's expedition to the west is mentioned in Chap. 22 of his saga
in *Heimskringla*. See also the *History of the Earls of Orkney*. Chap. 4.

[19]Jon Ogmundsson was Bishop of Holar 1106-21.

[20]No such bishop is known from any extant source, and it has been suggested
that this is an allusion to St. Patrick of Ireland (d. 461).

[21]St. Columba (d. 597) founded the Iona monastery c. 563 and from there he
and his fellow-monks preached the faith to the still pagan Picts. Christian settlers
from the Hebrides continued to venerate him in their new homes in Iceland.

they'd no idea where they were. Then Orlyg made a solemn vow to Bishop Patrick that if they made land he'd name the place after him. Shortly afterwards they sighted land, having drifted west of Iceland. They came ashore at a place now called Orlygshaven, but the fjord that cut into the land from there they called Patreksfjord. They stayed there over winter. In the spring Orlyg got his ship ready to sail, but some of his crew settled down there, as will be described later. Orlyg journeyed east round Bard, and once he'd gone beyond Snæfellsness Glacier and sailed into the bay he could see two mountains, each of them with a valley cutting into it. Then he knew this was the place he'd been guided to, so he made for the southern mountain. This was Kjalarness, which his cousin Helgi had already claimed. Orlyg stayed the first winter with him, and in the spring with Helgi's approval he laid claim to the land between Mogils River and Osvifs Brook, making his home at Esjuberg where he built a church as he had promised. Orlyg had a number of children. His sons were Valthjof, father of Valbrand, father of Torfi, and Geirmund, father of Halldora, mother of Thorleif, from whom the people of Esjuberg are descended.

Orlyg and his kinsmen put their faith in St. Columba. Orlyg the Old also had a daughter called Velaug, wife of Gunnlaug Adder-Tongue, son of Hromund of Thverarhlid. Their daughter was Thurid Sow-thistle, mother of Illugi the Black of Gilsbakki.

16. *Svartkel*

There was a man from Caithness called Svartkel. He took possession of land between Mogils and Eilifsdale Rivers. He lived first at Kidjafell, and later at Eyr. He was the father of Thorkel, father of Glum, whose prayer to the cross was,

> Good luck to the old.
> Good luck to the young.

Glum was the father of Thorarin, father of Glum.

17. *Valthjof Orlygsson*

Valthjof Orlygsson of Esjuberg took possession of the entire Kjos district, and made his home at Medalfell. From him are descended the Valthyfling kin. He was the father of Signy, mother of Gnup, father of Birning, father of Gnup, father of Bishop Eirik of Greenland.[22]

---

[22]According to *The Icelandic Annals* Bishop Eirik of Greenland went in search of Vinland in 1121. In the so-called Yale Map a mention is made of Bishop Henricus of Greenland who went to explore Vinland in 1117 and stayed there for a year before coming back to Greenland. See R. A. Skelton, Th. E. Marston and G. D. Painter *The Vinland Map and the Tartar Relation*, 1965, p. 140.

18. *Hvamm-Thorir*

Hvamm-Thorir took possession of land between Lax and Fors Rivers, and made his home at Hvamm. Thorir quarrelled with Ref the Old over a cow called Brynja. The valley Brynjudale takes its name from her. She used to roam there wild with forty head of cattle, all of them her offspring. Ref and Thorir fought at Thorishills and Thorir was killed there with eight of his men.

19. *Thorstein Solmundsson*

Thorstein, son of Solmund, son of Thorolf Butter, took possession of land between Botns and Fors River, including the whole of Brynjudale. He married Thorbjorg Katla, Helgi Cormorant's daughter, and their son was Ref the Old, from whom the Brynjudale people are descended.

Now we've listed all the settlers who lived to the west of Ingolf, within his original land-claim.

20. *Avang the Irishman*

There was a man called Avang, of Irish descent, the first settler at Botn. At that time there was such a great wood there he was able to build an ocean-going ship from the timber. Avang was the father of Thorleif, father of Thurid, wife of Thormod, son of Thjostar of Alftaness and of Idunn Molda-Gnup's-daughter. Thormod was the father of Bork, father of Thord, father of Audun of Brautarholt.

21. *Kolgrim the Old*

Kolgrim the Old, son of the chieftain Hrolf, took possession of land between Botns and Kalmans Rivers, and made his home at Ferstikla. Kolgrim married Gunnvor, daughter of Hrodgeir the Wise, and their two children were Thorhalli, father of Kolgrim, father of Stein, father of Kvist, from whom the Kvistlings are descended; and Bergthora, wife of Ref of Brynjudale.

22. *Thormod*

There were two brothers who took possession of the entire Akraness, between Kalmans and Aurrida Rivers. One of them, Thormod, owned land south of Reynir and lived at Holm. He was the father of Bresi, and of Thorlaug, mother of Tongue-Odd.

23. *Ketil*

The other brother, Ketil, owned the west side of Akraness, as far as Aurrida River. He was the father of Jorund the Christian, who lived at Gardar, then called Jorundarholt. Jorund was the father of Klepp, father of Einar, father of Narfi and Havar, father of Thorgeir.

24. *Asolf*

There was a man called Asolf who was related to Jorund of Gardar.
He came to Iceland and made land in the east at Osar. He was a
devout Christian and would have nothing to do with the heathen. He
wouldn't even accept food from them. He built himself a house in the
Eyjafell District at a place now called Eastern Asolfsskali and kept out
of people's way, so they tried to find out what he used for food, and
saw there was a lot of fish in the house. When they came to the stream
that flowed past the house it seemed to be teeming with fish, and people
were amazed, never having seen anything like it. When the local farmers
found out about it they drove Asolf away, not wanting him to reap the
benefit of this abundance. Then Asolf moved house west and went to
live at Midskali, but when people tried to fish in the stream, all the
fish had vanished. Then they came to Asolf's new house, only to find
the river which flowed there was now full of fish. Once more they drove
him away, and he moved over to Western Asolfsskali, where precisely
the same thing happened all over again. After he'd moved a second
time, he went to see his kinsman Jorund who invited him to stay, but
Asolf said he wanted to keep away from other people, so Jorund had a
separate house built for him at Inner Holm and provided him with
food. Asolf stayed there for the rest of his life, and there he lies buried.
The present church stands on his grave and people now think of him
as the holiest of men.

25. *Bekan*

There was a man called Bekan, who took possession of land in Ketil's
territory, between Berjadale and Urrida Rivers. He lived at Bekans-
stead.

26. *Finn the Wealthy*

Finn the Wealthy son of Halldor Hognason took possession of land
between Lax River in the south and Kalmans River, and lived at Mid-
fell. His son was Thorgeir, father of Jostein, father of Thorunn, mother
of Gudrun, mother of Sæmund, father of Bishop Brand.[23]

27. *Hafnar Orm*

Hafnar-Orm took possession of land in the Melar District, between
Urrida and Lax Rivers in the north, and Andakils River in the south;
he lived at Hofn. His son was Thorgeir Cheek-Wound, father of
Thorunn, mother of Thorunn, mother of Jostein, father of Sigurd,

---

[23]Brand Sæmundsson was Bishop of Holar 1163-1201.

father of Bjarnhedin. Thorgeir Cheek-Wound was a retainer of King
Hakon, fosterson of King Athelstan.[24] At the Battle of Fitjar he got a
wound on the cheek and a great reputation.

28. *Hrodgeir and Oddgeir*

There were two brothers called Hrodgeir the Wise of Saurby and
Oddgeir of Leir River, who lived in the territory claimed by Orm and
Finn the Wealthy. Finn and Orm thought themselves a bit cramped
there, so they paid the brothers money to go away. Hrodgeir and his
brother later took possession of some land in Hraungerdingahrepp in
the Floi district. Hrodgeir made his home at Hraungerdi, and Oddgeir
at Oddgeirshills. Oddgeir married the daughter of Ketil Gufa.

29. *Kveld-Ulf*

There was a man called Ulf, nicknamed Kveld-Ulf,[25] son of Brunda-
Bjalfi and Hallbera, daughter of Ulf the Brave of Hrafnista. Ulf
married Salbjorg Berdlu-Kari's-daughter, and their sons were Thorolf
and Skalla-Grim. King Harald Fine-Hair had Thorolf put to death up
north at Alost in Sandness because of slanderous talk by the Hildiridarsons, and refused to pay compensation for the killing. Then Skalla-
Grim and Kveld-Ulf got a trading ship ready for a voyage with the
idea of going to Iceland, as they'd heard their friend Ingolf was there.
They waited for a while at Solmund Isles before putting out to sea,
and there they took the ship King Harald had confiscated from Thorolf
just after Thorolf's men had returned with it from England, and killed
Hallvard the Hard Sailing, and Sigtrygg the Fast Sailing, who had
been in charge of confiscating the ship. They also put to death the sons
of Guthorm, Sigurd Hart's son, who were cousins of King Harald, and
killed the rest of the crew as well apart from two men they told to
carry the news to the king.

After that they got both ships ready for the voyage to Iceland each
with thirty men aboard. Kveld-Ulf took charge of the ship they had
captured and got Grim the Halogalander, son of Thorir, son of
Gunnlaug, son of Hrolf, son of Ketil Keeler, to join him in command of
it. The two ships kept in touch most of the time. When the crossing
was pretty well completed, Kveld-Ulf fell ill. He asked his men to make
a coffin for him should he die, and to tell his son Skalla-Grim to build
his home in Iceland near the spot where the coffin would come ashore,

---

[24]King Hakon ('the Good') was ruler of Norway c. 935-61. He had been
brought up by King Athelstan of England.

[25]Kveld-Ulf, literally "evening-wolf." He gained a reputation for surly conduct
towards evening, and was believed by some to be a were-wolf. See *Egils Saga*, Ch. 1.

if that were possible. Then Kveld-Ulf died and his coffin was thrown overboard.

Both ships sailed along the coast, as they'd heard that Ingolf was living in the south. They sailed west round Reykjaness, then straight up the bay, and there they lost sight of one another so neither knew where the other had got to. Grim the Halogalander and his crew sailed right up the bay till they had all the skerries behind them, and then they cast anchor. At high tide they moved the ship up into a certain estuary, hauling it along as far as they could—this is now known as Gufu River —then they carried their belongings ashore. They started exploring the land, and hadn't gone very far when they found Kveld-Ulf's coffin washed ashore in a creek there. They carried it over to the nearest headland and piled stones round it.

30. *Skalla-Grim*

Skalla-Grim put in at a place now called Knarrarness in Myrar. Then he started exploring and found extensive marshes and woodlands stretching from the mountains right down to the sea.

On their way east along the bay, they came to a headland where they found some swans, so they called it Alftaness.[26] They kept going till they found Grim the Halogalander and his men, who told them what had happened and repeated the message Kveld-Ulf had sent his son. Skalla-Grim went to see where the coffin had come ashore and nearby seemed to him a good place for a farmstead. Skalla-Grim spent the winter at the place where he had landed and explored the whole district. He took possession of all the land from Selalon in the west, north to Borgarhraun and south to Hafnarfell, using the rivers to mark his landclaim right down to the sea. He built a farm near the creek where Kveld-Ulf's coffin had come ashore, and called it Borg, and the fjord Borgarfjord. After that he granted land to his companions, and later plenty of others came to settle on his territory with his approval. Skalla-Grim granted land to Grim the Halogalander on the south side of the Fjord, between Andakils River and Grims River. Grim lived at Hvanneyr. He was the father of Ulf, father of Hrolf of Geitland.

31. *Thorbjorn the Black*

There was a man called Thorbjorn the Black. He bought land from Hafnar-Orm between Selseyr and Foss River, and lived at Skeljabrekka. His son was Thorvard, who married Thorunn, daughter of Thorbjorn

---

[26]Literally "Swan Ness."

of Arnarholt, and their sons were Thorarin the Blind and Thorgils the Orra-Poet, who stayed with Olaf Kvaran in Dublin.[27]

Skorri, Ketil Gufa's freedman, took possession of Skorradale above the lake, and was killed there.

32. *Bjorn the Gold-Bearer*
Bjorn the Gold-Bearer took possession of South-Reykjadale, and lived at Gullberastead. His first son was Grimkel the Priest of Blawoods who married Signy, daughter of Valbrand Valthjofsson, and their son was Hord, leader of the men of Holm. Bjorn the Gold-Bearer married Ljotunn, Kolgrim the Old's sister, and they had another son called Svarthofdi of Reydarfell who married Thurid Tongue-Odd's-daughter, and their daughter was Thordis, who married Gudlaug the Wealthy. Bjorn's third son was called Thjostolf, and the fourth Geirmund.

33. *Thorgeir Meldun*
Thorgeir Meldun was granted land by Bjorn above Grims River, and lived at Tungufell. Thorgeir married Geirbjorg, daughter of Balki of Hrutafjord, and their son was Veleif the Old.

34. *Floki*
Floki, Ketil Gufa's slave, took possession of Flokadale, and that's where he was killed.

35. *Oleif Hjalti*
There was a man of great distinction called Oleif Hjalti, who brought his ship to Borgarfjord, and stayed the first winter with Skalla-Grim. With Skalla-Grim's approval he took possession of land between Grims River and Geirs River, and lived at Varma Brook. His sons were Ragi of Laugardale, and Thorarin the Lawspeaker,[28] who married Thordis, daughter of Olaf Feilan, and they also had a daughter, Vigdis, who married Stein Thorfinnsson. Ragi had a son called Guthorm, father of Gunnvor, mother of Thorny, mother of Thorlak, father of Runolf, father of Bishop Thorlak.[29]

36. *Ketil Blund*
Ketil Blund and his son Geir came to Iceland and stayed the first winter with Skalla-Grim. Geir married Thorunn, Skalla-Grim's-daughter. In the spring Skalla-Grim told them where they should

---

[27]Olaf Kvaran ruled the Norse kingdom of Dublin c. 938-80.
[28]Thorarin ('Ragi's-brother') was Lawspeaker of the Althing c. 950-69.
[29]Thorlak Runolfsson was Bishop of Skalholt 1118-33.

settle, and they took possession of the tongue of land between Flokadale and Reykjadale Rivers, all the way up to Raudsgill, including Flokadale up as far as the slopes. Ketil lived first at Thrandarholt, and later at Blundswater, which takes its name from him.

His son Geir the Wealthy lived at Geirshlid and had another farm at Upper Reykir. His sons were Thorgeir Blund, Blund-Ketil, and Svardkel of Eyr. Geir had a daughter called Bergdis, who was married to Gnup Flokason of Hrisar. Thorodd Hrisa-Blund belonged to that family.

37. *Onund Broad-Beard*

Onund Broad-Beard son of Ulfar, son of Ulf Fitjar-Beard, son of Thorir the Clanger took possession of the whole tongue of land between Hvit River and Reykjadale River, and lived at Breidabolstead. He married Geirlaug, daughter of Thormod of Akraness and sister to Bersi, and they had a son called Tongue-Odd, and a daughter Thorodda who married Torfi, son of Valbrand, son of Valthjof Orlygsson of Esjuberg; her dowry was half of Breidabolstead and Hals lands. Torfi gave Signy, his sister, Signyjarstead, and that's where she farmed. Torfi killed the twelve men of Kropp, and he was mostly responsible for the killing of the men of Holm too. He was present at Hellisfitjar with Illugi the Black and Sturla the Priest when the eighteen cave-dwellers[30] were killed, and they burnt Audun Smidkelsson in his home at Thorvardsstead. Torfi had a son called Thorkel of Skaney.

Tongue-Odd married Jorunn, Helgi's-daughter, and their sons were Thorvald, who was responsible for the burning of Blund-Ketil, and Thorodd, who married Jofrid, Gunnar's-daughter whose daughter Hungerd married Sverting Hafur-Bjarnarson. Tongue-Odd's daughters were Thurid, who married Thorfinn Sel-Thorisson, and Hallgerd who married Hallbjorn, son of Odd of Kidjaberg.

Tongue-Odd had an aunt called Kjolvor, who lived at Kjolvararstead. She was the mother of Thorleif, Thurid's mother, and mother of Gunnhild, Kali's wife, and of Glum, the father of Thorarin, Glum of Vatnslausa's father.

38. *Raud*

A man called Raud took possession of land from Raudsgill up to Giljar, and lived at Raudsgill. His sons were Ulf of Ulfsstead and Aud of Audsstead north of the river, who was killed by Hord, which gave rise to *The Saga of Hord Grimkelsson and Geir*.

---

[30]Apparently outlaws, who had taken refuge in some caves.

39. *Grim*

There was a man called Grim, who took possession of land south of Giljar up to Grimsgill, and lived at Grimsgill. His sons were Thorgils Auga of Augastead and Hrani of Hranastead, father of Grim, who was nicknamed Prow-Grim and farmed at Stafngrimsstead, now called Sigmundarstead. His burial mound stands there, down by Hvit River on the north bank, and that's where he was killed.

40. *Thorkel Kornamuli*

Thorkel Kornamuli took possession of Southern As, from Kolls Brook up to Deildargill, and lived at As. His son was Thorberg Kornamuli, who married Alof Ellida-Shield, daughter of Ofeig and of Asgerd, Thorgeir Gollnir's sister. Their children were Eystein and Hafthora, who married Eid Skeggjason, who later farmed at As. That's where Midfjord-Skeggi died, and his burial mound stands just below the farm. Skeggi had another son called Koll, who lived at Kolls Brook. The sons of Eid were Eystein and Illugi.

41. *Ulf*

Ulf, son of Grim the Halogalander and of Svanlaug, daughter of Thormod of Akraness and Bersi's sister, took possession of land between Hvit River and the southern ice-fields, and lived at Geitland. His first son was Hrolf the Wealthy, father of Halldora, who married Gizur the White, and had a daughter Vilborg who married Hjalti Skeggjason; his second was Hroald, father of Hrolf the Younger, who married Thurid, daughter of Valthjof, son of Orlyg the Old; their children were Kjallak of Lund in South-Reykjadale, father of Koll, father of Bergthor; and Solvi of Geitland, father of Thord of Reykholt, father of Solvi, father of Thord, father of Magnus, father of Thord, father of Helga, mother of Helga, mother of Gudny, the mother of the Sturlu-sons.[31]

Hrolf had a third son who was called Illugi the Red, the first man to farm Hrauns Ridge. At that time he was married to Sigrid, daughter of Thorarin the Evil and sister to Mice-Bolverk. Illugi gave this farm to Bolverk and went himself to farm at Hofsstead in Reykjadale. The men of Geitland were supposed to pay for half the upkeep of the temple there, and Tongue-Odd the other half. Finally Illugi went to live at Outer-Holm on Akraness when he and Holm-Starri exchanged

---

[31]The Sturlusons, the sons of Hvamm-Sturla, were Snorri (1179-1241), author of *The Prose-Edda* and *Heimskringla*, Sighvat, (d. 1238), and Thord (d. 1237), father of Sturla (1214-84), the redactor of the present version of the *Book of Settlements*.

their property, farms, wives, livestock and all. Then Illugi married
Jorunn, daughter of Thormod Thjostarsson of Alftaness, but Sigrid
hanged herself in the temple because she couldn't bear the change of
husbands.

Hrolf the Younger gave his daughter Thorlaug the Priestess in marriage to Odd Yrarson. That's why Hrolf moved house west to Ballar
River and that's where he lived for a long time. He was called Hrolf
of Ballar River.

42. *Kalman*

Now we come to the settlement of the West Quarter, where very many
important people have lived.

There was a man called Kalman, a Hebridean by origin; he went to
Iceland and put into Hvalfjord, settling at Kalmans River, and there
in Hvalfjord two of his sons were drowned. Afterwards he took possession of land west of Hvit River as far as Fljot, including the whole
of Kalmanstongue, and eastwards up to the icefields as far as grass will
grow, and made his home at Kalmanstongue. Kalman was drowned
in Hvit River, on his way back from Hraun where he had been visiting
his concubine, and his grave mound stands at Hvitarbakki, south of
the river.

Kalman was the father of Sturla the Priest, who first lived at Sturlu-
stead just below Tungufell, east of Skaldskelmisdale, and later farmed
at Kalmanstongue. Sturla had a son called Bjarni, who quarrelled with
Hrolf the Younger and his sons over Lesser-Tongue. Then Bjarni
promised to become a Christian, and afterwards Hvit River changed
its course and made a new channel where it flows now, so Bjarni
gained possession of Lesser-Tongue down to Grind and Solmundarhofdi.

Kalman had a brother called Kylan, who lived at Kollshamar. He
was the father of Kari, who quarrelled over an ox with Karli Konalsson
of Karlastead, a freedman of Hrolf of Geitland, and it turned out to
belong to Karli. Then Kari egged his slave into killing Karli. The
slave behaved like a madman and ran south across the lava fields.
Karli was sitting at the doorstep of his house, and the slave gave him
his deathblow. Afterwards Kari killed the slave. Thjodolf, Karli's son,
killed Kylan Karason at Kylanshills. Then Thjodolf burnt Kari inside
his house at a place now called Brenna.

Bjarni Sturluson received baptism and lived at Bjarnastead in Lesser-
Tongue where he built a church.

43. *Hrosskel*

There was a great man called Thrand Nose, father of Thorstein who married Lopthæna, daughter of the chieftain Arinbjorn of Fjord Province. Lopthæna had a sister called Arnthrud, who was married to the chieftain Thorir Hroaldsson, and their son was the chieftain Arinbjorn. The mother of Lopthæna and Arnthrud was Astrid Slækidreng, daughter of Bragi the Poet and of Lopthæna, daughter of Erp the Stooping. Thorstein and Lopthæna had a son called Hrosskel, who married Joreid, daughter of Olvir, son of King Mottul of Lappland, and their son was Hallkel. Hrosskel went out to Iceland and put in at Grunnafjord. To begin with he lived at Akraness, but Ketil and his brothers wouldn't have him there, so he took possession of Hvitarsida between Kjarr River and Fljot. He lived at Hallkelsstead, as did his son Hallkel after him. Hallkel married Thurid Sowthistle, daughter of Gunnlaug of Thverarhlid and of Velaug Orlyg's-daughter of Esjuberg.

Hrosskel granted land to Thorvard, father of Smidkel and Audun, the leaders of the cave-dwellers. He lived at Thorvardsstead and owned the whole of Fljotsdale right up to Fljot. Hrosskel granted land to his shipmate Thorgaut down in Sida; he lived at Thorgautsstead, and had two sons both called Gisli.

Hallkel and Thurid had these children; Thorarin, Finnvard, Tind, Illugi the Black, and a daughter Grima who married Thorgils Arason. Mice-Bolverk killed Thorarin when he was living at Hrauns Ridge. Then he fortified the farm and diverted Hvit River through the ridge; before that it used to flow down through Melrakkadale. Illugi and Tind attacked Bolverk in the stronghold.

44. *Asbjorn the Wealthy*

Asbjorn Hardarson the Wealthy bought land south of Kjarr River, from Sleggju Brook north of Hvitborg, and lived at Asbjarnarstead. He married Thorbjorg, daughter of Midfjord-Skeggi, and their daughter was Ingibjorg, wife of Illugi the Black.

45. *Ornolf*

There was a man called Ornolf who took possession of Ornolfsdale and Kjarradale as far north as Hvitbjorg. Blund-Ketil bought all the land south of Klif from Ornolf and lived at Ornolfsdale. Ornolf made his first home in Kjarradale, at a place now known as Ornolfsstead. The area up from Klif is called Kjarradale,[32] because there used to be brush and copses between Kjarr and Thver Rivers, so the place was

---

[32]Kjarradale means literally 'Copse Valley'.

unsuitable for farming. Blund-Ketil was a wealthy man, and had lots of clearings made in the woods, where he started farming.

46. *Hromund*

Grim the Halogalander had a brother called Hromund, son of Thorir, son of Gunnlaug, son of Hrolf, son of Ketil Wake. Hromund brought his ship to Hvit River, and took possession of Thverardale and Thverarhlid, between Hallarmull and Thver River. He lived at Hromundarstead, or Karlsbrekka as they call it nowadays. He was the father of Gunnlaug Adder-Tongue, who lived at Gunnlaugsstead, south of Thver River, and married Velaug as was written earlier. One of Hromund's shipmates was a man called Hogni, who lived in Hognastead; he was the father of Helgi of Helgawater, father of Arngrim the Priest, who took part in the burning of Blund-Ketil. This Hogni was the brother of Finn the Wealthy.

47. *Isleif and Isrod*

Two brothers called Isleif and Isrod took possession of the land down from Sleggju Brook, between Ornolfsdale and Hvit Rivers, as far north as Rauda Brook and south to Hordahills. Isleif lived at Isleifsstead and Isrod, who owned land along Hvit River on the south side, at Isrodarstead; he was the father of Thorbjorn, father of Ljot of Veggjar, who was killed in the Moor-Battle.

48. *Asgeir*

One of Hromund's shipmates, a man called Asgeir, lived at Hamar north of Helgawater. He married Hild Star, daughter of Thorvald Thorgrimsson the Bleater, and their sons were Steinbjorn the Strong-Striker, and Thorvard, father of Mæva, wife of Hrifla; their third son was Thorstein, and the fourth Helgi, father of Thord, father of Poet-Helgi.

49. *Arnbjorg and Thorunn*

A woman called Arnbjorg lived at Arnbjargar Brook. Her sons were Eldgrim, who lived at Eldgrimsstead on the ridge above Arnbjargar Brook, and Thorgest, who was fatally wounded when he fought Hrani at a place now called Hranafall.

A woman called Thorunn lived at Thorunnarholt. She owned land down as far as Vidi Brook and up to the part belonging to Thurid the Prophetess, who lived at Grof. Thorunnar Pool in Thver River takes its name after her and the Hamar-Dwellers are her descendants.

50. *Thorbjorn*
Thorbjorn, son of Arnbjorn Oleifsson Long-Neck, was the brother of Lyting of Vapnafjord. Thorbjorn took possession of the entire Stafholts-Tongue between Nord and Thver Rivers, and lived at Arnarholt. His son was Teit of Stafaholt, father of Einar.

51. *Thorbjorn Blaze*
Thorbjorn Blaze took possession of land in Nordriverdale on the south side, up from Krok, including the whole of Hellisdale, and lived at Blesastead. He was the father of Gisli of Melar in Hellisdale who gave his name to the Gislawaters. Thorbjorn Blaze had another son called Thorfinn of Thorfinnsstead, father of Thorgerd Moor-Widow, mother of Thord Strife, father of Thorgerd, mother of Helgi of Lund.

52. *Geirmund*
Geirmund, son of Gunnbjorn Wand, took possession of the tongue of land between Nord and Sand Rivers, and lived at Tongue. His son was Bruni, father of Thorbjorn of Steinar, who was killed in the Moor-Battle.

53. *Orn the Old*
Orn the Old took possession of Sanddale, Mjovadale and Nordriverdale from Krok down to Arnarbæli, and lived at Hareksstead.

54. *Ore-Bjorn*
Ore-Bjorn took possession of Bjarnardale and all the valleys that branch off from it. He had one farm below Mælifellsgill, and another down in the settlement, as was written earlier.

55. *Karl*
Karl took possession of Karlsdale, above Hredawater, and lived at Karlsfell; he owned land down as far as Jafnaskard, on the way towards the land belonging to Grim.

56. *Gris and Grim*
There were two freedman of Skalla-Grim called Gris and Grim, to whom he granted land up near the mountains; to Gris he gave Grisartongue, and to Grim, Grimsdale.

57. *Bersi the Godless*
There was a man called Bersi the Godless, son of Balki Blæingsson of Hrutafjord. Bersi took possession of the whole of Langavatnsdale, and

that's where he farmed. He had a sister called Geirbjorg who was married to Thorgeir of Tungufell, and their son was Veleif the Old. Bersi the Godless married Thordis, daughter of Thorhadd of Hitardale, and along with her he got the Holmslands. Their son was Arngeir, father of Bjorn the Hitardale-Champion.

58. *Sigmund*
To one of his freedmen, Sigmund, Skalla-Grim granted land between Gljufur and Nord Rivers. Sigmund farmed first at Haugar, then moved house to Munadarness. Sigmundarness takes its name after him.

59. *Ore-Bjorn*
Ore-Bjorn bought land from Skalla-Grim between the Gljufur and Gufu Rivers, and lived at Raudabjarnarstead above Eskiholt. His sons were Thorkel Fringe of Skard, Helgi of Hvamm and Gunnvald, father of Thorkel, who married Thorgeir of Vidimyr.

60. *Thorbjorn and Thord*
There were two brothers called Thorbjorn the Bent, and Thord Beigaldi, to whom Skalla-Grim granted land west of Gufu River; Thorbjorn farmed at Holar and Thord at Beigaldi.

61. *Thorbjorg and her Brothers*
To Thorir Troll and Thorgeir Land-Long and their sister Thorbjorg Pole, Skalla-Grim granted land up beside Long River on the south bank. Thorir farmed at Thursstead, Thorgeir at Jardlangsstead, and Thorbjorg at Stangarholt.

62. *An*
To a man called An, Grim gave land between Long River and Hafs Brook. He lived at Anabrekka. His son was Onund Sjoni, father of Steinar and Dalla, Kormak's mother.

63. *Thorfinn the Strong*
Thorfinn the Strong was the standard-bearer of Thorolf Skalla-Grimson. Skalla-Grim gave his daughter to him as well as land west of Long River, out as far as Leiru Brook and up to the mountain. Thorfinn lived at Foss. Their daughter was Thordis, mother of Bjorn the Hitardale-Champion.

64. *Yngvar*
There was a man called Yngvar, father of Bera, Skalla-Grim's wife,

and Skalla-Grim granted Yngvar land between Leiru Brook and Straumfjord. Yngvar lived at Alftaness. He had another daughter called Thordis, wife of Thorgeir Lamb of Lambastead, father of Thord, whom the slaves of Ketil Gufa burnt inside his house. Thord had a son called Lambi the Strong.

65. *Steinolf*

A man called Steinolf took possession of the two Hraunsdales as far down as Grjot River, with Skalla-Grim's approval. He was the father of Thorleif, from whom the Hraundalers are descended.

66. *Thorhadd*

Thorhadd, son of Stein the Fast-Sailing, son of Vigbjod, son of Bodmod of the Cargo-Hold, took possession of Hitardale, from Grjot River in the south west of Kald River, and the whole region between Hitar and Kald Rivers down to the sea. He had a son called Thorgeir, father of Hafthor, father of Gudny, mother of Thorlak the Wealthy. Thorgeir had other sons called Grim of Skard, Thorarin, Finnbogi, Eystein, Gest and Torfi.

67. *Thorgils Knob*

Thorgils Knob, a freedman of Kolli Hroaldsson, took possession of Knappadale. He was the father of Ingjald and Thorarin of Akrar, and owned land between Hitar and Alft Rivers, bordering on Steinolf's property. Thorarin had a son called Thrand who married Steinunn, daughter of Hrut of Kambsness, and their sons were Thorir and Skum, father of Torfi, father of Tanni; Thorir had a son called Hrut, who married Kolfinna, the daughter of Illugi the Black.

Now we've listed all those who settled in Skalla-Grim's land-claim.

68. *Grim*

There was a man called Grim, son of Ingjald, son of Hroald of Haddingjadale and brother of the chieftain Asi. He went to Iceland looking for land and sailed to the north of the country. He spent a winter on Grims Isle in Steingrimsfjord. He had a wife called Bergdis, and a son called Thorir. In the autumn Grim went fishing with his farm hands and the boy Thorir lay in the prow tucked into a sealskin bag which was tied at the neck. Grim caught a merman, and when he got him to the surface, Grim asked "What can you tell us about our futures? Where in Iceland ought we to settle?"

"There's no point in my making prophesies about you," said the merman, "but that boy in the sealskin bag, he'll settle and claim land where

your mare Skalm lies down under her load." Not another word could
they get out of him. Later that winter Grim and his men went out
fishing. Only the boy stayed behind, and all the rest were drowned.

In the spring Bergdis and Thorir travelled from Grims Isle west
across the moor over to Breidafjord. Skalm went ahead of them but
never lay down. They spent the next winter at Skalmarness in Breida-
fjord, and when they set out the following summer they turned south.
Skalm was still in the lead, and coming down from the moor into
Borgarfjord District, just as they reached two red-coloured sand dunes,
Skalm lay down under her load beside the westermost dune. So Thorir
took possession of the land south of Gnup River to Kald River below
Knappadale, from the mountains and down to the sea. He lived at
Wester Raudamel and was a great chieftain.

When Thorir was old and blind, he went outside one evening and
saw a huge evil-looking man come rowing into Kald River Estuary in
a great iron boat, walk up to a farm called Hrip and start digging at
the gate of the sheep pen. During the night there was an eruption
there, and that's how the lava field at Borg started. The farm stood
where the mountain is now.

Sel-Thorir had a son called Thorfinn, who married Jofrid, the daughter of Tongue-Odd; their sons were Thorkel, Thorgils, Stein, Galti,
Orm, Thororm, and Thorir. Thorfinn had a daughter called Thorbjorg
who married Thorbrand of Alftafjord.

When they died Sel-Thorir and his pagan kinsmen went into Thoris
Cliff. Thorfinn's sons, Thorkel and Thorgils both married Unn, the
daughter of Alf of the Dales. Thorir's mare, Skalm, died at Skal-
markelda.

69. *Thord*

The brothers Thormod and Thord Peak, sons of Odd the Erect, son
of Thorvid, son of Freyvid, son of Alf of Vors, went to Iceland and
took possession of land between Gnup and Straumfjord Rivers. Thord
got Djupadale and that's where he farmed. His son was Skapti, father
of Hjorleif the Priest and Finna, who married Ref the Great, father of
Steinunn, mother of Hofgarda-Ref.

70. *Thormod the Priest*

Thormod lived at Raudkollsstead and was called Thormod the Priest.
He married Gerd, daughter of Kjallak the Old, and their son was
Gudlaug the Wealthy who married Thordis, daughter of Svarthofdi,
son of Bjorn the Gold-Bearer and Thurid the daughter of Tongue-Odd,
who was then living at Horgsholt.

Gudlaug the Wealthy realised that the Raudamels lands were better than any other in the district. He challenged Thorfinn to single combat for the lands and fought a duel with him. They were both struck down in the fight, but Thurid Tongue-Odd's-daughter healed and reconciled them both.

71. *Gudlaug*

Afterwards Gudlaug took possession of land between Straumfjord River and the Fura, from the mountains down to the sea. He lived at Borgarholt, and the Straumfjord men are descended from him. It was his son Gudleif who owned one of the ships—the other belonged to Thorolf, son of Loft the Old—when they fought with Earl Gyrd Sigvaldason. Gudlaug had another son called Thorfinn, father of Gudlaug, father of Thordis, mother of Thord, father of Sturla of Hvamm. Gudlaug the Wealthy had a daughter called Valgerd.

72. *Hlif and her Sons*

Vali the Strong, a retainer of King Harald Fine-Hair, killed a man in a sanctuary and was sentenced to outlawry. He went to the Hebrides and settled down there, but his three sons went to Iceland. Their mother was Hlif the Horse-Gelder. One of them was called Atli, the second Alfarin, and the third Audun the Stutterer.

Atli Valason and his son Asmund took possession of land between the Fura and the Lysa. Asmund lived at Thorutoft in Langaholt, and was married to Langaholt-Thora. When Asmund grew older, he started farming at Oxl, but Thora stayed behind, and had a hall built right across the road with the table always laid; she used to sit on a chair outside and invite every guest to come in for a meal. Asmund was buried in Asmund's Grave in a ship with his slave beside him. Someone who walked past the mound heard this verse being sung in the mound:

> On board my ship
> in this stony mound,
> no crew here
> crowding around me;
> far better solitude
> than feeble support.
> a fine sailor I was once;
> that won't be forgotten.

After that the mound was opened up and the slave taken from the ship.

73. *Hrolf the Stout*

Hrolf the Stout, son of Eyvind Oak-Hook took possession of land between Hraunhafnar River and the Lysa. His son was Helgi of Hofgardar, father of Finnbogi, Bjorn and Hrolf. This Bjorn was the father of Gest, father of Poet-Ref.

74. *Solvi*

A man called Solvi took possession of land between Hellir and Hraunhaven. He lived first at Brenning, but later at Solvahamar because he thought it better farmland.

75. *Sigmund*

Sigmund, son of Ketil Thistle who had settled north in Thistilfjord, was married to a woman called Hildigunn. Sigmund took possession of land between Hellishraun and Beruvikurhraun. He lived at Laugarbrekka and that's where he was buried in a mound. He had three sons: one was Einar who later farmed at Laugarbrekka. He and his father had sold the Lon lands to a man called Einar who then became known as Lon-Einar. After Sigmund died, Lon-Einar went over to Laugarbrekka with six companions and summoned Hildigunn for sorcery. Einar, her son, was away at the time and came back home just after Lon-Einar had left. Hildigunn told him what had happened and gave him a newly-made tunic. Einar took his shield and sword, mounted a carthorse and rode off after them. He broke the horse's wind at Thufu Cliff, but went on to Mannafallsbrekka, and that's where they fought. Four of Lon-Einar's men were killed, and two slaves ran away. The two Einars kept fighting for a long time, until Lon-Einar's trouser-belt broke and as he tried to grab it the other Einar gave him his death-blow. Einar of Laugarbrekka had a slave called Hreidar who gave chase. When he came to Thufu Cliff he could see Lon-Einar's slaves running, so he went for them and killed them both at Thrælavik. For this Einar gave him his freedom and as much land as he could fence off in three days. The place where he made his home is called Hreidarsgerdi nowadays.

Einar of Laugarbrekka married Unn, daughter of Thorir, Aslak of Langadale's brother. Their daughter was Hallveig who married Thorbjorn Vifilsson.

Sigmund had another son called Breid, who married Gunnhild, daughter of Aslak of Langadale, and their son was Thormod who married Helga Onund's-daughter, sister of Poet-Hrafn; their daughter was Herthrud, wife of Simon, whose daughter was Gunnhild. She married Thorgils and their daughter was Valgerd, mother of Finnbogi Geirsson the Learned.

Sigmund had yet another son, Thorkell, who married Joreid, daughter of Tind Hallkelsson.

Einar of Laugarbrekka was buried near Sigmund's Mound and his grave mound is always green, summer and winter.

Lon-Einar's son Thorkel married Grima Hallkel's-daughter, who later became the wife of Thorgils Arason; they had a son called Finnvard.

Einar of Laugarbrekka had another daughter called Arnora, who married Thorgeir Vifilsson. Their daughter was Yngvild who married Thorstein, son of Snorri the Priest, and their daughter Ingunn married Asbjorn Arnorsson.

76. *Grimkel*

There was a man called Grimkel, the son of Ulf, the son of Crow-Hreidar and brother to that Gunnbjorn the Gunnbjarnar Skerries[33] are named after. Grimkel took possession of land between Beruvikurhraun and Neshraun, including the whole of Ondverdarness. He lived at Saxahvoll and drove Saxi, son of Alfarinn Valason away from there. After that, Saxi farmed at Hraun near Saxahvoll.

Grimkel married Thorgerd, daughter of Valthjof the Old, and their son Thorarin Korni was a great sorcerer and lies buried in Kornahaug. Thorarin Korni married Jorunn, daughter of Einar of Stafaholt, and their daughter was Jarngerd who married Ulf Uggason.

Grimkel had another son called Klæng, who married Oddfrid, daughter of Helgi of Hvanneyr. Their son was Kolli, who married Thurid, Asbrand of Kamb's-daughter, and their son was Skeggi, father of Thorkatla, who married Illugi, son of Thorvald Tindsson, father of that Gils who killed Gjafvald.

Kolli had another son called Bard, who married Valgerd, Vidar's-daughter. Their daughter Vigdis married Thorbjorn the Stout, and their daughter Thordis married Thorbrand of Olfusswater. Their sons were Thorir, Bjarni of Breidabolstead and Torfi, and their daughter Valgerd married Runolf, the bishop's son.

Bard had another daughter called Asdis, who was first married to Thorbjorn Thorvaldsson, half-brother to Mana-Ljot by the same mother. Their daughter was Thurid, wife of Thorgrim Oddsson, and their children were Geirmund of Mavahlid and fourteen others besides. Later, Asdis married Skuli Jorundarson, and their daughter was Valgerd of Mosfell.

---

[33]The Gunnbjarnar Skerries have been tentatively identified with a group of rocky islets, off the east coast of Greenland near Angmagssalik.

77. *Alfarin*

Alfarin Valason first took possession of the headland between Beruvik-urhraun and Enni. His sons were Hoskuld who lived at Hoskulds Rivers, Ingjald of Ingjaldsvoll, Goti of Gota Brook, and Holmkell of Foss near Holmkels River.

78. *Olaf Belg*

There was a man called Olaf Belg, who took possession of all the land from Enni east to Frod River and lived at Olafsvik.

79. *Orm the Slender*

There was a man called Orm the Slender, who brought his ship to Frod River Estuary and lived at Brimilsvellir for a time. He drove away Olaf Belg, took possession of the Old Creek between Enni and Hofdi, and lived at Frod River. He had a son called Thorbjorn the Stout, who first married Thurid, daughter of Asbrand of Kamb, their children being Ketil the Champion, Hallstein and Gunnlaug, and a daughter Thorgerd who married Onund Sjoni. Later Thorbjorn married Thurid, daughter of Bork the Stout and Thordis Sur's-daughter.

Thorbjorn the Stout summoned Geirrid Thorolf Twist-Foot's-daughter on a charge of witchcraft after his son Gunnlaug died from an illness he caught when he went to Geirrid for lessons in sorcery. Geirrid was the mother of Thorarin of Mavahlid. Arngrim the Priest was asked by the twelve jurymen to give judgement in the case, and he dismissed the charge after Thorarin had invalidated the case by taking an oath at the sacred ring.

Afterwards Thorbjorn's herd of horses vanished from the mountain pastures, and he blamed Thorarin for it, went over to Mavahlid and held a door court there. He had eleven men with him, and there were seven against them: Thorarin, Alfgeir the Hebridean, Nagli, Bjorn the Easterner and three farmhands. They broke up the court, and fighting started in the home-meadow. Aud, Thorarin's wife, called the women to come and separate them. One of Thorarin's men was killed, and Thorbjorn lost two. Then Thorbjorn went away with his surviving men and they dressed their wounds under a certain haystack near Vogar. Aud's hand was found lying in the home-meadow and because of that Thorarin set out after them and found them at the haystack. Nagli ran in tears past them up the mountain. Thorarin killed Thorbjorn on the spot and wounded Hallstein fatally. Five of Thorbjorn's men were killed there. Arnkel and Vermund backed up Thorarin and kept a force of fighting men at Arnkel's. At the Thorsness Assembly, Snorri the Priest took action over Thorbjorn's killing, and had all the attackers sentenced to outlawry. After that he burnt Alfgeir's ship at Salteyrar Estuary. Arnkel bought them a ship at Dogurdarness and went with them beyond the islands. This started the enmity between Arnkel and Snorri the Priest.

Ketil the Champion was abroad at the time. He was the father of Hrodny who married Thorstein, son of Killer-Styr.

80. *Sigurd Hog's-Head*

Sigurd Hog's-Head was a great champion, and lived in Vaagastranden. His son Herjolf was only eight years old when he killed a brown bear which had bitten a goat of his. This verse was composed about it:

> The bear with a burnt arse
> bit Herjolf's goat,
> Herjolf with the bent arse
> paid the bear back.

Herjolf was the best of fighters and was only twelve years old when he avenged his father. In his old age, Herjolf went to Iceland and took possession of land between Bulandshofdi and Kirkjufjord. His son was Thorstein Coal-Beard, father of Thorolf, father of Thorarin the Black of Mavahlid and Gudny who married Vermund the Slender; their son was Brand the Open-handed.

81. *Vestar*

Vestar, son of Thorolf Bladder-Pate, married Svana Herraud's-daughter, and they had a son called Asgeir. Vestar went to Iceland with his aged father and took possession of the Eyrar lands and Kirkjufjord. He lived at Ondverdareyr, and they were both buried in a mound at Skallaness. Asgeir Vestarsson married Helga Kjallak's-daughter, and their son was Thorlak, who had these sons by Thurid, daughter of Audun the Stutterer: first of all Steinthor, then Thord Blig, who married Otkatla, daughter of Thorvald, son of Thormod the Priest; third was Thormod who married Thorgerd the daughter of Thorbrand of Alftafjord; and fourth, Bergthor who was killed at Vigrafjord. Their sister was Helga who married Asmund Thorgestsson. Steinthor mar- married Thurid, daughter of Thorgils Arason, and their son Gunnlaug married Thurid the Wise, Snorri the Priest's daughter.

82. *Kol*

There was a man called Kol, who took possession of land between Fjardarhorn and Trolla Ridge in the west, including Berserkseyr as far as Hraunsfjord. His sons were Thorarin and Thorgrim, and Kolsonafell takes its name after them. Father and sons lived at Kolgrafir, and the Kolgrafir men are descended from them.

83. *Audun the Stutterer*

Audun the Stutterer, son of Vali the Strong, took possession of the whole of Hraunsfjord above Hraun, between Svinawater and Trolla Ridge. He was a big powerful man and lived at Hraunsfjord. He married Myrun, daughter of King Maddad of Ireland.

One autumn, Audun saw a dapple-grey horse come racing down from Hjardarwater, make straight for his herd of horses and floor the stallion. Audun went and caught the grey horse, hitched him to a two-ox sledge and hauled home all the hay from his home-meadow. The horse was quite manageable till noon, but later in the day he began stamping into the ground right up to the fetlocks. After sunset he tore the harness apart, galloped back to the lake, and that was the last anyone ever saw of him. Audun had a son called Stein, father of Helga, who married An of Hraun; their son was Mar, father of Gudrid, mother of Kjartan and An of Kirkjufell. Audun had another son called Asbjorn, and a third, Svarthofdi. Audun's daughter Thurid married Asgeir of Eyr, and their son was Thorlak.

84. *Bjorn the Easterner*

Ketil Flatnose and Yngvild, daughter of Ketil Wether, chieftain in Ringerike, had a son called Bjorn, who stayed behind on his father's estate when Ketil went to the Hebrides. After Ketil refused to hand over the tribute to King Harald Fine-Hair, the king drove Bjorn Ketilson away from the estate and took it over. After that Bjorn went west over the sea, but wouldn't settle there, and that's why he was nicknamed Bjorn the Easterner. He married Gjaflaug Kjallak's-daughter sister of Bjorn the Strong.

Bjorn the Easterner went to Iceland and took possession of land between Hraunsfjord River and Staf River. He ran a splendid farm at Borgarholt in Bjarnarhaven, and had a shieling at Seljar. He died at Bjarnarhaven and was laid in a grave mound at Borgar Brook, the only one of Ketil Flatnose's children never to be baptized.

Bjorn and Gjaflaug had a son called Kjallak the Old, who farmed at Bjarnarhaven after his father, and another son called Ottar, father of Bjorn, father of Vigfus of Drapuhlid, whom Snorri the Priest had put to death. Ottar had yet another son called Helgi who raided in Scotland, where he captured Nidbjorg, daughter of King Bjolan and of Kadlin Ganger-Hrolf's-daughter. Ottar made Nidbjorg his wife, and their sons were Osvif the Wise and Einar Scales-Clatterer. Einar was drowned at Einarsskerry in Selasound, but his shield was washed ashore at Skjald Island and his cloak on Feldarholm.[34]

Einar was the father of Thorgerd, mother of Herdis, mother of Stein the Poet. Osvif married Thordis, daughter of Thjodolf of Hofn; their children were Ospak, father of Ulf the Marshal, Thorolf, Torrad, Einar, Thorbjorn and Thorkel—all of whom were outlawed for the killing of Kjartan Olafsson—and also Gudrun, mother of Gellir, Bolli, Thorleik and Thord Cat.

Bjorn the Easterner had a son called Vilgeir.

Kjallak the Old married Astrid, daughter of the chieftain Hrolf and of Ondott, sister of Olvir the Child-Sparer. Their son was Thorgrim the Priest who married Thorhild, and their sons were Killer-Styr, Vermund the Slender and Brand, father of Thorleik.

Kjallak the Old's daughters were Gerd, who married Thormod the Priest, and Helga, wife of Asgeir of Eyr.

85. *Thorolf Mostur-Beard*

Thorolf, son of Ornolf the Fish-Driver, lived on Mostur Island, and that's why he was called Mostur-Beard. He was a great sacrificer and worshipped Thor. He fled to Iceland because of the oppression of King Harald Fine-Hair, and made landfall in the south, and when he'd come west as far as Breidafjord, he threw his high-seat pillars overboard. They had an image of Thor carved on them. Thorolf declared that Thor would come ashore where he wanted Thorolf to make his home, and he promised to dedicate his entire land-claim to Thor and call it after him.

Thorolf sailed up the fjord and gave it the name of Breidafjord. He made land on the southern side, halfway up, and there on a headland, now called Thorsness, he found Thor washed ashore. They put into the creek, and Thorolf called it Hofs Creek.[35] He built a farm there and a big temple which he dedicated to Thor. Nowadays the farm is called Hofsstead. Along the fjord at that time there was still little or nothing in the way of settlements.

Thorolf took possession of land between Staf River and Thors River, and called it Thorsness. He held the mountain on that headland so sacred that he called it Helgafell[36] and no one was allowed even to look at it unless he'd washed himself first. So holy was the mountain, no living creature there, man or beast, could be harmed until they left

---

[34]*Skjaldarey* and *Feldarholm*, literally "Shield Island" and "Cloak Isle".
[35]*Hof* means "a temple."
[36]Literally "Holy Fell."

of their own accord. Thorolf and his kinsmen all believed that they would go into the mountain when they died.

On the headland where Thor had come ashore, Thorolf used to hold all his courts, and established the district assembly there with the approval of all the people in the neighbourhood. When people attended the assembly it was agreed no one should ease himself on that piece of land, and a special rock called Dirt Skerry was set aside for it, because they didn't want to defile such a holy place. After Thorolf's death when his son Thorstein was still young, Thorgrim Kjallaksson and his brother-in-law Asgeir refused to go out to the rock to ease themselves. The Thorsnessings wouldn't stand for their desecrating a place as holy as that, which is why Thorstein Cod-Biter and Thorgeir the Bent fought over the rock against Thorgrim and Asgeir at the assembly. Several men were killed there and a good many wounded before they could be separated. Thord Gellir took charge of the reconciliation, and since neither would give way, the field was considered to be defiled by the spilling of blood in enmity. So it was resolved that the assembly should be moved from there to the eastern part of the headland, where it still is. This became a very sacred place too, and Thor's Boulder that was used for the killing of those who were to be sacrificed, still stands there. Beside it is the court circle where people were sentenced to be sacrificed. This is where Thord Gellir also established the Quarter Court, with the approval of all the people in the Quarter. The son of Thorolf Mostur-Beard was Hallstein the Priest of Thorskafjord, father of Thorstein Surt the Wise. The mother of Thorstein Surt was Osk, daughter of Thorstein the Red. Thorolf had another son called Thorstein Cod-Biter, who married Thora, daughter of Olaf Feilan and sister of Thord Gellir; their sons were Thorgrim, father of Snorri the Priest, and Bork the Stout, father of Sam whom Asgeir killed.

86. *Geirrod and Geirrid*

There was a man called Geirrod who went to Iceland and with him Finngeir, son of Thorstein Snow-Shoe, and Ulfar the Champion. They put out from Halogaland for Iceland. Geirrod took possession of land between Thors and Langadale Rivers, and made his home at Eyr. Geirrod granted land to his companion Ulfar on either side of Ulfarsfell, and also behind the mountain. To Geirrod, Finngeir granted land in Alftafjord, and that's where he farmed at the place now called Karsstead. Finngeir was the father of Thorfinn, father of Thorbrand of Alftafjord, who married Thorbjorg, daughter of Thorfinn Sel-Thorisson.

Geirrod had a sister called Geirrid who had been married to Bolverk

Blind-Snout, and they had a son called Thorolf. After Bjorn died, mother and son emigrated to Iceland and spent the first winter at Eyr. In the spring Geirrod gave his sister a farmstead in Borgardale, but Thorolf set out on a viking expedition. Geirrid was very free with food. She built a hall right across the road and she used to sit outside on a chair and ask travellers to come inside, where there was always food on the table.

Thorolf came back to Iceland after his mother died. He challenged Ulfar to single combat for the lands he owned. Ulfar was old and childless, and was killed in the fight, but Thorolf was wounded in the leg and walked with a limp for the rest of his life, so he was nick-named Twist-Foot. Thorolf took some of Ulfar's lands, but some went to Thorfinn of Alftafjord, who settled his freedmen there, Ulfar and Orlyg.

Geirrod of Eyr was the father of Thorgeir the Bent, who moved house from the spit of land up to below the mountain. He was the father of Thord, Atli's father.

Thorolf Twist-Foot was the father of Arnkel the Priest and of Geirrid, who married Thorolf of Mavahlid. The sons of Thorbrand of Alftafjord were Thorleif Kimbi, Thorodd, Snorri, Thorfinn, Illugi, and Thormod. They quarrelled with Arnkel over the inheritance left by his freedmen and along with Snorri the Priest they were fighting him when he was killed at Orlygsstead.

Thorleif Kimbi went abroad, and later he was struck with a ladle by Arnbjorn, son of Asbrand of Breiduvik. Kimbi didn't take it serious-ly, but Thord Blig poked fun at him for it at the Thorsness Assembly, when Kimbi asked for the hand of Thord's sister Helga. It was because of Kimbi that Thord got hit by a piece of sandy turf on this occasion, and this sparked off the quarrels between the men of Eyr on one hand, and the Thorbrandssons and Snorri the Priest on the other. They fought battles at Alftafjord and on Vigrafjord.

87. Thorberg

There was a man called Thorberg, who went from Iafjord to Iceland, took possession of the two Langadales, and made his home in the valley to the west. His son Aslak married Arnleif, daughter of Thord Gellir, and their children were Illugi the Mighty and Gunnhild, who first married Breid and later Halldor of Holmslatur. Illugi the Mighty married Gudleif daughter of Ketil Smith's-Bellows, and their sons were Eyjolf, Eindridi, Koll, and Gellir. Their daughters were Herthrud, whom Thorgrim the son of Vermund the Slender married, Fridgerd whom Odd Draflason married, Gudrid who first married Bergthor, son of Thormod Thorlaksson and later Jorund of Skorradale, Jodis who married Mar, son of Illugi Arason, and Arnleif who married Koll, son of Thord Blig. The Langadale men are descended from Illugi.

88. *Stein the Hard-Sailing*

Stein Vigbjodsson the Hard-Sailing, brother of Thorir Autumn-Dusk took possession of Skogarstrand as far as Thorberg's land-claim and east to Lax River, and farmed at Breidabolstead. His sons were Thorhadd of Hitardale and Thorgest, who married Arnora, Thord Gellir's daughter, whose sons were Stein the Lawspeaker,[37] Asmund, Haflidi and Thorhadd.

89. *Eirik the Red*

Thorvald, son of Asvald, son of Ulf Oxen-Thorisson, had to leave Jæderen, along with Eirik the Red, his son, because of killings they were involved in, and they took possession of land in the Hornstrands. They made their home at Drangar, where Thorvald died. Afterwards Eirik married Thjodhild, the daughter of Jorund Atlason and Thorbjorg Ship-Breast, who by that time was the wife of Thorbjorn the Haukadaler. Then Eirik moved house from the north down to Haukadale and cleared some land for farming. He lived at Eiriksstead near Vatnshorn.

After that Eirik's slaves launched a landslide onto the farm of Valthjof of Valthjofsstead, but his kinsman Eyjolf Saur killed the slaves near Skeidsbrekkur up above Vatnshorn. This was why Eirik killed Eyjolf Saur, besides killing Dueller-Hrafn at Leikskalar. Geirstein and Odd of Jorva, Eyjolf's kinsman, went to law over the killing, and after that Eirik was banished from Haukadale.

Eirik took possession of Brok Isle and Oxen Isle, but spent the first year at Todur on South Isle; that was when he lent his bench-boards to Thorgest. Afterwards Eirik moved house to Oxen Isle and lived at Eiriksstead. Then he asked to have the bench-boards back, but didn't get them, so he went over to Breidabolstead and fetched them himself. Thorgest set out after him, and they fought near the farm at Drangar. Two of Thorgest's sons and some other men were killed there.

After that both sides kept a force of fighting men. On his side Eirik had Styr, Eyjolf of Svin Isle, the sons of Thorbrand of Alftafjord and Thorbjorn Vifilsson, and on Thorgest's side were the sons of Thord Gellir, Thorgeir of Hitardale, and Aslak of Langadale and his son Illugi. Eirik and his men were sentenced to outlawry at the Thorsness

---

[37]Stein Thorgestsson was Lawspeaker of the Althing 1031-33.

Assembly. He got his ship ready at Eirik's Creek, and Eyjolf hid him at Dimun Creek while Thorgest and his men were scouring the islands for him. Thorbjorn, Eyjolf and Styr went beyond the islands along with Eirik, and he told them he meant to search for the land Gunnbjorn, son of Ulf Crow, had sighted when he drifted west beyond Iceland, the time he discovered the Gunnbjorn Skerries. Eirik said he'd come back to see his friends, if he ever found this land.

Eirik put out from Snæfellsness, and made landfall at Mid-Glacier, called Blaserk[38] nowadays. From there he sailed south along the coast looking for somewhere inhabitable, and stayed the first winter on Eirik's Isle, near the middle part of the Western Settlement. Next spring he went over to Eiriksfjord and set up house there. Over summer he travelled west to the wilderness and named a good many places there. He spent the next winter at Eiriksholms near Hvarf's Peak and the third summer he travelled all the way north as far as Snæfell and up into Hrafnsfjord. Then he decided he'd reached a point level with the head of Eiriksfjord. After that he turned back and spent the third winter on Eirik's Isle at the mouth of Eiriksfjord.

The next summer he went back to Iceland and put in at Breidafjord. He spent the winter at Holmslatur with Ingolf. In the spring Eirik and Thorgest fought a battle and Eirik was the loser. After this they were reconciled. That summer Eirik set out to colonize the country he'd discovered; he called it Greenland because he thought people would be more keen to go there if the place had an attractive name.

90. *Sailings to Greenland*

According to learned men,[39] about twenty-five ships set out for Greenland that summer from Breidafjord and Borgarfjord, but only fourteen completed the voyage. Some of them were driven back, and others were lost at sea. This was fifteen years before Christianity was adopted by law in Iceland.[40]

91. *Herjolf*

There was a man called Herjolf, son of Bard, son of Herjolf, a kinsman

---

[38]Blaserk ('Blue Shirt') has been tentatively identified with Ingolfsfjeld, a glacier peak near Angmagssalik.

For this, and other place names in Greenland mentioned here, see *The Vinland Sagas*. Penguin Classics, pp. 114-18.

[39]This refers to Ari Thorgilsson's *Book of the Icelanders*, Ch. 6.

[40]According to Ari Thorgilsson, Eirik's colonization of Greenland took place in A.D. 985 or 986.

of Ingolf the Settler. To Herjolf and his family Ingolf granted land between Vog and Reykjaness. Herjolf the Younger went to Greenland when Eirik colonized it. Aboard with him was a Christian Hebridean who composed the *Hafgerdinga Lay* which has this refrain:

> I beseech the immaculate Master of monks
> To steer my journeys;
> May the Lord of the lofty heavens
> Hold his strong hand over me.

Herjolf took possession of Herjolfsfjord, made his home at Herjolfsness, and became a man of great consequence.

92. *Eirik's Settlement*

After that Eirik took possession of Eiriksfjord, and lived at Brattahlid, and his son Leif after him. The following men who went abroad with Eirik took possession of land in Greenland: Herjolf took Herjolfsfjord, and made his home at Herjolfsness; Ketil took Ketilsfjord; Hrafn, Hrafnsfjord; Solvi, Solvadale; Helgi Thorbrandsson, Alftafjord; Thorbjorn Glora, Siglufjord; Einar, Einarsfjord; Hafgrim, Hafgrimsfjord and Vatna District; and Arnlaug, Arnlaugsfjord. Others went to the Western Settlement.

93. *Thorkel Farserk*

There was a man called Thorkel Farserk, a cousin of Eirik the Red, who went to Greenland with Eirik. He took possession of Hvalseyjarfjord and of the region between Eiriksfjord and Einarsfjord, and lived at Hvalseyjarfjord. The men of Hvalseyjarfjord are descended from him. He was a man of unusual powers. Once when he wanted to welcome his cousin Eirik, but had no seaworthy boat at home, he swam out to Hvals Isle for an old sheep, and carried it on his back to the mainland, a distance of well over a mile. Thorkel was buried in the enclosure of Hvalseyjarfjord, and has been there, round about the house, ever since.

94. *Ingolf the Strong*

Ingolf the Strong took possession of land from Lax River east to Skraumuhlaups River and lived at Holmslatur. He was brother to Thorvald, Thorleif's father, who farmed there afterwards.

95. *Aud the Deep-Minded*

There was a warrior king called Olaf the White, the son of King Ingjald, son of Helgi, son of Olaf, son of Gudrod, son of Halfdan

White-Leg, King of the Uplands. Olaf went on a viking expedition to the British Isles, conquered Dublin in Ireland and the region round about, and made himself king over it. He married Aud the Deep-Minded, Ketil Flat-Nose's daughter, and they had a son called Thorstein the Red. Olaf was killed fighting in Ireland, and after that Aud and Thorstein went to the Hebrides, where Thorstein married Thurid, daughter of Eyvind the Easterner, and sister of Helgi the Lean. They had a good many children. Their son was Olaf Feilan, and Groa, Alof, Osk, Thorhild, Thorgerd and Vigdis were their daughters.

Thorstein the Red became a warrior king, and joined forces with Earl Sigurd the Powerful, son of Eystein the Clatterer; they conquered Caithness, Sutherland, Ross and Moray, and more than half of Argyll.[41] Thorstein ruled over these territories as King until he was betrayed by the Scots and killed there in battle.

Aud was in Caithness when she learned of Thorstein's death; she had a ship built secretly in a forest, and when it was ready she sailed away to Orkney. There she married off Groa, daughter of Thorstein the Red. Groa was the mother of Grelod, who married Thorfinn the Skull-Splitter. After that, Aud set out for Iceland with twenty free-born men aboard her ship.

96. *Dala-Koll*

There was a man called Koll, son of Wether-Grim, son of the chieftain Asi, who was Aud's leading and most respected man. Koll was married to Thorgerd, daughter of Thorstein the Red.

Aud had freed a slave called Erp, son of Earl Meldun of Argyll who'd been killed by Earl Sigurd; Erp's mother was Muirgeal, daughter of King Gljomal of Ireland. Earl Sigurd took them captive and enslaved them. Muirgeal became the bondmaid of Earl Sigurd's wife, and served her faithfully. She was a clever woman. She made sure the queen's illegitimate[42] child was alright when the queen was taking her bath. Afterwards Aud bought Muirgeal for a high price and promised her freedom if she would serve Thurid, Thorstein the Red's wife, as faithfully as she'd served the queen. Muirgeal and her son Erp went to Iceland with Aud.

97. *Aud comes to Iceland*

Aud went first to the Faroes, where she married off Alof, daughter of

---

[41]*Argyll*. The Icelandic text has *Skotland* "the land of the Scots" which evidently refers to the Gaelic Kingdom of Dalriada.

[42]*Óborit*. Literally 'unborn', but apparently referring to a child unacknowledged by its father.

Thorstein the Red. From her the Gotuskeggjar kin are descended.
After that Aud carried on to Iceland, and made land at Vikarskeid,
where her ship was wrecked. Then she travelled to Kjalarness to visit
her brother Helgi Bjolan. He invited her to stay there with half of her
company, but she thought this a poor offer and said he would always
be mean-minded. Then she travelled west to Breidafjord to her brother
Bjorn, who went out to welcome her with all his servants. He said
he knew what a noble-minded woman his sister was and invited her to
stay with him with all her men, and she accepted.

In the spring Aud set out to look for land in Breidafjord, and her
companions went with her. They took their breakfast towards the
south of Breidafjord, at a place that's now called Dogurdarness.[43]
Then they sailed up past the islands in the sound and landed at a
certain headland where Aud lost her comb, so she called it Kambsness.

Aud took possession of the entire Dales district at the head of the
fjord, between the Dogurdar and Skraumuhlaups Rivers. She made
her home at Hvamm near Aurrida River Estuary, at a place now
called Audartoft. She used to say prayers at Kross Hills; she had
crosses erected there, for she'd been baptized and was a devout Christian. Later her kinsmen worshipped these hills, then when sacrifices
began, a pagan temple was built there. They believed they would go
into the hills when they died. Thord Gellir was led to the hills before
he took over the chieftaincy, as is told in his saga.

98. *Ketil*

Aud made grants of land to her ship-mates and freed men. There was
a man called Ketil, to whom she granted land between the Skraumuhlaups and Hordadale Rivers, and he made his home at Ketilsstead. He
was the father of Vestlidi and Einar whose children were Kleppjarn,
and Thorbjorn who was killed by Styr, and Thordis, mother of
Thorgest.

99. *Hord*

To one of her ship-mates called Hord, Aud gave Hordadale. He was
the father of Asbjorn, who married Thorbjorg, daughter of Midfjord-
Skeggi, and their children were Hnaki, who married Thorgerd,
daughter of Thorgeir Cheek-Wound, and Ingibjorg, who married Illugi
the Black.

100. *Vifil*

Aud had a freedman called Vifil. He asked her why she didn't give

---

[43]Literally 'Breakfast Head'.

him a farm like the others. Aud said it wasn't all that important and that he'd be thought a man of quality wherever he was; but all the same she gave him Vifilsdale. He settled there and quarrelled with Hord. Vifil had a son called Thorbjorn, the father of that Gudrid who was first married to Thorstein, Eirik the Red's son, and later to Thorfinn Karlsefni; the bishops Bjorn, Thorlak and Brand[44] were descended from them. Vifil had another son called Thorgeir, who married Arnora, Lon-Einar's daughter, and their daughter was Yngvild, who married Thorstein, son of Snorri the Priest.

101. *Hundi*
To one of her freedmen, a Scot called Hundi, Aud gave Hundadale, and he lived there for a long time.

102. *Sokkolf*
To one of her freedmen, a Scot called Hundi, Aud gave Hundadale, made his home at Breidabolstead, and many people are descended from him.

103. *Erp Meldunsson*
To Erp, Earl Meldun's son who was mentioned earlier, Aud gave his freedom and the Saudafell lands; the Erplings are descended from him. Erp had a son called Orm, and another called Gunnbjorn, father of Arnora who married Kolbein Thordarson; a third son was Asgeir, father of Thorarna, who married Sumarlidi Hrappsson. Erp had a daughter called Halldis, who married Alf of the Dales. Erp had another son, called Dufnall, father of Thorkel, father of Hjalti, father of Beinir, and yet another called Skati, father of Thord, father of Gisli, father of Thorgerd.

104. *Thorbjorn*
There was a man called Thorbjorn, who farmed at Vatn in Haukadale. He was married and he and his wife had a daughter called Hallfrid, who married Hoskuld of Laxriverdale. They had a large family; their sons were Bard and Thorleik. Thorleik's son Bolli married Gudrun Osvif's-daughter, and their sons were Thorleik, Hosku'd, Surt and Bolli, and their daughters Herdis and Thorgerd. Before that Gudrun had been married to Thord Ingunnarson, and their children were Thord Cat and Arnkatla. Thorkel Eyjolfsson was Gudrun's last hus-

---

[44]Bjorn Gilsson was Bishop of Holar 1147-62; Thorlak Runolfsson Bishop of Skalholt 1118-33; Brand Sæmundsson Bishop of Holar 1163-1201.

band, and their children were Gellir and Rjupa. Bard Hoskuldsson
was the father of Hallbjorg, who married Hall, son of Killer-Styr.
Hoskuld's daughters were Hallgerd Twist-Breeks, Thorgerd and
Thurid.

105. *Koll of the Dales*

Koll, called Koll of the Dales, took possession of the whole of Laxriverdale as far as Haukadale River. He married Thorgerd the
daughter of Thorstein the Red, and their children were Hoskuld, Groa
who married Veleif the Old, and Thorkatla who married Thorgeir
the Priest. Hoskuld married Hallfrid, daughter of Thorbjorn of Vatn,
and their son was Thorleik, who married Thurid, daughter of Arnbjorn
Strife-Bjarnarson, and their son in turn was Bolli. Hoskuld bought
Melkorka, the daughter of King Myrkjartan of Ireland, and their
sons were Olaf the Peacock and Helgi; Hoskuld's daughters were
Thurid, Thorgerd and Hallgerd Twist-Breeks. Olaf married Thorgerd, daughter of Egil Skalla-Grimsson, and their sons were Kjartan,
Halldor, Steinthor and Thorberg, and Olaf's daughters were Thurid,
Thorbjorg the Stout and Bergthora. Kjartan married Hrafna, the
daughter of Asgeir the Hasty, and their sons were Asgeir and Skum.

106. *Hrut Herjolfsson*

Afterwards, Herjolf, son of Eyvind Fire, married Thorgerd, Thorstein
the Red's daughter, and their son was Hrut, to whom Hoskuld gave
as his share in their mother's estate the Kambsness lands, between
Haukadale River and the ridge which extends from the mountain
there down to the sea. Hrut made his home at Hrutsstead, and married Hallveig, daughter of Thorgrim of Thykkvawood, sister of Armod
the Old. They had a lot of children; one of their sons was Thorhall,
father of Halldora, mother of Gudlaug, father of Thordis, mother of
Thord, father of Hvamm-Sturla. Hrut's other sons were called Grim,
Mar, Eindridi, Stein, Thorljot, Jorund, Thorkel, Steingrim, Thorberg,
Atli, Arnor, Ivar, Kar and Kugaldi; and Hrut's daughters were Bergthora, Steinunn, Rjupa, Finna and Astrid.

107. *Eystein Foul-Fart*

Aud gave Thorstein the Red's daughter Thorhild in marriage to Eystein
Foul-Fart, son of Alf of Osta. Their sons were Alf of the Dales and
Thord, father of Kolbein, father of Thord the Poet.

Alf married Halldis, Erp's daughter, and their son was Snorri,
father of Thorgils Holluson. Alf of the Dales had these daughters:
Thorgerd who married Ari Masson, and Thorelf who married Havar,

son of Einar Kleppsson, and had a son Thorgeir. Eystein had a third
son called Thorolf Fox, who was killed at the Thorsness Assembly
when he was fighting on the side of Thord Gellir against Tongue-Odd.
A fourth son of Eystein was called Hrapp.

108. *Osk*

Aud gave Thorstein the Red's daughter Osk in marriage to Hallstein
the Priest, and their son was Thorstein Surt. Aud gave Vigdis Thorstein's-daughter in marriage to Kampa-Grim, and their daughter was
Arnbjorg, who married Asolf Flosi of Hofdi. Their children were Odd,
and Vigdis, who married Thorgeir Kadalsson.

109. *Olaf Feilan*

Aud reared Olaf Feilan, son of Thorstein the Red, and he married
Alfdis of Barra, daughter of Konal, son of Steinmod, son of Olvir the
Child-Sparer. Konal had a son called Steinmod, the father of Halldora
who married Eilif, son of Ketil One-Hand. Their children were Thord
Gellir, and Thora, mother of Thorgrim, father of Snorri the Priest.
Thora was also the mother of Bork the Stout and of Mar Hallvards-
son. Olaf Feilan's sons were called Ingjald and Grani, and his daughter
Vigdis. Olaf's third daughter Helga married Gunnar Hlifarson, and
their daughter was Jofrid, who married first Thorodd Tongue-Oddsson
and later Thorstein Egilsson. Gunnar had another daughter, Thorunn,
who married Herstein, son of Blund-Ketil. The sons of Gunnar were
called Raud and Hoggvandil. The fourth daughter of Olaf Feilan,
Thordis, married Thorarin Ragi's-brother, and their daughter was
Vigdis, who married Stein Thorfinnsson of Raudamel.

110. *Aud dies*

Aud was a woman of great dignity. When she was growing weary with
old age, she invited her kinsmen and relatives by marriage to a magnificent feast, and when the feast had been celebrated for three days,
she chose fine gifts for her friends and gave them sound advice. She
declared that the feast would go on for another three days and that it
would be her funeral feast. That very night she died, and she was
buried at the high water mark as she'd ordered, because having been
baptized, she didn't wish to lie in unconsecrated earth. Afterwards her
kinsmen lost the faith.

111. *Kjallak*

There was a man called Kjallak, son of Bjorn the Strong and brother
to Gjaflaug the wife of Bjorn the Easterner. He went to Iceland, took

possession of land between Dogurdar River and Klofningar, and lived
at Kjallaksstead. His sons were Helgi Roe, Thorgrim Tangle-Weed of
Fell, Eilif the Proud, Asbjorn Muscle of Orrastead, Bjorn Whale-
Belly of Tungard, Thorstein the Thinner, Gizur the Gleeful of Skora-
vik and Thorbjorn the Chatterer of Ketilsstead. Kjallak had a
daughter called Æsa of Svin Isle, mother of Eyjolf and Tin-Forni.

There was a man called Ljotolf, to whom Kjallak gave farmland
at Ljotolfsstead, east of Kaldakinn. His sons were Thorstein, Bjorn and
Hrafsi, who was descended from giants on his mother's side. Ljotolf
was a blacksmith; he and his men moved over to Ljotolfsstead in
Fellswood. Vifil who lived at Vifilstoft was a friend of theirs. Thorunn
of Thorunnartoft was the mother of Oddmar and fostermother to
Kjallak, son of Bjorn Whale-Belly.

Alof, the daughter of Thorgrim of Fell, went insane. People blamed
Hrafsi, but he caught Oddmar beside her bed and said that Oddmar
was responsible. After that Thorgrim gave Hrafsi Deildar Isle. Hrafsi
said that he would kill Oddmar and put the blame on Bjorn unless he
paid him compensation. Kjallak refused to hand over the island, and
Hrafsi carried off their money from a boatshed. The Kjallakssons went
after him, but couldn't get the money back. After that Eilif and Hrafsi
went to the island. Eilif the Greyish was hit by an arrow in the groin,
and went into a frenzy. Bjorn Whale-Belly killed Bjorn Ljotolfsson in
a game and Ljotolf and his men paid money to Oddmar to lure Bjorn
so that they could get at him. Kjallak the Younger ran after him, but
they couldn't overcome him, until they had taken the boy. They killed
Kjallak at Kjallakshill. After that the Kjallakssons attacked Ljotolf
and Thorstein in an underground chamber at Fellswoods. Eilif found
one of the openings and crept up behind them and killed them both.
Dressed as a woman, Hrafsi walked into the hall at Orrastead when
people were feasting there. Kjallak was sitting on the dais with a shield.
Hrafsi gave Asbjorn his deathblow and went out through the wall.
Thord Vifilsson told Hrafsi that his oxen were bogged down in a
quagmire, and brought him his shield. Hrafsi threw him over a cliff
when he saw the Kjallakssons. They couldn't get at him until they'd
crowded round him with boards. Eilif sat by idle when they attacked
Hrafsi.

112. *Geirmund Hell-Skin*

King Hjorleif of Hordaland married Æsa the Fair, and their son was
Otrygg, father of Oblaud, father of Hogni the White, father of Ulf the
Squint-Eyed. Another son of Hjorleif was Half, the leader of Half's
Band; his mother was Hild the Slender, daughter of Hogni of Næroy

Island. King Half was the father of King Hjor who avenged his father along with Solvi Hognason. Hjor plundered in Permia, and there he took captive Ljufvina, daughter of the king of Permia. She stayed behind in Rogaland when King Hjor set out on a viking expedition, and later gave birth to twins, one called Geirmund and the other Hamund. Both of them were very swarthy. At the same time her bond-maid gave birth to a boy called Leif, whose father was the slave Lod-hott. Leif was very fair, and that's why the queen exchanged the boys with her bondmaid and claimed Leif as her son. When the king came back home, he took a strong dislike to Leif and said he was a puny-looking thing.

When the king set out on his next viking expedition, the queen invited Bragi the Poet and asked him to take a look at the boys. They were three years old at the time. She locked the boys in a room with Bragi and hid herself under the dais. Bragi composed this verse:

> There are two in this room
> I trust them well:
> Hamund and Geirmund,
> Hjor's own sons.
> The third's Leif,
> Lodhott's son.
> Feed him, woman,
> he'll grow worse.

Then he struck with his wand at the dais under which the queen was hiding. When the king came back home, the queen told him everything and showed him the boys. He said he'd never seen such hell-skins, and that's what the brothers were called ever after.

Geirmund Hell-Skin became a warrior-king. He went on viking expeditions to the British Isles, but ruled a kingdom in Rogaland. When he came back after a long absence, King Harald had fought the Battle of Hafursfjord against King Eirik of Hordaland, King Sulki of Rogaland and Kjotvi the Wealthy, and had defeated them. He'd conquered the whole of Rogaland and driven a good many farmers from their estates. Geirmund realized he had no choice but to emigrate, because he had no standing there any more, so he decided to sail to Iceland. On that journey he was joined by his kinsman Ulf the Squint-Eyed and Steinolf the Short, son of the chieftain Hrolf of Agder and of Ondott, sister of Olvir the Child-Sparer.

113. *Geirmund and Steinolf*
Geirmund and his companions sailed in a convoy, each in charge of

his own ship. They made land at Breidafjord and lay at anchor off Ellida Isle. Then they were told the south coast of the fjord was fully settled, but the north coast was still unoccupied, or only very slightly so. Geirmund sailed up to Medalfells Strand and took possession of land between Fabeins River and Klofastones. He put into Geirmundar Creek, and spent the first winter at Budardale.

Steinolf took possession of land east of Klofastones, and Ulf settled on the west side of the fjord, as will be described later. Geirmund thought his land-claim too small, because he ran a splendid farm and had a large number of men with him, including eighty freedmen. He made his home at Geirmundarstead below Skard.

114. *Thrand Slender-Leg*

There was a man called Thrand Slender-Leg whose family belonged to Agder. He went to Iceland with Geirmund Hell-Skin, took possession of the islands west of Bjarn Isle Bay and made his home on Flat Isle. He married the daughter of Gils Ship-Nose and their son was Hergils Knob-Buttocks, who lived on Hergils Isle. Hergils had a daughter called Thorkatla, who married Mar of Reykjahills. Hergils married Thorarna, daughter of Ketil Broad-Sole, and their son was Ingjald who lived on Hergils Isle and supported Gisli Sursson. Because Ingjald had given this aid, Bork the Stout took the islands from him. After that Ingjald bought Hlid in Thorskafjord. His son was Thorarin who married Thorgerd, the daughter of Glum Geirason, and their son was Helgu-Steinar. Thorarin was with Kjartan in Svinadale, when he was killed.

At the time Odd the Showy and his son Thorir came to Iceland, Thrand Slender-Leg was living on Flat Isle. They took possession of land in Thorskafjord. Odd made his home at Skogar, and Thorir went abroad on viking expeditions, picking up plenty of gold in Lappland. With him were the sons of Hall of Hofstead. When they came back to Iceland, Hall insisted the gold was his, and so a great quarrel began; that's how the events in *Thorskfirdinga Saga* came about. Gold-Thorir lived at Thorisstead and married Ingibjorg, daughter of Gils Ship-Nose; their son was called Gudmund. Thorir was the most outstanding of men.

115. *Geirmund's land-claim*

Geirmund went west to the Strands and took possession of land from Rytagnup west as far as Horn and all the way east to Straumness. He started four farms there: one, at Adalvik, was run by his steward, another at Kjaransvik by his slave Kjaran, and a third, in Western

Commons, by his slave Bjorn. This Bjorn was found guilty of sheep-stealing after Geirmund died, and what is now common land was a portion of his fine. The fourth farm at Bardvik, was in charge of his slave Atli, who had fourteen slaves under him. Whenever Geirmund travelled between his estates, he used to have eighty men with him. He had a great deal of money, and plenty of livestock. People say his pigs used to roam on Svinaness and his sheep on Hjardarness,[45] and he had a shieling in Bitra. It's also said he had a farm in Steingrimsfjord, at Geirmundarstead in Selriverdale.

According to learned men, he was the noblest born of all the original settlers of Iceland. He was getting on in years when he emigrated, and didn't quarrel much with anyone after he came to Iceland. He and Kjallak quarrelled over the land between Klofningar and Fabeins River, and they fought at the cornfield north of Klofningar where they both wanted to grow corn. Geirmund had the better of it. Bjorn the Easterner and Vestar of Eyr reconciled them. Vestar landed at Vestarsness on his way to the peace meeting. Geirmund hid a lot of his money in Andar Bog below Skard. He married Herrid, daughter of Gaut Gautreksson, and their daughter was Yr. Later he married Thorkatla, the daughter of Ofeig Thorolfsson, and one of their children was Geirrid. Geirmund died at Geirmundarstead, and was given a ship burial in the wood north of the farm.

116. *Steinolf the Short*

Steinolf the Short, son of the chieftain Hrolf of Agder, took possession of land from Klofastones east to Grjotvallarmull, and lived at Steinolfshjalli in Fagradale. He climbed the mountain above and saw on the other side a broad valley, with trees growing everywhere. He saw there was a clearing in the valley, and that's where he built a farm. He called it Saurby,[46] because it was very boggy, and he gave the same name to the whole valley. Nowadays the place where he built his farm is called Torfness. Steinolf married Eirny Thidrandi's-daughter. Their son was Thorstein the Farmer, and their daughter Arndis the Wealthy, mother of Thord, father of Thorgerd, who married Odd, and their son was Hrafn Limerick-Farer, who married Vigdis, daughter of Thorarin Foal-Brow; their son was Snort, father of Jodis, wife of Eyjolf Hallbjarnarson, and their daughter was Halla, wife of Atli Tannason, whose daughter was Yngvild, wife of Snorri Hunbogason.[47]

---

[45]Literally 'Herd Headland'.
[46]Literally 'Mud Farm'.
[47]Snorri Hunbogason was Lawspeaker of the Althing 1166-70.

Steinolf lost three pigs which were found two years later in Svinadale, by which time there were thirty of them. Steinolf also took possession of Steinolfsdale in Kroksfjord.

117. *Strife-Bjorn*

There was a man called Strife-Bjorn, who married Thurid, daughter of Steinolf the Short. With Steinolf's approval he took possession of the western valley in Saurby and lived at Strifebjarnarstead above Thverfell. His son was Thjodrek, who married Arngerd, daughter of Thorbjorn Shield-Bjarnarson; their sons were Killer-Sturla who built the farm at Stadarhill, Knott, Thorgeir's father, Thorbjorn and Thjodrek, after whom the hill on Kollafjardar Moor takes its name. Thjodrek Strife-Bjarnarson thought it too crowded in Saurby, so he moved house to Isafjord. That's where the events of the *Saga of Thorbjorn and Havard the Lame* took place.

118. *Olaf Belg*

Olaf Belg, whom Orm the Slender drove away from Olafsvik, took possession of Belgsdale and lived at Belgsstead, until Thjodrek and his men drove him out. Afterwards he took possession of land east of Grjotarvallarmull, and lived at Olafsdale. His son was Thorvald, the one who handed over to Ogmund Volu-Steinsson a court action about stolen sheep, against Thorarin Gjallandi, and that's why Thorarin killed Ogmund at the Thorsness Assembly.

119. *Gils Ship-Nose*

Gils Ship-Nose took possession of Gilsfjord, between Olafsdale and Kroksfjardarmull, and lived at Kleifar. His son was Hedin, the father of Halldor Garpsdale-Priest, father of Thorvald of Garpsdale who married Gudrun Osvif's-daughter.

120. *Thorarin Hook*

Thorarin Hook took possession of Kroksfjord between Hafrafell and Kroksfjardarness. He quarrelled with Steinolf the Short over Steinolfsdale and set out after him in a boat with nine men when Steinolf was coming back from his shieling with only six. They started fighting on the sandspit near Fagradale Estuary, and then some men came from the farm to help Steinthor. Thorarin was killed there along with three of his men, but seven of Steinolf's, and their graves are still there.

121. *Ketil Broad-Sole*

Ketil Broad-Sole, son of Thorbjorn Talkni, took possession of Berufjord.

His daughter Thorarna married Hergils Knob-Buttocks, son of Thrand Slender-Leg, and their son was Ingjald, father of Thorarin who married Thorgerd, daughter of Glum Geirason. Their son in turn was Helgu-Steinar. Thrand Slender-Leg married the daughter of Gils Ship-Nose, and their daughter was Thorarna who married Hrolf, Helgi the Lean's son. Thorbjorg Ship-Breast was another daughter of Gils Ship-Nose. He also had a son called Herfinn, who lived at Kroksfjord.

122. *Ulf the Squint-Eyed*

Ulf the Squint-Eyed, son of Hogni the White, took possession of all the land between Thorskafjord and Hafrafell. He married Bjorg, daughter of Eyvind the Easterner and sister of Helgi the Lean. Their son was Atli the Red, who married Thorbjorg, sister of Steinolf the Short. Their son was Mar of Reykjahills who married Thorkatla, daughter of Hergils Knob-Buttocks. Their son was Ari who drifted to White Men's Land, which some people call Greater Ireland. It lies in the ocean to westward, near Vinland the Good, said to be a six day sail west from Ireland. Ari couldn't get away, and was baptized there. This story was first told by Hrafn Limerick-Farer who spent a long time at Limerick in Ireland. Thorkel Gellisson quoted some Icelanders who had heard Earl Thorfinn of Orkney say that Ari had been recognized in White Men's Land, and couldn't get away from there, but was thought very highly of.[48] Ari married Thorgerd, daughter of Alf of the Dales, and their sons were Thorgils, Gudleif, and Illugi. This is the Reykjaness line.

Ulf the Squint-Eyed had a son called Jorund, who married Thorbjorg Ship-Breast. Their daughter was Thjodhild who married Eirik the Red, and their son was Leif the Lucky of Greenland. Atli the Red had a son called Jorund, who married Thordis the daughter of Thorgeir the Boiler, and their daughter was Otkatla who married Thorgils Kollsson. Jorund had another son called Snorri.

123. *Hallstein Thorolfsson*

Hallstein, son of Thorolf Mostur-Beard, took possession of Thorska-

---

[48]In Ch. 12 of Eirik's Saga (see *The Vinland Sagas*, tr. M. Magnusson and H. Pálsson, Penguin Classics 1965, p. 103) a similar reference is made. The name *Hvítramannaland* (White Men's Land) seems to reflect Medieval European ideas of geography. An 'Albania-Land' i.e. Land of White Men, is mentioned in Latin sources. There may be a connection with the *Tir na BhFear BhFionn* (Land of the White Men) of Irish Legend, particularly in view of the reference to 'Greater Ireland'. The story about Ari is reminiscent of the one told in *Eyrbyggja Saga* of Bjorn the Breidavik-Champion, (see Ch. 64). It should be noted that Thorkel Gellison was the uncle of Ari Thorgilsson the Learned, who may have heard this story from him directly.

fjord, and lived at Hallsteinsness. He held sacrifices so that Thor would send him high-seat pillars. Then a tree was washed ashore on his land, sixty three ells long and two fathoms thick, and this was used for making high-seat pillars for almost every farm there in the fjords. The place where the tree came ashore is now called Greni-treesness. Hallstein had raided in Scotland and taken some slaves there captive. He sent them out to Svefn Isles to make salt. They were kept as slaves there.[49]

Hallstein married Osk, daughter of Thorstein the Red, and their son was Thorstein Surt who discovered the principle of the intercalary week.[50] Thorstein Surt married and he and his wife had a son called Thorarin, and two daughters, one called Thordis, who married Thorkel Fringe, and another called Osk, who married Stein the Fast-Sailing, and whose son was Thorstein the White. Thorstein Surt had an illegitimate son called Sam. He quarrelled over Thorstein's inheritance with Thorkel Fringe, who sided with Thorarin's children.

124. *Thorbjorn Loki*

There was a man called Thorbjorn Loki, son of Bodmod of Skut. He went to Iceland and took possession of Djupafjord and Groness as far as Gufufjord. His son was Thorgils of Thorgilsstead in Djupafjord, the father of Koll who married Thurid, daughter of Thorir, son of Earl Hallad, son of Earl Rognvald of More. They had a son called Thorgils who married Otkatla, daughter of Jorund, son of Atli the Red, and their son was Jorund who married Hallveig, daughter of Oddi, son of Yr and Ketil Gufa.

Snorri Jorundsson married Asny, daughter of Killer-Sturla, and their son was Gils who married Thordis, daughter of Gudlaug and of Thorkatla, daughter of Halldor, son of Snorri the Priest. Gils had a son called Thord who married Vigdis Sverting's-daughter, and their son was Hvamm-Sturla.

125. *Ketil Gufa*

There was a man called Ketil Gufa, son of Orlyg, son of Bodvar

---

[49]The meaning of the last sentence in the original is obscure.

[50]*Sumarauki.* "In early times, the Icelanders reckoned 364 days, or fifty-two weeks, in the year, and thus the year was a day and a quarter short. The year was divided into two seasons of equal length—summer and winter; and as time went by the Icelanders realised that the year was too short, as the calendar year no longer matched the solar year. At Thorstein Surt's suggestion, shortly after the middle of the tenth century, an intercalary week was added to the summer season every seventh year". See *Laxdœla Saga*, tr. M. Magnusson and H. Pálsson, Penguin 1969, p. 55, footnote 1.

Vigsterksson. Orlyg married Signy Oblaud's-daughter, sister of Hogni the White. Their son Ketil came to Iceland late in the Settlement Period. He had been on viking expeditions in the British Isles and brought Irish slaves from there. One of them was called Thormod, the second Floki, the third Kori, the fourth Svart, and there were two called Skorri. Ketil made land at Rosmhvalaness, and stayed the first winter at Gufuskalar, but travelled over in spring to Ness and spent the following winter at Gufuness. Then the older of the two Skorris and Floki absconded with two women and a lot of money. They went into hiding in Skorradale at Skorraholt, and were all killed in Flokadale and Skorradale.

Ketil could get no farmland in the Nesses, so he travelled over to Borgarfjord and spent the third winter at Gufuskalar near Gufu River. Early in the spring he went west to Breidafjord looking for land. He came to Geirmundarstead and asked for, and got, the hand of Yr, Geirmund's daughter. Geirmund advised Ketil to go west for land, across the fjord.

While Ketil was away in the west, his slaves ran off and arrived one night at Lambastead. The farmer there was Thord, son of Thorgeir Lamb and Thordis Yngvar's-daughter, aunt of Egil Skalla-Grimsson. The slaves set fire to the house and burnt Thord and his entire household inside. Then they broke into a store-house, and took a lot of goods and money. They rounded up some horses, loaded them with packs, and headed for Alftaness. Later that morning, after they'd gone, Lambi the Strong, Thord's son, came home from the Assembly and set out after them. Then the neighbouring farmers joined him. As soon as the slaves saw this, they scattered in all directions. Kori was captured in Koraness, and the others swam out to sea. Svart was captured on Svart Skerry, Skorri on Skorra Isle off Myrar, and Thormod on Thormod's Skerry, a mile off the coast.

When Ketil came back, he travelled to the west of Myrar and spent the fourth winter at Gufuskalar in Snæfellsness. Afterwards he took possession of Gufufjord and Skalaness, as far as Kollafjord. Ketil and Yr had two sons; one was called Thorhall, father of Hallvor who married Bork, son of Thormod Thjostarsson, and the other Oddi, who married Thorlaug, daughter of Hrolf of Ballar River and Thurid, daughter of Valthjof Orlygsson of Esjuberg.

126. *Kolli Hroaldsson*
Kolli Hroaldsson took possession of Kollafjord and Kvigandafjord, but sold off his land to various settlers.

127. *Knjuk Thorolfsson*

Thorolf Sparrow who came to Iceland with Orlyg had a son called
Knjuk, whom they used to call Ness-Knjuk. He took possession of
all the headlands on Bardastrand from Kvigandafjord. One of Knjuk's
sons was Einar, father of Steinolf, father of Salgerd, mother of Bard
the Black, and he had a daughter called Thora. She married Thorvald,
son of Thord Vikingsson, and their son was Swamp-Knjuk, father of
Thorgaut, father of Steinolf, father of Halla, mother of Steinunn,
mother of Hrafn of Eyr. Knjuk married Eyja, daughter of Ingjald,
son of Helgi the Lean, and their son was Eyjolf, father of Thorgrim
Katla's son. This Katla had previously been married to Glum, and
their daughter was Thorbjorg Coal-Brow, to whom Thormod address-
ed his poems. Thorgrim had a son called Steingrim, father of Yngvild,
who married Ulfhedin of Vidimyri.

128. *Geirstein Kjalki*

Geirstein Kjalki took possession of Kjalkafjord and Hjardarness, with
Knjuk's approval. His son was Thorgils who married Thora, daughter
of Vestar of Eyr, and their son was Stein the Dane who married
Hallgerd, daughter of Ornolf, Armod the Red's son. Ornolf was married to a woman called Vigdis. Stein the Dane and Hallgerd had a
daughter called Vigdis who married Illugi Steinbjarnarson. Their
daughter Thorunn, was the mother of Thorgeir Long-Head.

129. *Geirleif*

Geirleif, son of Eirik, Hogni the White's son, took possession of Bard-
astrand, between Vatnsfjord and Berghlidar. He was the father of
Oddleif and Helgi Cormorant. Oddleif was the father of Gest the Wise,
Thorstein, and Æsa who married Thorgils Grimsson of Grimsness.
Their sons were Jorund of Midengi and Thorarin of Burfell. Gest was
married and his children were: Thord, Halla who married Snorri
Dale-Alfsson and whose son was Thorgils, and another daughter
Thorey, who married a man called Thorgils, and whose son was
Thorarin, father of Jodis, mother of Illugi, father of Birna, mother of
Illugi, Arnor and Eyvind. Helgi Cormorant was the father of Thor-
bjorg Katla, who married Thorstein Solmundarson, and their sons
were Ref of Brynjudale and Thord, father of Illugi, father of
Hrodny, who married Thorgrim the Scorcher. Helgi Cormorant had
another daughter called Thordis who married Thorstein Asbjarnarson
of Kirkby in the east, and their son was Surt, father of Sighvat the
Lawspeaker.[51] Geirleif married Jora Helgi's-daughter. Geirleif's third

---

[51]Sighvat was Lawspeaker of the Althing from 1076 to 1083.

son was Thorfinn who married Gudrun Asolf's-daughter, and their son was called Asmund who married Halkatla, daughter of Bjorn, son of Mar Asmundarson. They had a son called Hlenni who married Ægileif, daughter of Thorstein Krofluson, and their son in turn was Thorfinn, father of Thorgeir Long-Head. Thorstein Oddleifsson was the father of Isgerd who married Bolverk, Eyjolf the Grey's son, and their son was Gellir the Lawspeaker.[52] Thorstein had yet another daughter called Veny, mother of Thord Crow-Beak, from whom the Krakneflings are descended.

130. *Armod the Red*
Armod Thorbjarnarson the Red, Geirleif's blood-brother, took possession of Raudasand; he was the father of Ornolf and Thorbjorn, father of Hrolf of Raudasand.

131. *Thorolf Sparrow*
Thorolf Sparrow came to Iceland with Orlyg and took possession of Patreksfjord on the west side, including the creeks west of Bard, except for Kollsvik, where Orlyg's blood-brother Koll lived. Thorolf also took possession of Keflavik south of Bard, and made his home at Hvallatur. Ness-Knjuk, Ingolf the Strong and Geirthjof were the sons of Thorolf Sparrow. Ingolf had a daughter called Thorarna who married Thorstein Oddleifsson.

132. *Thorbjorn Talkni*
Thorbjorn Talkni and Thorbjorn Skuma, sons of Bodvar Bladder-Bald, came to Iceland with Orlyg and took possession of half of Patreksfjord and the whole of Talknafjord as far as Kopaness.

133. *Ketil Broad-Sole*
Ketil Broad-Sole, son of Thorbjorn Talkni, took possession of all the valleys between Kopaness and Dufansdale. He gave his daughter Thorarna in marriage to Hergils Knob-Buttocks, and then he moved house south to Breidafjord and took possession of Berufjord near Reykjaness.

134. *Orn*
There was a famous man called Orn, a kinsman of Geirmund Hell-Skin; the oppression of King Harald forced him to leave Rogaland, and he took possession of all the land that he wanted in Arnarfjord. He spent the winter at Tjaldaness because the sun could still be seen up there, even at winter solstice.

---

[52]Gellir was Lawspeaker of the Althing from 1054 to 1062.

135. *An Red-Cloak*

An Red-Cloak, son of Grim Hairy-Cheek of Hrafnista and Helga, An Bow-Bender's daughter, fell out with King Harald Fine-Hair. That's why he left Norway and set out on a viking expedition to the British Isles. He raided in Ireland and there he married Grelod, Earl Bjartmar's daughter. They went to Iceland and came to Arnarfjord a year later than Orn. An spent the first winter at Dufansdale, but Grelod thought there was a nasty smell coming up from the earth.

Orn got news of his kinsman Hamund Hell-Skin north in Eyjafjord, and wanted to move house there. So he sold An Red-Cloak all the lands between Langaness and Stapi. An made his home at Eyr, and there Grelod thought the grass smelt as sweet as honey. An had a freedman called Dufan, who stayed behind at Dufansdale.

An had a son called Bjartmar, father of the two Vegests, and of Helgi, father of Thurid Arnkatla who married Hergils. Their daughter was Thurid Arnkatla, wife of Helgi Eythjofsson. Bjartmar had another daughter called Thorhild who married Vestein Vegeirsson, and their children were Vestein and Aud. An had a freedman called Hjallkar, father of Bjorn, Bjartmar's slave. He gave Bjorn his freedom and soon Bjorn started making money. Vegest didn't like it and ran him through with a spear, but Bjorn struck him dead with a spade.

136. *Geirthjof*

Geirthjof Valthjofsson was yet another settler in Arnarfjord and he also took possession of Fossfjord, Reykjarfjord, Trostanfjord and Geirthjofsfjord. He made his home at Geirthjofsfjord and married Salgerd, daughter of Ulf the Squint-Eyed. Their son was Hogni who married Aud, daughter of Olaf Jafnakoll and Thora Gunnstein's-daughter, and their son Atli married Thurid, daughter of Thorleif, son of Eyvind Knee and Thurid Grunt-Sow. Thorleif married Gro, daughter of Thorolf Brækir. Atli was the father of Hoskuld, father of Atli, father of Bard the Black.

137. *Eirik*

There was a man called Eirik who took possession of Dyrafjord and Slettaness as far as Stapi and Outer Hals in Dyrafjord. He was the father of Thorkel, father of Thord, father of Thorkel, father of Steinolf, father of Thorleif, mother of Thorgerd, mother of Thora, mother of Gudmund Gris. Thorleif was the mother of Lina, mother of Cecily, mother of Bard and Thorgerd who married Bjorn the Englishman and their children were Abbot Arnis and Thora who married Amundi Thorgeirsson.

138. *Vestein and Thorbjorn Sur*

Vestein Vegeirsson, brother of Vebjorn the Sogn-Champion, took possession of land between the ridges in Dyrafjord, and lived at Haukadale. He married Thorhild Bjartmar's-daughter, and their children were Vestein and Aud.

Thorbjorn Sur came to Iceland after the country was fully settled, and Vestein granted him half of Haukadale. The sons of Thorbjorn Sur were Gisli, Thorkel and Ari, and his daughter was Thordis, who married Thorgrim. Their son was Snorri the Priest. Afterwards Thordis married Bork the Stout, and their daughter was Thurid who married, first, Thorbjorn the Stout, and later Thorodd the Tribute-Trader. Their son was Kjartan of Frod River.

139. *Dyri*

There was a famous man called Dyri who went from South-More to Iceland with the approval of Earl Rognvald and because of the oppression of King Harald Fine-Hair. Dyri took possession of Dyrafjord and lived at Halsar. His son was Hrafn of Ketilseyr, father of Thurid who married Vestein Vesteinsson, and their sons were Berg and Helgi.

140. *Thord Vikingsson*

There was a man called Thord, who was either the son of a man called Viking or of King Harald Fine-Hair. He went to Iceland and took possession of land between Thufa in Hjallaness and Jardfallsgill, and made his home at Alvidra. Thord married Thjodhild, daughter of Eyvind the Easterner and sister of Helgi the Lean, and their son was Thorkel Alvidra-Champion the Wealthy. Thorkel married, and his sons by his wife were Thord and Eyjolf, father of Gisli who married Hallgerd, daughter of Vermund the Slender. Their son was Brand, father of Priest Gudmund of Hjardarholt, and their daughter was Thora. Thora married Brand Thorhaddsson, and their daughter in turn was Steinvor, mother of Rannveig, mother of Sæhild who married Gizur.[53] Eyjolf had another son called Helgi, and his children were Olaf and Gudleif who married Fjarska-Finn. Thord Vikingsson had another son called Thorvald the White who married Thora, daughter of Ness-Knjuk, and their son was Swamp-Knjuk, father of Thorgaut, father of Steinolf who married Herdis Tind's-daughter. Their children were Thorkel of Myrar, and Halla who married Thord Oddleifsson. Thorvald the White had another son called Thord the Left-Handed who married Asdis, daughter of Thorgrim Hardrefsson. Asdis' mother

---

[53]Gizur Hallsson was Lawspeaker of the Althing 1181-1202.

was Rannveig, daughter of Earl Grjotgard of Lade. Asdis was the
mother of Ulf the Marshal, and sister of Ljot the Wise and of Halldis
who married Thorbjorn Thjodreksson. Thord the Left-Handed and
his wife had a daughter called Otkatla who married Sturla Thjodreksson, and their son was Thord who married Hallbera, daughter of
Snorri the Priest, whose daughter Thurid married Haflidi Masson.
Thord Sturluson had a son called Snorri who married Oddbjorg,
daughter of Grim Lodmundarson, and their children were Fly-Grim
and Hallbera who married Mag-Snorri. Sturla had six daughters. One
called Asny married Snorri Jorundsson, and their daughter was Thordis, mother of Hoskuld the Physician. Snorri and Asny had a son
called Gils, father of Thord, father of Hvamm-Sturla.

141. *Ingjald*

Ingjald Brunason took possession of Ingjaldssand between Hjallasand
and Ofæra. He was the father of Hardref, father of Thorgrim, father
of Ljot the Wise and others, as has already been written.

142. *Ljot the Wise*

Ljot the Wise lived at Ingjaldssand. He was the son of Thorgrim
Hardrefsson and his mother was Rannveig, Earl Grjotgard's daughter.
Ljot had a son called Thorgrim Gagar. One of Ljot's sisters, Halldis,
was married to Thorbjorn Thjodreksson, and another sister of his,
Asdis, was abducted by Ospak Osvifsson. For this offence Ljot had
Ospak sentenced to outlawry. They had a son called Ulf, and Ljot
brought him up.

Grim Kogur lived at Brekka, and his sons were Sigurd and Thorkel,
small puny men.

Ljot had a fosterson called Thorarin. Ljot bought meat from Grim
to the value of twenty hundreds and paid for it with the stream that
flowed between their farms. It was called Osomi, and Grim used it
to irrigate his meadows and dug a ditch through Ljot's land. Ljot
took Grim to court over this and it caused friction between them.
Ljot took in a Norwegian who had landed at Vadil, and this man fell
in love with Asdis.

Gest Oddleifsson attended an autumn feast at Ljot's. When Egil
Volu-Steinsson came there and asked Gest to advise him how his
father could get over the grief he suffered because of the death of his
son Ogmund, Gest composed the beginning of *Ogmund's Lay*. Ljot
asked Gest what sort of man Thorgrim Gagar would turn out to be.
Gest replied that Ljot's fosterson Thorarin would be the more famous
of the two, and told Thorarin to be on his guard and not to let his

smooth tongue get twisted round his neck. Ljot took offence, but asked again next morning what the future held for Thorgrim. Gest said that his nephew Ulf would be the more famous of the two. Then Ljot got angry, but still he went to see Gest off, and asked "How will my death come about?"

Gest said he couldn't see Ljot's future, and advised him to be kind to his neighbours.

Ljot asked, "Will the earth-lice, the sons of Grim Kogur cause my death?"

"A hungry louse can give a nasty bite," said Gest.

"Where will that happen?" said Ljot.

"Not far from here," said Gest.

A Norwegian rode with Gest up to the moor, and steadied Gest in the saddle when his horse stumbled. Then Gest said. "This is a sign of luck for you, and you'll soon be lucky again. But take good care your luck doesn't go bad on you."

On his way back home the Norwegian found some silver buried in the ground and took twenty coins from it, assuming he'd find the treasure again. But when he went to look for it he couldn't find it. Ljot caught him when he was digging for it and forced the Norwegian to pay him three hundreds for each coin he'd taken.

That autumn Thorbjorn Thjodreksson was killed. One spring day Ljot was sitting on a certain hill keeping an eye on his slaves. He was wearing a coat with the hood tied round the neck and with a single sleeve. The sons of Grim Kogur came running up the hill and struck him both at the same time. Then Thorkel pulled the hood up over his head. Ljot told them to act like good neighbours, and then they tumbled down to the same path where Gest had once ridden. That's where Ljot died. The Grimssons went to see Havard the Lame. Eyjolf the Grey and his son Steingrim supported them all.

143. *Onund*

Onund Vikingsson, brother of Thord of Alvidra, took possession of the whole of Onundarfjord and lived at Eyr.

144. *Hallvard Sugandi*

Hallvard Sugandi took part in the Battle of Hafursfjord against King Harald, and that was why he went to Iceland. He took possession of Sugandafjord and Skalavik as far as Stigi, and made his home there.

145. *Thurid*

Thurid the Sound-Filler and her son Volu-Stein went from Halogaland to Iceland and took possession of Bolungarvik. They made their home at Vatnsness. The reason why she was called the Sound-Filler was that during a famine in Halogaland she filled every sound with fish by means of witchcraft. She also marked out the Kviar fishing ground in Isafjord Bay, and took a hornless ewe in return from every farmer in Isafjord. Volu-Stein had two sons called Ogmund and Egil.

146. *Helgi Hrolfsson*

Hrolf of Gnupufell had a son called Helgi, who was born in the east and was an Uplander on his mother's side. Helgi went to Iceland to visit his kinsmen. He made landfall in Eyjafjord, which by that time was completely settled. Then he wanted to go back to Norway, but was driven off course and got to Sugandafjord. He stayed the winter with Hallvard, and in the spring he set out to look for a place to farm. He came upon a certain fjord and found a harpoon on the shore. He called the place Skutilsfjord[54] and lived there for the rest of his life. He had a son called Thorstein Ill-Luck, who went abroad and killed one of the retainers of Earl Hakon Grjotgardsson, and so the Earl's counsellor, Eyvind, sent Thorstein to Vebjorn Sygnatrausti for protection. He took him in, though his sister Vedis warned against it. That's why Vebjorn sold his possessions and went to Iceland. He didn't feel safe with Thorstein on his hands.

147. *Thorolf*

Thorolf Brækir took possession of parts of Skutilsfjord and Skalavik, and made his home there.

148. *Eyvind Knee*

Eyvind Knee and his wife Thurid Grunt-Sow went from Agder to Iceland. They took possession of Alftafjord and Seydisfjord and made their home there. Their sons were Thorleif, who's been mentioned already, and Valbrand, father of Hallgrim, Gunnar and Bjargey. Bjargey married Havard the Lame and their son was Olaf.

149. *Vegeir*

There was a famous man in Sogn called Geir, and he became known as Vegeir, because he was a great sacrificer.[55] He had a large number of children. Vebjorn the Sogn-Champion was his eldest son, and after him came Vestein, Vethorm, Vemund, Vegest, and Vethorn; his

---

[54]Literally "Harpoon-fjord".
[55]The word *vé* means a sacred place, such as a sanctuary or a temple.

daughter was called Vedis. After Vegeir died, Vebjorn fell out with Earl Hakon as has been mentioned already, and that's why the brothers and their sister went to Iceland. They had a long and difficult voyage, and made land in the autumn at Hloduvik, west of Horn. Then Vebjorn held a great sacrifice, but said that Earl Hakon, too, was holding sacrifices that same day, to bring them bad luck. All the while he was at the sacrifice, his brothers kept urging him to come away, so he abandoned it and they put out to sea again. That day they wrecked their ship in foul weather under a certain high cliff. They just managed to scramble up the cliff, with Vebjorn in the lead. Now it's called Sygnacliff.[56] Atli of Fljot, Geirmund Hell-Skin's slave, took them all in for the winter, and when Geirmund learned what Atli had done, he gave him his freedom and the farm he was in charge of as well, and Atli became a man of some importance.

In the spring Vebjorn took possession of land between Skotufjord and Hestfjord, as much as he could walk across in a day, and in addition a plot he called Folafot. Vebjorn was a great fighter, and there's a long saga about him. He gave his sister Vedis in marriage to Grimolf of Unadsdale. The brothers-in-law fell out, and Vebjorn killed Grimolf near Grimolfswater. Because of this, Vebjorn was killed at the Quarter Court at Thorsness, and three other men with him.

150. *Gunnstein and Halldor*

Gunnstein and Halldor were the sons of Gunnbjorn, Ulf Crow's son, who discovered the Gunnbjarnar Skerries. They took possession of Skotufjord, Laugardale, and Ogurvik as far as Mjovafjord. Halldor had a son called Bersi, father of Thormod the Coal-Brow-Poet. Afterwards Laugardale was farmed by Thorbjorn Thjodreksson, who killed Olaf son of Havard the Lame, and Bjargey, Valbrand's-daughter. That brought about the killing of Thorbjorn and the events related in the *Saga of the Isfirdings*.

151. *Snæbjorn*

Snæbjorn, son of Eyvind the Easterner and brother of Helgi the Lean, took possession of land between Mjovafjord and Langadale River, and lived at Vatnsfjord. He was the father of Holmstein, father of Snæbjorn Galti. Snæbjorn's mother was Kjalvor, so that he and Tongue-Odd were cousins on their mothers' side. Snæbjorn was brought up by Thorodd of Thingness.

---

[56]Literally 'Sogn-people's Cliff'.

152. *Hallbjorn*

Hallbjorn, son of Odd of Kidjaberg, son of Hallkel who was the brother of Ketilbjorn the Old, married Hallgerd, (Tongue-Odd's-daughter). They stayed the first winter with Odd, and Snæbjorn was also there at the time. There was no love lost between husband and wife. In the spring at Removal Days[57] Hallbjorn got ready to leave, and while he was making his preparations, Odd set out from home over to the baths at Reykholt, where his sheep sheds were. He didn't want to be around when Hallbjorn left because he was afraid that Hallgerd wouldn't go with him. Odd had always tried to put things right between husband and wife.

When Hallbjorn had saddled their horses, he came back into Hallgerd's room where she was sitting on the dais, combing herself. Her hair flowed round her body right down to the floor; she had the finest hair of all the women in Iceland, apart from Hallgerd Twist-Breeks. Hallbjorn told her to get up and come along, but she sat still and didn't say a word. Then he gave her a pull, but didn't budge her. This happened three times. Hallbjorn stood in front of her and said:

> The linen-clad lady
> loves making a fool of me
> this is what turns
> my face away from her.
> Saddened forever
> by the sorrow she's caused me;
> grief makes me pale,
> pain grips the heart's root.

Then he twisted her hair round his hand and tried to pull her off the dais, but she sat still and didn't budge. He drew his sword, sliced off her head and then went out and rode away. There were three of them together, with two pack-horses.

There were few men at home at the time, and right away they sent someone to tell Odd. Snæbjorn was at Kjalvararstead, and Odd sent someone to ask him to take over the pursuit, adding that on no account would he go himself.

Snæbjorn set out at once with eleven companions. When Hallbjorn and his men saw the pursuers, the men asked him to ride off, but he wouldn't. Snæbjorn and his men caught up with them at the hills now called Hallbjarnar Cairns. Hallbjorn and his men went up the

---

[57]'Removal Days' was a legal term for the period of four days, late in May, during which farms could change hands.

hill and took their stand. Three of Snæbjorn's men and both Hallbjorn's companions were killed there. Then Snæbjorn sliced through
Hallbjorn's leg at the ankle, and Hallbjorn fell back as far as the
southernmost hill and killed two of Snæbjorn's men there before he
was killed himself. That's why there are three cairns on that hill,
and five on the other. After that Snæbjorn went back home.

Snæbjorn owned a ship at Grimsriver Estuary, and Hrolf of Raudasand bought a half-share in it. Each of them had eleven men with
him. With Snæbjorn were Thorkel and Sumarlidi, the sons of Thorgeir
the Red, son of Einar of Stafaholt. Snæbjorn took on Thorodd of
Thinganess, his fosterfather, and Thorodd's wife, and Hrolf took on
Styrbjorn, the one who made this verse after a dream he'd had:

> I can see death
> in a dread place,
> yours and mine,
> north-west in the waves,
> with frost and cold,
> and countless wonders;
> that's why Snæbjorn, I see,
> will lose his life.

They set out to search for the Gunnbjarnar Skerries, and reached
land. Snæbjorn wouldn't let them explore it during the night. Styrbjorn
left the ship, found money in a grave and hid it. Snæbjorn struck
him with an axe, and then the purse fell to the ground. After they
built themselves a house, it was snowed under. Thorkel, Thorgeir
the Red's son, noticed there was a drop of water on a fork sticking
out through the skylight; this was about late winter.[58] Then they
dug themselves out. Snæbjorn started repairing the ship, putting
Thorodd and his wife in charge of the house. Hrolf left Styrbjorn
and others to look after his share. The rest of the men were out
hunting. Styrbjorn killed Thorodd, and then Hrolf and Styrbjorn
killed Snæbjorn. To save their lives the sons of Thorgeir the Red
swore oaths of loyalty, and then everyone else did the same. They
sailed to Halogaland, and from there to Iceland, putting in at Vadil.
Thorkel Fringe guessed what had happened to the sons of Thorgeir
the Red. Hrolf built a stronghold on Strandar Moor, and Thorkel
Fringe sent Sveinung to kill him. First he went over to see Hermund
of Myri, then Olaf of Drangar, and finally Gest of Hagi who sent
him to his friend Hrolf. Sveinung killed Hrolf and Styrbjorn, and

---

[58]*Góa*: This was the name of one of the months in the Icelandic calendar, from
about mid-February to mid-March.

after that he went back to Hagi. Gest exchanged a sword for an axe with him, gave him two saddled horses and sent someone riding with him through Vadil and over to Kollafjord. He sent Thorbjorn the Strong for the horses, and Thorbjorn killed Sveinung at Svein-ungseyr, for the sword broke off at the hilt. When people were compar-ing the intelligence of Thorkel Fringe and Gest, Thorkel boasted to Gest that he'd tricked Gest into sending someone to kill his own friends.

153. *Olaf Jafnakoll*

Olaf Jafnakoll took possession of land between Langadale and Sandeyrar Rivers, and lived at Unadsdale. He married Thora Gunn-stein's-daughter, and their son was Grimolf who married Vedis, Vebjorn's sister.

154. *Thorolf Hard-Grip*

There was a man called Thorolf Hard-Grip who lived in Sogn. He fell out with Earl Hakon Grjotgardsson and went to Iceland with King Harald's approval. He took possession of land between Sandeyrar River and Gygjarspors River in Hrafnsfjord, and lived at Snæfells. He was the father of Ofeig who married Otkatla.

155. *Orlyg*

Orlyg, son of Bodvar Vigsterksson, went to Iceland because of the oppression of King Harald Fine-Hair. He stayed the first winter with Geirmund Hell-Skin, and in the spring Geirmund granted him farm-land in Adalvik, together with all the lands belonging to it. Orlyg married Signy Oblaud's-daughter, sister of Hogni the White, and their son was Ketil Gufa who married Yr Geirmund's-daughter.

The land-claim of Geirmund starts at this point and extends to Straumsness east of Horn, as was written earlier. Orlyg got possession of Sletta and the Jokulsfjords.

156. *Hella-Bjorn*

Hella-Bjorn, son of Herfinn and Halla, was a great viking and a constant enemy of King Harald Fine-Hair. He went to Iceland and put in at Bjarnarfjord in a ship lined with shields. Afterwards he was called Shield-Bjorn. He took possession of land between Straumsness and Drangar, and made his home at Skaldabjarnarvik but had another farm at Bjarnarness where the extensive ruins of his hall can still be seen. He was the father of Thorbjorn, father of Arngerd who married Thjodrek Sleitu-Bjorn's son, and their sons were Thorbjorn, Sturla and Thjodrek.

157. *Geirolf*

There was a man called Geirolf who wrecked his ship at Geirolfsgnup. Afterwards with the approval of Bjorn he made his home below the mountain.

158. *Thorvald*

Thorvald, son of Asvald, son óf Ulf, son of Oxen-Thorir, took possession of Drangar and Drangavik as far as Enginess, and farmed at Drangar for the rest of his life. He was the father of Eirik the Red, who colonized Greenland as was written earlier.

159. *Eyvind and his brothers*

There was a famous man called Herrod White-Cloud. King Harald had him put to death, but his three sons went to Iceland and took possession of land in the Strands: Eyvind settled at Eyvindarfjord, Ofeig at Ofeigsfjord, and Ingolf at Ingolfsfjord. They farmed at these places for the rest of their lives.

160. *Eirik Snare*

There was a man called Eirik Snare, who took possession of land between Ingolfsfjord and Veidilaus, and lived at Trekyllisvik. He married Alof, daughter of Ingolf of Ingolfsfjord, and their son was Flosi. Flosi was living at Vik when some Norwegians were shipwrecked there and built a new ship from the wreckage which they called the Tree-Tub. Flosi sailed out on this ship, but was driven back into Oxarfjord, and what happened afterwards is told in the *Saga of Bodmod Gerpir and Grimolf*.

161. *Onund Tree-Foot*

Onund Tree-Foot, son of Ofeig Club-Foot, son of Ivar Prick, fought against King Harald at Hafursfjord and lost his leg there. Afterwards he went to Iceland and took possession of land from Kleifar to Ofæra, including Kaldbaksvik, Kolbeinsvik and Byrgisvik. He lived to a ripe old age at Kaldbak. He was the brother of Gudbjorg, mother of Gudbrand Globe, father of Asta, mother of King Olaf.[59] Onund had four sons; one was called Grettir, the second Thorgeir Flask-Back, and the third Asgeir the Hasty, father of Kalf, father of Hrefna who married Kjartan, and of Thurid who first married Thorkel Kuggi and later Steinthor Olafsson; Onund's fourth son was Thorgrim Hoary-Head, father of Asmund, father of Grettir the Strong.

---

[59]King Olaf the Saint, ruler of Norway 1016-1030.

162. *Bjorn*

There was a man called Bjorn who took possession of Bjarnarfjord.
He married a woman called Ljufa, and their son was Svan of Svanshill.

163. *Steingrim*

Steingrim took possession of the whole of Steingrimsfjord, and lived
at Trollatongue. He was the father of Thorir, father of Halldor,
father of Thorvald the Aur-Priest, father of Bitru-Oddi, father of
Steindor, father of Odd, father of Snorri the Tall, father of Odd the
Monk,[60] Thorolf, and Thorarin Rosti.

164. *Kolli*

There was a man called Kolli, who took possession of Kollafjord, and
lived at Fell for the rest of his life.

165. *Thorbjorn Bitra*

There was a man called Thorbjorn Bitra, a viking and a criminal.
He went to Iceland with his family, took possession of the fjord now
known as Bitrufjord and made his home there. A little later Gudlaug,
the brother of Gils Ship-Nose, wrecked his ship there, on the headland
now called Gudlaugshofdi. Gudlaug managed to get ashore with his
wife and daughter, but the rest of the crew were drowned. Then
Thorbjorn Bitra came and killed the husband and wife but took the
girl and brought her up. When Gils Ship-Nose heard about this, he
set out to avenge his brother, killing Thorbjorn Bitra and other men
besides. Gudlaugsvik takes its name from Gudlaug.

166. *Balki*

There was a man called Balki, the son of Blæng Sotason of Sotaness.
He fought against King Harald at Hafursfjord. After that he went
to Iceland and took possession of the whole of Hrutafjord. He farmed
at the two Balkasteads, and eventually at Bær where he died. He was
the father of Bersi the Godless, who first farmed at Bersastead in
Hrutafjord and later he took possession of Langavatnsdale where he
had another farm until he married Thordis, daughter of Thorhadd of
Hitardale, and got Holmsland as her dowry. Their son was Arngeir,
father of Bjorn the Hitardale-Champion. Balki had a daughter called
Geirbjorg, mother of Veleif the Old.

---

[60]Odd Snorrason was a monk in the Benedictine Monastery at Thingeyrar in the
late 12th century. He wrote (in Latin) a biography of King Olaf Tryggvason. The
Latin original is lost but the work survives in two Icelandic versions.

167. *Arndis the Wealthy*

Afterwards, Arndis the Wealthy, daughter of Steinolf the Short, took possession of land in Hrutafjord, north of Bordeyr and made her home at Bær. She was the mother of Thord, who first lived at Muli in Saurby.

168. *Throst and Grenjad*

Throst and Grenjad, the sons of Hermund the Bent, took possession of land in Hrutafjord, south of Bordeyr, and farmed at Melar. The Priest Horse-Gellir is descended from Grenjad, and Orm from Throst. Throst had a son called Thorkel of Kerseyr, father of Gudrun who married Thorbjorn Thyna, son of Hromund the Lame; they lived at Fagrabrekka, and their son was Thorleif, who was brought up by Hromund. Hromund had another son called Hastein; all these men worked closely together. Thorkel Throst's son had a son called Thorir who lived at Melar. He had a daughter called Helga.

Then Strife-Helgi came to Iceland with his brother Jorund and put in at Bordeyr. There were twelve vikings altogether as well as servants. They went to Melar, and Helgi married Helga Thorir's-daughter. Some of Hromund's horses went missing, and Helgi got the blame for their disappearance. Midfjord-Skeggi summoned them to the Althing on a charge of theft. Hromund and his men were left in charge of the district and built a strong fortification at Brekka. The Norwegians started getting their ship ready.

One morning a raven came to the skylight at Brekka and gave a loud scream. Then Hromund said:

> I hear the blue-feathered
> carrion-bird calling
> at daybreak, roused
> and ravening for prey.
> That's the cry it would raise
> when other ravens
> were making their prophecy
> of doom for men."

Thorbjorn said:

> The hail-beaten
> bird of carrion
> comes exulting,
> eager for blood.
> That's how the ravens cried,

> cawing from an ancient tree
> when their desire
> was for a blood-draught."

At that moment the Norwegians broke into the stronghold, because the farmhands had failed to close it properly. The brothers went outside, but the women said Hromund was too old and Thorleif too young to go; he was only fifteen.

Then Hromund said:

> I'm not doomed to die
> today or yesterday,
> I'm getting ready
> to go to war.
> The soldiers don't worry me,
> waving their red shields,
> long ago our destiny
> was decided."

Six of the Norwegians were killed in the stronghold, and the remaining six fled. When Thorbjorn was trying to shut the stronghold, he was pierced by a flying halberd. Thorbjorn pulled the halberd out of the wound and drove it straight through Jorund between the shoulder blades. Helgi lifted him on to his back and ran off with him. Hromund had fallen, and Thorleif was sorely wounded. Hastein kept chasing after them until Helgi threw down Jorund's body, then he went back. The women asked what had happened.

Hastein said:

> Six sword-wielding
> warriors lie dead,
> unmourned, on the pavement,
> put down by sword-strokes.
> Half those lawbreakers
> must be lying back there,
> I gave the runaways
> some racking sword-wounds."

The women asked how many there were. Hamund said:

> Few supporters
> I had at the sword-play;
> Just us four kinsmen,
> accused of aggression,

against the twelve fearless
fighters from ship-board,
keen to come against us,
dye their cold blades crimson."

The women asked how many of the vikings had fallen. Hastein said:

Seven fighters have stuck
their faces in the soil,
warm blood falls
like dew on the battlefield:
not so many
mariners will sail
the ship back home
across the sea.

Here you can see
all the signs
of a weary day,
the work of us four.
Little the peace
we proffered the truce-breakers,
from the dead the raven
ripped his food.

We soaked the rogues'
shirts in red blood,
my sword is fighting-sharp,
fierce work the slaughter.
Soldiers bore swords
behind their shields;
ravens gratified
their ravening greed.

Loud din of sharp attack,
showering stones,
armour split in the fray,
till men fell back for rest.
Stones and spears
were striking the shield,
more deaths their side
suffered than did ours.

Hear the ravens
where wounded heroes fell,

cawing over the dead,
drinking the blood:
and a draught for the eagle too,
clawing at the corpses,
where Strife-Helgi the outlaw's
head wore the blood-cap.

Battle-keen heroes
had on their helmets
as they set out to meet us
from the splendid ship:
but the gods hated
these hard sailors,
bloodstained the hair they wore
when they went.

Helgi and his men put out the same day, and all were drowned at Helga Skerry off Skridinsenni. Thorleif's wounds healed, and he made his home at Brekka. Hastein went abroad and was killed aboard the Long Serpent.[61]

169. *The West Quarter: Conclusion*

So now we've written about most of the settlements in the West Quarter, according to the accounts of learned men. As you can see, there've been a good many important people living in that Quarter, and a good many distinguished families have come from them, as you've already heard.

170. *The Great Settlers*

These were the leading settlers of the West Quarter: Hrosskel, Skalla-Grim, Sel-Thorir, Bjorn the Easterner, Thorolf Mostur-Beard, Aud the Deep-Minded, Geirmund Hell-Skin, Ulf the Squint-Eyed and Thord Vikingsson. Even so, there were still nobler forbears in some other family-lines.

When the farmers of Iceland were counted, there were about 1080 of them in this Quarter.[62]

---

[61]The Long Serpent was the famous ship of King Olaf Tryggvason, in which he lost his life at the Battle of Svoldur in 1000 A.D.

[62]This refers to the list of taxpaying farmers drawn up towards the end of the 11th century in connection with the institution of the tithe system (1097 A.D.).

171. *The North Quarter*

Now we begin with the settlements in the North Quarter, the most
densely populated part of Iceland where the greatest sagas have been
set, both in earlier and in more recent times, as we are about to write
and as the facts show.

172. *Eystein Foul-Fart*

Eystein Foul-Fart, son of Alf of Osta, took possession of the eastern
side of Hrutafjord after Balki. He lived there for several years, before
he married Thorhild, daughter of Thorstein the Red, and then he
moved house west to the Dales and farmed there. Their sons were Alf
of the Dales, Thord, Thorolf Fox and Hrapp.

173. *Thorodd*

There was a man called Thorodd who took possession of land in
Hrutafjord and lived at Thoroddsstead. He was the father of Arnor
Hairy-Nose who married Gerd, daughter of Bodvar of Bodvarshills.
Their sons were Thorbjorn, whom Grettir killed, and Thorodd Poem-
Piece, father of Valgerd, who married Skeggi Short-Hand, son of
Gamli, son of Thord, son of Eyjolf, son of Eyjar, son of Thorolf
Hard-Grip of Snæfells. Skeggi Short-Hand had a son called Gamli,
father of Alfdis, mother of Odd the Monk.

174. *Skutad-Skeggi*

A famous man in Norway called Skutad-Skeggi had a son Bjorn,
nick-named Fur-Bjorn because he used to go trading to Novgorod.
When Bjorn got tired of trading voyages, he went to Iceland and took
possession of Midfjord and Linakradale. He was the father of Midfjord-Skeggi, a great fighting man and sea-going trader. He went to
plunder in the Baltic, and on his way back from the east he was
lying at anchor off Zealand in Denmark. He went ashore and broke
into Hrolf Kraki's burial mound, taking away King Hrolf's sword,
Skofnung, Hjalti's axe and a good many other treasures besides; but
he couldn't get the sword Laufi.

Skeggi lived at Reykir in Midfjord. He was married and he and
his wife had several children. One was Eid, who married Hafthora,
daughter of Thorberg Kornamuli and Alof Ship-Shield, sister of
Thorgeir Gollnir, and they had a number of children. Skeggi had
another son called Koll, father of Halldor, father of Thorkatla and
of Thordis who married Poet-Helgi. Skeggi's daughters were Hrodny
who married Thord Gellir, and Thorbjorg who married Asbjorn
Hardarson the Wealthy; their daughter was Ingibjorg who married

Illugi the Black, and their sons were Gunnlaug Adder-Tongue, Hermund and Ketil.

175. *Harald Ring*

There was a man of distinguished birth called Harald Ring, who brought his ship to Vesturhop and spent his first winter in Iceland near the place where he'd landed, now called Hringsstead. He took possession of the whole of Vatnsness, north of Ambattar River on the west side, and on the east as far south as Thver River and from there straight across over to Bjarga Estuary, all the land on that side of the cliffs right down to the sea. He lived at Holar. He was the father of Thorbrand, father of Asbrand, father of Solvi the Proud of Ægissida, and of Thorgeir who lived at Holar. Thorgeir had a daughter called Astrid, who married Arnmod Hedinsson, and their son was Hedin. Thorgeir had another daughter called Thorgerd who married Thorgrim, son of Petur of Os.

176. *Soti*

There was a man called Soti who took possession of Vesturhop and lived at Sotafell.

177. *Audun Shaft*

There was an Earl in England called Hunda-Steinar. He married Alof, Ragnar Hairy-Breek's daughter, and their children were Bjorn, father of Audun Shaft, Eirik, father of Sigurd Bjodaskalli, and Isgerd who married Earl Thorir of Vermaland.

Audun Shaft went to Iceland, took possession of Vididale and lived at Audunsstead. His comrade Thorgils Gjallandi, father of Thorarin the Priest, came to Iceland with him.

Audun Shaft was the father of Thora Moss-Neck, mother of Ulfhild, mother of Asta, mother of King Olaf the Holy. Audun had a son called Asgeir of Asgeirs River, who married Jorunn, daughter of Ingimund the Old. Their children were Thorvald, father of Dalla, mother of Bishop Gizur, and Audun, father of Asgeir, father of Audun, father of Egil who married Ulfheid, daughter of Eyjolf Gudmundarson, and their son was Eyjolf, who was killed at the Althing, the father of Bishop Thorlak's[63] chaplain, Orm. Audun Shaft had another son called Eystein, father of Thorstein, father of Helgi, father of Thororm, father of Odd, father of Hallbjorn, father of Sighvat the Priest. Asgeir of Asgeirs River had a daughter called Thorbjorg Bekkjarbot.

---

[63]Thorlak Thorhallsson the Holy was Bishop of Skalholt 1178-1193.

178. *Orm*

There was a man called Orm who took possession of Ormsdale and farmed there. He was the father of Odd, father of Thorodd, father of Helgi, father of Harri, father of Jora, father of Thordis, mother of Tanni, father of Skapti.

179. *Ingimund*

There was a famous chieftain in Romsdale in Norway called Ketil Raum. He was the son of Orm Shell-Piece, son of Horse-Bjorn, son of Raum, son of Giant-Bjorn of North-Norway. Ketil married Mjoll, daughter of An the Bow-Bender. They had a son called Thorstein who, on his father's instigation, brought about the death of Jokul, son of Earl Ingimund of Gautland, in the forest near the Uplands. Jokul would not take his life in return.[64] Afterwards Thorstein married Jokul's sister, Thordis, and their son was Ingimund the Old. He was brought up on Hefni Island by Thorir, father of Grim and Hromund. The seeress Heid made the prophecy that all three would settle in a still undiscovered country, west in the ocean. Ingimund said he would make sure that would never happen. The seeress told him he couldn't prevent it, and as a proof she said that something had vanished from his purse and wouldn't be found till he started digging for his high-seat pillars in the new country.

Ingimund was a great viking and was always going on plundering expeditions to the British Isles. He had a partner called Sæmund, from the Hebrides. They came back from a viking expedition just about the time King Harald, who was forcing his way to power in Norway, was setting out to take on Thorir Long-Chin and his allies at the Battle of Hafursfjord. Ingimund wanted to support the king, but Sæmund wouldn't have it, so their partnership broke up. After the battle the King gave Ingimund Vigdis, the daughter of Earl Thorir the Silent, as his wife. Vigdis and Jorund Neck were Thorir's illegitimate children. Ingimund couldn't settle down happily anywhere, and that's why King Harald encouraged him to seek his fortune in Iceland. Ingimund said he'd never intended to go there, but all the same he sent two Lapps on a magic ride to Iceland to look for the object he'd lost. It was an image of Frey, made of silver. The Lapps came back— they'd found the image but couldn't get it—and told Ingimund that it was in a certain valley between two hillocks. They described to him in detail how the land lay, and all about where he was to make his home.

---

[64]The incident alluded to is described in *Vatnsdæla Saga*, Chapter 3.

After that Ingimund set out for Iceland, along with Jorund Neck, his brother-in-law, and his friends Eyvind Sorkvir, Asmund and Hvati and his slaves Fridmund, Bodvar, Thorir Fox-Beard and Ulfkel. They put in at Grims River Estuary in the south, and all spent the winter at Hvanneyr with Grim, Ingimund's blood-brother. In the spring they travelled north across the moors and came to a fjord where they saw two rams, so they called it Hrutafjord.[65] Then they travelled on northwards through the districts, naming places everywhere. Ingimund spent the following winter at Ingimundarholt in Vididale, and from there they could see snow-free mountains to the south-east, so they travelled there in the spring, and there Ingimund recognized the land he'd been guided to. His daughter Thordis was born at Thordisarholt. Ingimund took possession of the whole of Vatnsdale, down to Helga-water and Urdarwater on the east side. He made his home at Hof, and found his amulet when he started digging for his high-seat pillars. His sons by Vigdis were Thorstein Jokul, Thorir Buck-Bottom and Hogni, and he had a son called Smid by a bondmaid. Ingimund had two daughters called Jorunn and Thordis.

Jorund Neck took possession of land between Urdarwater and Mogils Brook, and made his home at Grund below Jorundarfell. He was the father of Mar of Masstead. Hvati took possession of land between Mogils Brook and Gilja River, and lived at Hvatastead. Asmund took possession of the Thingeyrar District north of Helgawater, and lived at Gnup. Fridmund took possession of Forsaeludale. Eyvind Sorkvir took possession of Blondudale, and his sons were Hermund and Hromund the Lame.

Ingimund found a she-bear with two cubs on Hunawater.[66] Afterwards he went abroad and gave these animals to King Harald. People in Norway had never seen polar bears before. Then King Harald gave Ingimund a ship with a cargo of timber, and Ingimund travelled back with two ships, the first man to sail north of Iceland round Skagi. He brought his ships into Hunawater, and there's a place near Thingeyrar called Stigandi's Shed.[67] Later, Hrafn the Easterner came to stay with Ingimund. He had a fine sword. He carried it into the temple, and that's why Ingimund took it from him.

There were two brothers called Hallorm and Thororm who came to Iceland and stayed with Ingimund. Hallorm married Ingimund's daughter Thordis, and got the Karnsriver lands as her dowry.

---

[65]Literally "Rams' Fjord".
[66]Literally "Bear Cubs' Lake".
[67]*Stigandi* was the name of Ingimund's ship, see *Vatnsdæla Saga*.

Their son was Thorgrim the Karnsriver-Priest. Thororm farmed at Thorormstongue.

Ingimund lost ten pigs, and when they were found the following autumn they numbered a hundred and twenty. The boar was called Beigad, and he plunged into Svinawater and kept swimming till his hoofs came off. He died of exhaustion on Beigadarhill.

180. *Hrolleif and Ljot*

Hrolleif the Tall and Ljot, his mother, came to Iceland and landed at Borgarfjord. They travelled north through the countryside and couldn't find any land to farm until they came to Sæmund of Skaga-fjord. Since Hrolleif was the son of Arnald, Sæmund's brother, Sæmund told them to go north to see Thord at Hofdastrand. Thord gave them land in Hrolleifsdale, where Hrolleif made his home. Hrolleif seduced Hrodny, daughter of Uni of Unadale. Odd Unason ambushed Hrolleif, killed his cousin Ljot and wounded Hrolleif in the leg, though no iron could bite his tunic. Hrolleif killed Odd and two others, but two got away. That's why Hofda-Thord banished him from the district, beyond the watersheds of Skagafjord. Then Sæmund sent Hrolleif to Ingimund the Old, and Ingimund set him up at Odds-ridge, opposite Hof. He shared the fishing rights in Vatnsdale River with Ingimund, though he was supposed to keep away from the river when the men of Hof were there. But Hrolleif wouldn't go away when Ingimund's sons came to fish, so they started fighting over the river. Ingimund was told about this. He was blind by then, and ordered his shepherd to lead the horse he was riding into the river, to separate them. Hrolleif hurled a spear at him, and it went right through him. Then Ingimund and the shepherd went back home, and Ingimund sent the boy to warn Hrolleif. When his sons came home, Ingimund was sitting on his high-seat, dead. Hrolleif told his mother, and she said they would soon find out which was more powerful, the luck of Ingimund's sons or her witchcraft. She told him to go away at once.

Thorstein was supposed to set upon Hrolleif and get his choice of the inheritance if he killed him. The sons of Ingimund didn't sit on their father's high-seat. They went north to Geirmund and gave him sixty ounces of silver to send Hrolleif away. They followed Hrolleif's tracks south across the ridges over to Vatnsdale. Thorstein sent a servant over to As to see what was going on there, and he recited twelve verses before anyone came to the door. He saw a heap of clothes lying on the firewood, with a piece of red cloth sticking out from it. Thorstein said that must have been Hrolleif. "Ljot must have made sacrifices to give him a longer life," he said. They went over to As, and Thorstein wanted

to lie in wait above the door, but Jokul wouldn't let him and insisted on
being there himself. Someone came outside and looked around, and
then another man came, walking ahead of Hrolleif. Jokul jumped up
and knocked over a wood pile, but managed to throw a stick to his
brothers to warn them. Then he set on Hrolleif, and the two of them
started rolling down the slope, with Jokul finishing up on top. Thorstein came up, and the brothers seized their weapons. By this time
Ljot had come outside, walking backwards, with her head between
her legs and her clothes thrown over her back. Jokul cut off Hrolleif's
head and hurled it right in Ljot's face. She said she'd been too slow,
"otherwise I'd have made the earth turn upside down with the power
of my gaze, and every one of you would have gone raving mad."

After that Thorstein chose the farm at Hof, and Jokul got the
sword and made his home at Tongue. Thorir received the chieftaincy
and lived at Undunfell. He used to suffer from berserk fits. Hogni got
the ship Stigandi and became a sea-going trader. Smid lived at Smids-
stead. Thorstein married Thurid the Priestess, daughter of Solmund
of Asbjarnarness; their sons were Ingolf the Handsome and Gudbrand.

Bard Jokulsson had a son called Jokul, who was put to death by
King Olaf the Holy. Jokul the outlaw had predicted that the family
would be cursed with unlucky deaths for many a year.

Thorgrim the Karnsriver-Priest was the father of Thorkel Krafla.

181. *Eyvind Audkula*

There was a man called Eyvind Audkula, who took possession of the
whole of Svinadale and lived at Audkulustead. Thorgils Gjallandi who
came to Iceland with Audun Shaft lived at Svinawater; his sons, including Stout-Orm, killed Skarphedin Vefrodarson.

182. *Thorbjorn Kolka*

There was a man called Thorbjorn Kolka, who took possession of
Kolkumyrar and lived there for the rest of his life.

183. *Eyvind Sorkvir*

Eyvind Sorkvir took possession of Blondudale, as was said earlier. His
son was Hromund the Lame who killed Hogni Ingimundarson when
Mar and the Ingimundarsons fought over Deildarhjalli; for this killing
he was banished from the North Quarter. His sons were Hastein and
Thorbjorn who fought against Strife-Helgi in Hrutafjord. Eyvind had
another son called Hermund, father of Hild who married Avaldi
Ingjaldsson. Their children were Kolfinna, whom Gris Sæmingsson
married, and Brand, who killed Galti Ottarsson at the Hunawater Assembly because of Hallfred's slanderous verses.

1. A page from an old manuscript of *The Book of Settlements*
(see chapters 373-377)

2. View from Thingvellir
— South Quarter

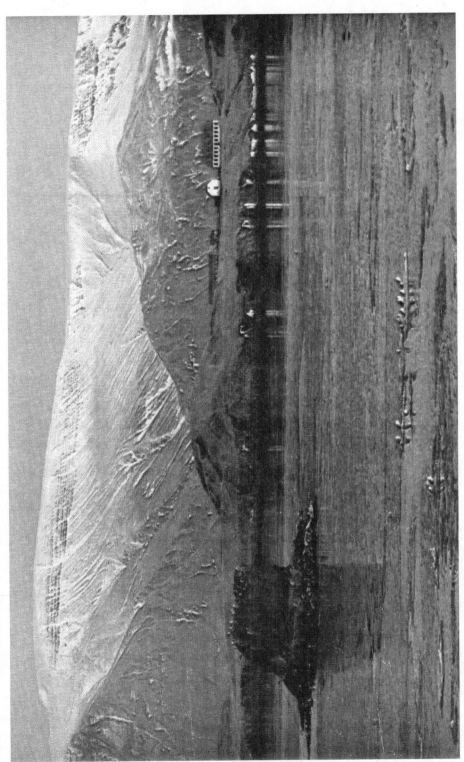

3. View from Reykjavík — South Quarter

4. Hvalfjord — South Quarter

Photography by G. HANNESSON

5. View of Snæfellsness — West Quarter

6. Hvamm in the Dales — West Quarter

Photography by P. JÓNSSON

7. View from Dyrafjord — West Quarter

Photography by P. JÓNSSON

Photography by P. JÓNSSON

8. View from Vatnsdale
— North Quarter

Photography by P. JÓNSSON

9. Miklibær in Skagafjord
— North Quarter

Photography by P. JÓNSSON

10. View from Svarfadardale
— North Quarter

11. View from Vopnafjord — East Quarter

Photography by P. JÓNSSON

12. View of Lagarwater — East Quarter

Photography by G. HANNESSON

Photography by G. HANNESSON

13. View of a glacier in South-East Iceland — East Quarter

14. Lomagnup — East Quarter

Photography by G. HANNESSON

15. View from the Eyjafell District — South Quarter

Photography by G. HANNESSON

16. Hlidarend in Fljotshlid — South Quarter

Photography by G. HANNESSON

184. *Ævar*

There was a man called Ævar, son of Ketil Slab-Flake and Thurid, daughter of King Harald Gold-Beard of Sogn. Ævar was married and by his wife he had a son called Vefrod. Ævar had illegitimate sons called Karli, Thorbjorn Bile and Thord the Tall. Ævar went to Iceland from a viking expedition with all his sons, except Vefrod. Along with Ævar came his kinsmen Gunnstein and Audolf and Gaut, but Vefrod carried on with his viking career. Ævar brought his ship into Blondu Estuary; by this time all the land west of the Blondu had been settled. He travelled up along the river looking for land, and when he came to the place known as Mobergsbrekkur, he set up a tall pole and said he was staking this claim for Vefrod to farm. Then he took possession of the whole of Langadale south of there and also some land north of the ridge. He divided his land-claim among his ship mates and made his home at Ævarsskard.

Later, Vefrod came to Iceland and landed at Gonguskards River Estuary. He travelled south to his father, who didn't recognize him. They set on each other so fiercely, every beam in the house was torn away, before Vefrod revealed who he was. He made his home at Moberg, as had been planned. Thorstein Bile lived at Strugsstead, Gunnstein at Gunnsteinsstead, Karli at Karlastead, Thord at Mikilsstead, and Audolf at Audolfsstead. Gaut settled in Gautsdale; he was one-handed. He and Eyvind Sorkvir did away with themselves because they didn't wish to live after Ingimund the Old had died. Hauk lived at a place now called Hauksgraves. Vefrod married Gunnhild, daughter of Eirik of Goddales, and sister to Dueller-Starri. Their sons were Ulfhedin, whom Thjostolf and his brother killed at Grinda Brook, Skarphedin, whom Stout-Orm and others killed at Vatnsskard, and Hunrod, father of Mar, father of Haflidi.

185. *Holti*

There was a man called Holti, who took possession of Langadale north of Moberg and lived at Holtastead. He was the father of Isrod, father of Isleif, father of Thorvald, father of Thorarin the Wise. Thorvald's daughter, Thordis, was married to Halldor, son of Snorri the Priest, and their daughters were Thorkatla, whom Gudlaug Thorfinnsson of Straumsfjord married—from them come the Sturlungs and the men of Oddi—and Gudrun, who married Kjartan Asgeirsson of Vatnsfjord. Their children were Thorvald, and Ingirid, whom Gudlaug the Priest married.

186. *Dueller-Mani*

There was a man called Dueller-Mani who took possession of Skagastrand on the west side as far south as Fors River, and south to Manathufa on the east side. He lived at Manavik. His daughter was married
to Thorbrand of the Dales, father of Mani, father of the Poet Kalf.

187. *Eilif Eagle*

There was a man called Eilif Eagle, son of Atli the Old, son of Skidi,
son of Bard of Al. Eilif Eagle's sons were Kodran of Gilja River, and
Thjodolf the Priest of Hof in Skagastrand, and Eystein the father
of Thorvald Tin-Bar, Thorstein Moor-Man and Orn of Fljot. Eilif
took possession of the region between Manathufa and Gonguskards
River, including Laxriverdale where he made his home. Eilif married
Thorlaug, daughter of Sæmund of Hlid, and their sons were Solmund,
father of Gudmund, father of Killer-Bardi and his brothers; and Atli
the Strong who married Herdis, daughter of Thord of Hofdi. Their
children were Thorlaug, who married Gudmund the Powerful, and
Thorarin, who married Halla, daughter of Jorund Neck. Thorarin
and Halla had a son Styrbjorn, who married Ingvild, daughter of
Steinrod Hedinsson of Hedinshofdi, and they in turn had a daughter
Arndis who married Hamal, son of Thormod, son of Thorkel Moon.

188. *Sæmund the Hebridean*

Sæmund the Hebridean, the partner of Ingimund the Old mentioned
earlier, brought his ship to Gonguskards River Estuary. Sæmund took
possession of the whole of Sæmundarhlid between Vatnsskard and
Sæmundar Brook and lived at Sæmundarstead; his son Geirmund
farmed there after him. Sæmund had a daughter called Reginleif who
married Thorodd Helmet, and their daughter was Hallbera, mother
of Gudmund the Powerful, father of Eyjolf, father of Thorey, mother
of Sæmund the Learned. Sæmund had another son called Arnald,
father of Rjupa who married Thorgeir, son of Thord of Hofdi, and
their son was Halldor of Hof.

189. *Skefil*

There was a man called Skefil who brought his ship into Gonguskards
River Estuary the same week as Sæmund. While Sæmund was carrying
fire around his land-claim, Skefil took possession of the entire region
north of Sauda River, which he took from Sæmund's land without
his approval, but Sæmund made no objection.

190. *Ulfljot*
There was a man called Ulfljot who took possession of the whole of Langaholt below Sæmundar Brook.

191. *Thorkel Prick*
Thorkel Prick, son of Skidi the Old, took possession of the whole of Vatnsskard and Svartriverdale. His son was Arnmod the Squint-Eyed, father of Galti, father of Thorgeir, father of Styrmir, father of Hall, father of Kolfinna.

192. *Alfgeir*
There was a man called Alfgeir who took possession of land around Alfgeirsvellir up to Mælifells River, and lived at Alfgeirsvellir.

193. *Thorvid*
There was a man called Thorvid who took possession of land between Mælifells and Gilja Rivers.

194. *Hrosskel*
With Eirik's approval, a man called Hrosskel took possession of the whole of Svartriverdale and the entire Yrarfellslands. His land-claim stretched north to Gilhagi and he made his home at Yrarfell. Hrosskel sent a slave of his called Rodrek south through Mælifellsdale and up to the mountains in search of land. He came to a ravine south of Mælifell called Rodreksgill nowadays, and there he set up a freshly cut birch pole—people called it the Explorer. After that he turned back.

195. *Eirik Hroaldsson*
A leading man from Norway, Eirik the son of Hroald, son of Geirmund, son of Eirik Bristle-Beard, went to Iceland and took possession of land from Gill River, including the entire Goddales, down as far as Nordur River. He lived at Hof in Goddales. Eirik married Thurid, the daughter of Thord Beard and sister of Helga, wife of Ketilbjorn the Old of Mosfell. The children of Eirik and his wife were Thorkel, Hroald, Thorgeir, Dueller-Starri and Gunnhild. Thorgeir Eiriksson married Yngvild Thorgeir's-daughter, and their daughter was Rannveig whom Bjarni Brodd-Helgason married. Gunnhild Eirik's-daughter married Vefrod Ævarsson.

196. *Vekell*
There was a man called Vekell the Shape-Changer who took possession

of land between Gill and Mælifells Rivers and lived at Mælifell. He
heard about Rodrek's trip and a little later set off south to the
mountains to explore the land for himself. He came to those mounds
called Vekel's Howes nowadays and shot an arrow between them; then
he turned back home. When Eirik of Goddales heard about this, he
sent his slave Rongud south to the mountains to explore the land
further. He came south to the Blanda tributaries and followed the
river which flows west of Hvinverjadale and then westward into the
lava field between Reykjavallir and Kjol, where he came across human
tracks and realized they came from the south. He built a cairn there,
now called Rongudar Cairn. Then he went back home, and Eirik
rewarded him for the trip by giving him his freedom. After that
people began to travel across the mountains between the North and
South Quarters.

197. *Crow-Hreidar*

There was a man called Crow-Hreidar, the son of Ofeig Dangle-
Beard, son of Oxen-Thorir. Hreidar and his father got their ship
ready and sailed for Iceland. When they made landfall Hreidar went
up to the mast and said he wasn't going to throw his high-seat pillars
overboard as he thought it a stupid way to make one's decisions.
Instead, he said he would ask for Thor's guidance on where to settle,
and that if it was settled there already, he was ready to fight for the
land. He put into Skagafjord and sailed up to Borgarsand where he
wrecked his ship. Havard the Heron came and invited Hreidar to
stay with him, so he spent the following winter at Hegraness.

In the spring Havard asked him what he planned to do. Hreidar
said he was going to fight Sæmund for land, but Havard discouraged
him saying that sort of thing had always turned out badly, and recom-
mended him to ask the advice of Eirik of Goddales. "He's the wisest
man in the district," he said. Hreidar did as Havard suggested, and
saw Eirik, who was against any fighting and said it was absurd for men
to quarrel when the land was so thinly populated. Instead he offered
to give Hreidar the entire tongue of land below Skalamyri, and said
Thor must have guided Hreidar there, seeing that the prow had been
pointing in that direction when he sailed up to Borgarsand. Eirik said
he thought this was quite enough land for Hreidar and his sons.
Hreidar accepted the offer and made his home at Steinsstead; he
chose to go into Mælifell when he died. His son was Ofeig Thin-
Beard, father of Bjorn, father of Tongue-Stein.

198. *Onund the Sage*

There was a man called Onund the Sage, who took possession of land above Merkilgill, including the eastermost valley. When Eirik was going to take possession of the valley to the west, Onund cast the divining rod to find out when Eirik would set out to make his claim. Onund got in first, shot a tinder-arrow across the river to claim the land west of it, and made his home between the rivers.

199. *Kari*

There was a man called Kari, who claimed possession of land between Nordur River and Merkigill. He made his home at Flatatongue, and was nick-named Tongue-Kari. The men of Silfrastead are descended from him.

200. *Thorbrand Orrek*

Thorbrand Orrek claimed possession of land above Bolstadar River, including the whole of Silfrastadahlid and the north side of Nordur-riverdale. He made his home at Thorbrandsstead where he built a hall so large that all those who travelled on that side of the river had to ride through it with their packhorses, and everyone was welcome to eat there. Orreksmoor above Hokustead takes its name from him. He was a greatly respected man and had a fine progeny.

201. *Hjalmolf*

There was a man called Hjalmolf, who claimed land down in Blonduhlid. His son was Thorgrim Kuggi, father of Odd of Axlarhagi, father of Sela-Kalf, from whom the men of Axlarhagi are descended.

202. *Thorir Dove-Nose*

Oxen-Thorir had a freedman called Thorir Dove-Nose who brought his ship to Gonguskards River Estuary after the west side of the district had been fully settled. Thorir travelled north across Jokuls River at Landbrot and took possession of land between Glodafeykis and Djup Rivers, making his home at Flugumyri. About this time a ship with a cargo of livestock put in at Kolbeins River Estuary and the crew lost a young mare at Brimness Woods. Thorir Dove-Nose bought the chance of finding the mare, and find her he did. She was an exceptionally fast horse and her name was Fluga.

There was a man called Orn, a sorcerer, who used to wander from one part of the country to another. He lay in wait for Thorir at Hvinverjadale when he was on his way south across Kjol, and made a bet with him as to which had the faster horse. Orn himself

had a particularly fine one. Each of them staked a hundred marks of
silver. They rode together south across Kjol until they came to the
level stretch of land known nowadays as Dufunefsskeid. Orn was only
half way up the course by the time Thorir met him on his way back,
so great was the difference between the two horses. Orn took the loss
of his money so badly he just didn't want to live any more. He went
up to the mountain known nowadays as Arnarfell, and there he killed
himself. Fluga had to be left behind, exhausted, and by the time
Thorir came back from the Althing he found there was a grey black-
maned stallion with the mare. She had a foal by him, and from their
line sprang the horse Eidfaxi, the one that was taken abroad and
killed seven men at Mjors in a single day before he was killed himself. Fluga lost her life in a swamp at Flugumyri.

203. *Kollsvein the Strong*
There was a man called Kollsvein the Strong who took possession of
land between Thver and Gljufur Rivers and made his home at Kolls-
veinsstead above Thver River. He used to hold his sacrifices at Hofsstead.

204. *Gunnolf*
There was a man called Gunnolf who took possession of land between
Thver and Glodafeykis Rivers and lived at Hvamm.

205. *Strife-Bjorn*
A great chieftain in Sweden called Gorm was married to Thora,
daughter of King Eirik of Uppsala. They had a son called Thorgils
who married Elin, daughter of King Boleslaw of Russia and Ingigerd,
sister of Dagstygg, king of the giants. Their sons were Hergrim and
Herfinn, who married Halla, daughter of Hedin and Arndis Hedin's-
daughter. Herfinn and Halla had a daughter called Groa, whom
Hroar married, and their son was Strife-Bjorn, the first man to settle
between Grjot and Deildar Rivers, before Hjalti and Kolbein came
to Iceland. Strife-Bjorn lived at Sleitu-Bjarnarstead. He was married
and had these children by his wife: Ornolf, who married Thorljot,
daughter of Hjalti Skalpsson; Arnbjorn who married Thorlaug,
daughter of Thord of Hofdi; Arnodd who married Thorny, daughter
of Sigmund Thorkelsson, whom Glum killed; and Arnfrid, who married Wisdom-Bodvar Ondottsson.

Ondott put in at Kolbeins River Estuary, and bought land from
Strife-Bjorn, below Halsgrof on the east side down to Kolbeins River
Estuary, and on the west side from the brook north of Nautabu south
to Gljufur River. He made his home at Vidvik.

206. *Kolbein*

Sigmund of Vestfold married Ingibjorg, daughter of Raud Rugga of Namdalen and sister of Thorstein Svarfad. Their son was Kolbein who went to Iceland and took possession of land between Grjot and Deildar Rivers, including Kolbeinsdale and Hjaltadale.

207. *Hjalti*

Hjalti, son of Thord Skalp, came to Iceland, took possession of Hjaltadale with Kolbein's approval, and made his home at Hof. His sons were Thorvald and Thord, both of them men of some note. The most magnificent funeral feast ever to be held in Iceland was the one his sons celebrated in honour of their father; there were about 1440 guests, and all the important people were presented with gifts when they left. At this feast Odd of Breidafjord declaimed a dirge he'd composed in honour of Hjalti. Previously, Glum Geirason had cited Odd to the Thorskafjord Assembly, and then the Hjaltasons sailed from the north over to Steingrimsfjord and walked south across the moor through a dell now known as Hjaltadælalaut. When they arrived at the Assembly they were so elegantly dressed that people thought the gods had come. This verse was made about it:

> None of the battle-seasoned
> warriors believed
> it could be anyone
> but the honoured gods,
> when staunch Hjalti's sons
> with gleaming helmets
> came to join the throng
> at Thorskafjord.

From the Hjaltasons stems a numerous and distinguished line.

208. *Thord*

There was a famous man called Thord, the son of Bjorn Butter-Box, son of Hroald Spine, son of Bjorn Ironside, son of Ragnar Hairy-Breeks. Thord went to Iceland, took possession of Hofdastrand in Skagafjord, between Unadale and Hrolleifsdale Rivers, and made his home at Hofdi. He married Thorgerd, daughter of Thorir Slouch and Fridgerd, daughter of King Kjarval of Ireland. They had nineteen children. Their son Bjorn married Thurid, daughter of Ref of Bard. The children of Bjorn and Thurid were Arnor Hag-Nose and Thordis, mother of Orm, father of Thordis, mother of Botolf, father of Thordis, mother of Helga, mother of Gudny, mother of the Sturlusons. Thord

had another son called Thorgeir, who married Rjupa, daughter of
Arnald Sæmundarson, and their son was Halldor of Hof. Thord had
a third son called Snorri, who married Thorhild the Ptarmigan,
daughter of Thord Gellir, and their son was Thord Horse-Head. A
fourth son was called Thorvald Hollow-Throat. One autumn he came
to Smidkel at Thorvardsstead and stayed there for a while. Then he
travelled up to Surt's Cave and declaimed a poem there that he'd
composed about the giant living in the cave. Afterwards he married
Smidkel's daughter, and their daughter was Jorunn, mother of Thorbrand of Skarfsness. Thord's fifth son was called Bard, who married
Thorarna, Thorodd Hjalm's daughter, and their son was the poet
Dadi. Thord's sixth son was called Soxolf, the seventh Thorgrim, the
eighth Hroar, the ninth Knor, the tenth Thormod the Bald, and the
eleventh Stein. Thord had a daughter called Thorlaug, who married
Arnbjorn Strife-Bjorn's son, and their daughter was Gudlaug who
married Thorleik Hoskuldsson. Their son was Bolli. Thord had another
daughter called Herdis, who married Atli the Strong. His third daughter was Thorgrima Ship-Cheek, his fourth Arnbjorg, his fifth Arnleif,
his sixth Asgerd, his seventh Thurid, and his eighth Fridgerd of
Hvamm.

Hrolleif the Tall settled in Hrolleifsdale, as was written earlier.
Thord banished him from the north for the killing of Odd Unason,
and that was when he moved house to Vatnsdale.

209. *Fridleif*
There was a man called Fridleif, a Gotlander on his father's side, but
with a Flemish mother called Bryngerd. Fridleif took possession of
the whole of Slettahlid and Fridleifsdale between Fridleifsdale and
Staf Rivers, and lived at Holt. His son was Thjodar, father of Ari
and Bryngerd, mother of Tongue-Stein.

210. *Floki*
Floki, son of Vilgerd Horda-Kari's daughter, went to Iceland and
took possession of Flokadale between Flokadale River and Reykjarhill.
He made his home at Mo. Floki married Gro, sister of Thord of
Hofdi, and their son was Oddleif Staff who lived at Stafshill and
quarrelled with the Hjaltasons. Floki's daughter was Thjodgerd,
mother of Kodran, father of Thjodgerd, mother of Kodran, father of
Kar of Vatnsdale.

211. *Thord Knob and Gimlet-Helgi*
In Sogn there were two men, one called Thord Knob, son of Bjorn of

Haug, and another called Gimlet-Helgi. They sailed in convoy to Iceland and put in at Haganess. Thord took possession of land between Stifla and Tungu River, and made his home at Knappsstead. He married Æsa, daughter of Ljotolf the Priest, and their son was Hafur who married Thurid, daughter of Thorkel of Goddales. Their son was Thorarin, father of Ofeig. Gimlet-Helgi took possession of land east from Haganess as far as Flokadale River below Bard and up to Tungu River, and lived at Grindil. He married Gro the Second-Sighted, and their children were Thorolf, Arnor who fought Fridleif at Stafshill, Thorgerd who married Geirmund Sæmundarson, and Ulfhild who married Arnor Skefilsson of Gonguskard. Their son was Thorgeir the Swaggerer who killed Sacrifice-Mar at Moberg. Gimlet-Helgi had a daughter too, called Thorunn Blue-Cheek.

212. *Bard the Hebridean*
Bard the Hebridean took possession of land between Stifla and Mjovadale River. His son was Hall of Mjovadale, father of Thurid who married Arnor Hag-Nose.

213. *Bruni the White*
There was a famous man called Bruni the White, son of Earl Harek of the Uplands. He had a great desire to go to Iceland and took possession of land between Mjovadale River and Ulfsdale. He made his home at Brunastead, and married Arnora, daughter of Thorgeir the Frenzied, son of Ljotolf the Priest. Their sons were Ketil and Ulfhedin, from whom the men of Bard are descended.

214. *Ulf and Olaf*
Ulf the Viking and Olaf Brook sailed to Iceland in convoy. Ulf took possession of Ulfsdales and lived there. Olaf Brook was the son of Karl of Bjark Island in Halogaland. He killed Thorir the Black and was outlawed for it. Olaf took possession of all the valleys to the west, as well as part of Olafsfjord up to Thormod's land-claim, and made his home at Kviabekk. His sons were Steinmod Bjorn's father, Grimolf and Arnodd, father of Vilborg, mother of Karl the Red.

215. *Thormod the Strong*
There was a man called Thormod the Strong. He killed Gyrd, uncle of Skjalg of Jæderen, and for that reason he had to get out of Norway, so he went to Iceland. He brought his ship into Siglufjord, and sailed it up to Thormodseyr; and it was he who named it Siglufjord. He took possession of the entire fjord, from Ulfsdale to Hvanndale, and

made his home at Sigluness. He quarrelled with Olaf Brook over Hvanndales and killed sixteen men before they were reconciled on the terms that each was to have the dales every other summer. Thormod was the son of Harald the Viking and was married to Arngerd, sister of Skidi of Skidadale. Their sons were Arngeir the Sharp and Narfi, father of Thrand, father of Hris-Isle Narfi, and Alrek, who fought Knor Thordarson at Slettuhlid.

216. *Gunnolf the Old*

Gunnolf the Old, son of Thorbjorn the Rushing of Sogn, killed Vegeir, father of Vebjorn the Sogn Champion, and afterwards went to Iceland. He took possession of the east side of Olafsfjord between Reykja River and Vamull and lived at Gunnolfs River. He married Gro, daughter of Thorvard of Urdir, and their sons were Steinolf, Thorir and Thorgrim.

217. *Bjorn Hrolfsson and his son Eyvind the Easterner*

There was a famous man in Gotaland called Bjorn, son of Hrolf of Ar. He married Hlif, daughter of Hrolf, son of Ingjald, son of King Frodi. They had a son called Eyvind. Bjorn quarrelled over some land with Sigfast, who was the father-in-law of King Solvar of Gotaland. Bjorn burnt him to death inside his own house and thirty others with him. Then Bjorn went to Norway with eleven companions, was given hospitality by the chieftain Grim, son of Kolbjorn the Slighter, and stayed with him for a year, but Grim wanted to kill Bjorn for money. That's why Bjorn went to Ondott Crow who lived at Hvinisfjord in Agder, and Ondott took him in. Bjorn spent his summers in the British Isles on viking expeditions, and wintered with Ondott, but when his wife Hlif died in Gotaland, his son Eyvind came from the east and took charge of his father's warships. Then Bjorn married Helga, Ondott Crow's sister, and their son was Thrand. Eyvind went on viking expeditions to the British Isles and was particularly active off the coast of Ireland. He married Rafarta, daughter of King Kjarval of Ireland, and settled there, and that's why he was called Eyvind the Easterner. Eyvind and Rafarta had a son called Helgi. They gave him into fosterage in the Hebrides, but when they came back to see him two years later he'd been so starved they didn't recognize him. They took him away with them and called him Helgi the Lean; he was brought up in Ireland. When he was grown up, he became a very important man, and married Thorunn Hyrna, daugher of Ketil

Flat-Nose. They had a number of children. Their sons were called Hrolf and Ingjald.

218. *Helgi the Lean*

Helgi the Lean went to Iceland with his wife and children and his son-in-law Hamund Hell-Skin as well. Hamund was married to Ingunn, Helgi's daughter. Helgi's faith was very much mixed: he believed in Christ but invoked Thor when it came to voyages and difficult times. When Helgi sighted Iceland, he consulted Thor as to where he should put in, and the oracle guided him north of the island. Then his son Hrolf asked Helgi whether he was planning to sail to the Arctic Ocean if Thor told him to go there? It was late summer, he said, and the crew thought it time to get ashore. Helgi made land north of Hris Isle, just south of Svarfadardale, and spent the first winter at Hamundarstead. The winter was very severe. In the spring Helgi climbed Solarfells, and saw that everything seemed much less white up towards the head of the fjord, which they called Eyjafjord because of the islands further out. Then Helgi carried all his possessions on board, but Hamund stayed behind. Helgi landed at Galtarhamar, and there he put two pigs ashore—the boar was called Solvi. The pigs were found three years later in Solvadale, and by that time there were seventy of them. Helgi spent the summer exploring the neighbourhood, and took possession of the whole of Eyjafjord, between Sigluness and Reynisness. He built fires at every estuary to hallow his land-claim. He spent next winter at Bilds River, but in the spring he moved house over to Kristness and lived there for the rest of his life. During the removal, Thorunn had a baby on Thorunnar Isle in Eyjafjord River, and that's where she gave birth to Thorbjorg Island-Sun. Helgi believed in Christ and called his home after him. Afterwards other settlers began to live within his land-claim, with Helgi's approval.

219. *Thorstein Svarfad*

There was a man called Thorstein Svarfad, son of Raud Rugga of Namdalen. He married Hild, daughter of Thrain Black-Troll. Thorstein went to Iceland and took possession of Svarfadardale with Helgi's approval. His children were Karl the Red of Karls River and Gudrun, wife of Hafthor the Viking; and their children were Klaufi and Groa, who was married to Gris the Gay.

There was a man called Atli the Evil. He killed Hafthor and put Karl in shackles. Then Klaufi came up unexpectedly, killed Atli and set Karl free. Klaufi married Yngvild Fair-Cheek, daughter of Asgeir Red-Cloak and sister of Olaf the Witch-Breaker and Thorleif. He slit

the bag of dyeing moss they'd collected in his land. Then Thorleif
made this verse:

> Boggvir cut
> my short-haired bag,
> and Olaf's belt
> and cloak besides.
> He'll never be safe
> from the slayer's hand
> as long as we live,
> this man of mischief.

This led to the events in *Svarfdæla Saga*.

220. *Karl*

There was a man called Karl who took possession of the entire Strand,
from Upsir to Migandi.

221. *Orn*

When his kinsman Orn, who had taken possession of Arnarfjord, came
from the west, Hamund Hell-Skin, son of King Hjor, gave him land.
Orn made his home at Arnarness. His daughter was Idunn, who
married Asgeir Red-Cloak, and his son was Narfi after whom Narfa
Skerry is named. He married Ulfheid, daughter of Ingjald of Gnupufell, and their sons were Asbrand, father of Hellu-Narfi, Eyjolf
father of Thorvald of Hagi, and Helgi father of Grim of Kalfskinn.

222. *Galm*

There was a man called Galm, who took possession of Galmansstrand
between Thorvaldsdale and Reistar Rivers. His son was Thorvald,
father of Orm, father of Children-Thorodd, father of Thorunn, mother
of Dyrfinna, mother of the smith Thorstein Skeggjason. To Thorvald,
Hamund gave land between Reistar and Horg Rivers, but before
that he'd lived at Thorvaldsdale.

223. *Geirleif*

There was a man called Geirleif, who took possession of Horgriverdale
up to Myrk River. He was Hrapp's son and lived at Old Hagi. His
son was Bjorn the Wealthy, from whom the men of Audbrekka are
descended.

224. *Thord the Tearer*

There was a man called Thord the Tearer, who took possession of
Horgriverdale above Myrk River and down to Drangar on the other

side. His son was Ornolf who married Yngvild All-Men's-Sister.[68]
Their sons were Thord, Thorvard of Kristness, and Steingrim of Kropp.
Thord the Tearer gave his kinsman Skolm part of his land-claim.
Skolm's son was Thoralf the Strong, who lived at Myrk River.

225. *Thorir the Troll-Burster*

There was a man called Thorir the Troll-Burster. He was reared on
Omd Island in Halogaland and fell out with Earl Hakon Grjotgardsson, so he had to go to Iceland. He took possession of the whole of
Oxnadale and lived at Vatns River. His son was Steinrod the Strong,
who saved a good many people when they were attacked by monsters.
There was a vile sorceress called Geirhild, and people with second
sight saw Steinrod going for her, taking her by surprise; but she
changed herself into a bull's hide bag filled with water. Steinrod was
a blacksmith and went after her with a huge iron pike in his hand.
This verse was made about their encounter:

> The hammering smith
> strikes at Geirhild
> with a long iron pike,
> piling on the blows.
> The rod attacks hard
> the hag's flank at Hjaltaeyr.
> The witch must have suffered
> from sore ribs after.

The daughter of Steinrod was Thorljot, who married Thorvard of
Kristness.

226. *Audolf*

There was a man called Audolf who went from Jæderen to Iceland
and took possession of Oxnadale, from Thver River down to Bægis
River, making his home at South Bægis River. He married Thorhild,
Helgi the Lean's daughter, and their daughter was Yngvild, wife of
Thorodd Helmet, father of Arnljot, father of Halldor.

227. *Eystein*

Eystein, son of Raudulf Oxen-Thorisson, took possession of land from
Bægis River down to Kræklingahlid and lived at Lon. His son Gunn-

---

[68]Her nickname may well have been given her because her mother and father
had both been married before, and she had a large number of half-brothers and
sisters.

stein married Hlif, daughter of Hedin of Mjola. Their children were Halldora who married Killer-Glum, Thorgrim, and Grim Sand-Leg.

228. *Eyvind Cock*

There was a famous man called Eyvind Cock, who came to Iceland towards the end of The Age of Settlements. He owned a ship jointly with Thorgrim Hlifarson. Eyvind was related to the Ondottssons, and they granted him land. He made his home at Hanatun, and was called Tun-Hani.[69] Nowadays the farm is called Marbæli. Eyvind married Thorny, daughter of Storolf Oxen-Thorisson, and his son was Snorri the Hlidamen-Priest.

229. *Thrand the Fast-Sailing*

Ondott Crow who was mentioned earlier became a wealthy man. But when Bjorn his brother-in-law died, the chieftain Grim claimed all his inheritance for the king, on the grounds that Grim was a foreigner and his sons were living in the British Isles. Ondott managed to hold onto the money for his nephew Thrand, and when Thrand heard his father had died, he put out from the Hebrides and sailed so fast, he was nicknamed the Fast-Sailing. After he'd collected his inheritance, Thrand went to Iceland and settled in the south, as will be told later.

That's why Grim killed Ondott but he failed to get the money even though he had the backing of the king. On the same night, Ondott's wife Signy carried all her movables on board a ship and put out, taking along her sons Asgrim and Asmund to her father Sighvat. She sent her sons to her fosterfather Hedin of Soknadale, but they weren't happy there and wanted to go back to their mother. At Christmas they came to Ingjald Trausti at Hvin. He took them in, because his wife Gyda wanted him to. Next summer chieftain Grim was preparing a feast in honour of Audun, King Harald's earl, but during the night when the ale-brewing was taking place at Grim's, the Ondottssons burnt him in his house, then took their foster-father Ingjald's boat and rowed away. Audun came to the feast as planned and found his friend missing. Then the Ondottssons came early one morning to the sleeping hall where Audun was resting, and rammed the door with a log. Asmund stood guard over the earl's two servants, while Asgrim put his spear's point to the earl's chest and told him to pay compensation for their father. The earl handed over three gold bracelets and a tunic of costly material. Asgrim gave the earl a nickname and called him Audun Nanny-Goat.

---

[69]Literally "Field-Cock".

After this the brothers travelled to Surnadale to Eirik Ale-Lover, who was a landholder, and he took them in. Another important man, Hallstein Horse, farmed there too, and each invited the other to a drinking party. Eirik was the first host and entertained well and truly, but then Hallstein was host and he was mean with his drink. He struck at Eirik with a drinking horn, and after that Eirik went back home, while Hallstein stayed behind with his servants. Then Asgrim went into the house alone and wounded Hallstein badly, but Hallstein's men thought they'd killed Asgrim. However, Asgrim got away into the forest, and a certain woman nursed him in an underground chamber, healing him completely.

That same summer Asmund went to Iceland, thinking his brother Asgrim was dead. Helgi the Lean gave Asmund Kræklingahlid, and he farmed at South Gler River.

When Asgrim was fully recovered, Eirik gave him a longship and he went on a viking expedition to the British Isles. Hallstein died of his wounds. When Asgrim came back from the raid, Eirik gave him his daughter Geirhild in marriage. Then Asgrim went to Iceland, and made his home at North Gler River. King Harald sent Thorgeir of Hvin to Iceland to kill Asgrim. He spent the winter at Hvinverjadale in Kjol, but got nowhere with the revenge. Asgrim's son was Ellida-Grim, father of Asgrim and of Sigfus, father of Thorgerd, mother of Grim, father of Sverting, father of Vigdis, mother of Sturla of Hvamm.

230. *Hamund*

Helgi the Lean granted land to Hamund, his son-in-law, between Merkigill and Skjalgdale River, and Hamund farmed at South Espihill. His son Thorir farmed there after him. Thorir married Thordis Kadal's daughter, and their sons were Thorarin of North Espihill and Thorvald Hook of Grund, but Thorgrim of Modrufell was not her son. They had a daughter called Vigdis.

231. *Gunnar*

Helgi gave his daughter Thora in marriage to Gunnar, son of Ulfljot who brought the laws to Iceland, and granted him land between Skjalgdale River and Hals. Gunnar made his home at Djupadale, and these were his children by his wife: Thorstein, Ketil and Steinmod, and two daughters, Yngvild and Thorlaug.

232. *Audun the Rotten*

Helgi gave his daughter Helga in marriage to Audun the Rotten, son

of Thorolf Butter, son of Thorstein Skrofa, son of Grim Kamban, and
he granted Audun land between Hals and Villingadale. Audun lived
at Saurby. Their children were Einar, father of Eyjolf Valgerdarson,
and Vigdis, mother of Halli the White, father of Orm, father of
Gellir, father of Orm, father of Halli, father of Thorgeir, father of
Thorvard, and of Ari, father of Bishop Gudmund. Hamund Hell-Skin
married Helga Helgi's-daughter after her sister Ingunn died, and their
daughter was Yngvild, nicknamed All-Men's-Sister, whom Ornolf
married.

233. *Hrolf*

To his son Hrolf, Helgi granted all the lands east of Eyjafjord River
above Arnarhill. Hrolf made his home at Gnupufell and built a large
temple there. He married Thorarna, daughter of Thrand Slender-
Leg. Their children were Haflidi the Generous, Valthjof, Vidar,
Grani, Bodvar, Ingjald and Eyvind, and one daughter, Gudlaug,
whom Thorkel the Black married. Valthjof was the father of Helgi,
father of Thorir, father of Arnor, father of Thurid, mother of Vigdis,
mother of Sturla of Hvamm.

234. *Ingjald*

To his son Ingjald, Helgi granted land between Arnarhill and North
Thver River. Ingjald made his home at Upper Thver River where he
built a large temple. He married Salgerd Steinolf's-daughter, and their
sons were Eyjolf, father of Killer-Glum, and Steinolf, father of Thorarin the Wicked and Arnor the Good of Raud River. Killer-Glum was
the father of Mar, father of Thorkatla, mother of Thord, father of
Sturla.

235. *Thorgeir*

Helgi gave his daughter Hlif in marriage to Thorgeir, Thord Bjalki's
son, and granted him land between Thver River and Vard Ravine.
They lived at Fiski Brook, and their children were Thord and Helga.

236. *Skagi Skoptason*

There was a famous man in More called Skagi Skoptason, who fell
out with Eystein the Clatterer and had to go to Iceland because of it.
With Helgi's approval he took possession of the east side of Eyjafjord,
from Vard Ravine north to Fnjoskadale River, and made his home
at Sigluvik. His son was Thorbjorn, father of Hedin the Generous
who built a farm at Svalbard sixteen years before Christianity was
adopted. He married Ragnheid, daughter of Eyjolf Valgerdarson.

237. *Thorir Flap*

A man called Thorir Flap, son of Ketil Seal got ready for a voyage to Iceland. One of his crew was called Gaut. As they were putting out to sea, vikings came at them intending to rob them, but Gaut struck at the forecastleman with a rudder, so the vikings sailed off. After this he was nicknamed Rudder-Gaut. Thorir and Gaut went to Iceland and brought their ship in to Skjalfandi Estuary. Thorir took possession of Kaldakinn, the land between Skuggacliffs and Ljosawater Pass, but he wasn't happy there and went away. Then he made this verse:

> Kaldakinn will lie here
> for everlasting, sailor,
> but Rudder-Gaut and I
> will go away unharmed.

Afterwards Thorir took possession of the whole of Fnjoskadale, as far as Odeila. He made his home at Lund,[70] and held the grove sacred. His sons were Orm Basket-Back, father of Hlenni the Old, and Thorkel the Black of Hleidrargard. Thorkel married Gudlaug Hrolf's-daughter. Their sons were Ongul the Black and Hrafn, father of Thord of Stokkahladir, and their daughter was Gudrid, whom Thorgeir the Ljosawater-Priest married.[71]

238. *Thengil the Fast-Sailing*

Thengil the Fast-Sailing went from Halogaland to Iceland, and with Helgi's approval took possession of land from Fnjosk River north to Grenivik, making his home at Hofdi. His sons were Vemund, father of Asolf of Hofdi, and Hallstein who made this verse as he was sailing in to land and heard of his father's death:

> Hofdi's drooping,
> Thengil's dead;
> the hillsides smile
> at Hallstein.

239. *Thormod*

There was a man called Thormod who took possession of Grenivik, Hvallatur and all the coast north to Thorgeirsfjord. His son was Snort, from whom the Snertlings are descended.

---

[70]*Lund* means 'a grove'.
[71]Thorgeir the Ljosawater-Priest was Lawspeaker of the Althing 985-1001.

240. *Thorgeir*

There was a man called Thorgeir, who took possession of Thorgeirs-fjord and Hvalvatnsfjord.

241. *Eyvind*

There was a man called Lodin Fishing-Hook, who was born on En-geloy in Halogaland. Oppressed by Earl Hakon Grjotgardsson, he set out for Iceland but died on the voyage. His son Eyvind took possession of Flateyjardale up to Gunnsteinar, and held the boulders there sacred. The stream Odeila separated his land-claim from that of Thorir Flap. Eyvind's son was Asbjorn Falling-Beam, father of Finnbogi the Strong.

242. *Bard*

Bard, son of Heyjangur-Bjorn, brought his ship in to Skjalfandi Estuary and took possession of the whole of Bardardale south of Kalfborgar and Eyjardale Rivers. For a while he lived at Lundarbrekka, then he noticed that the wind from the land was warmer than the wind from the sea, and that's why he decided the land south of the moors must be better. He sent his sons south one midwinter to explore, and they found horse-tails and other kinds of plants. Next spring Bard made a sled for every walking beast he had, and had each one haul its own fodder as well as all his goods. He travelled through Vonar Pass, by a route known ever since as Bard's Path. Afterwards he took possession of Fljotshverfi and made his home at Gnupar, and after that he was called Gnupa-Bard. He had a lot of children. One of his sons was called Sigmund, the father of Thorstein, who married Æsa, Hrolf Red-Beard's daughter, and their daughter was Thorunn whom Thorkel Leif married, and whose son was Thorgeir the Priest of Ljosawater. Bard had another son, Thorstein, father of Thorir, who fought at Fitjar on the side of King Hakon when he cut a hole in an oxhide and used it for protection; that's why he was nicknamed Leather-Neck. Thorstein married Fjorleif Eyvind's-daughter, and their sons were Havard of Fellsmull, Herjolf of Mywater, Ketil of Husavik, Vemund Fringe, who married Halldora, Thorkel the Black's daughter, Askel, and Hals, who farmed at Helgustead.

243. *Thorfinn Moon*

There was a man called Thorfinn Moon, son of Askel Torfi. He took possession of land below Eyjardale River down to Landamot and part of Ljosawater Pass, and made his home at Oxar River.

244. *Thorir Grimsson*

Thorir, son of Grim Greycloak-Mull of Rogaland took possession of parts of Ljosawater Pass. His son was Thorkel Leif the Tall, father of Thorgeir the Priest. Thorgeir's first wife was Gudrid, Thorkel the Black's daughter. Their sons were Thorkel Braggart, Hoskuld, Tjorvi, Kolgrim, Thorstein, and Thorvard, and their daughter was Sigrid. Later Thorgeir married Alfgerd, daughter of Arngeir the Easterner. Thorgeir also married Thorkatla, daughter of Dala-Koll. His sons by these wives were Thorgrim, Thorgils and Ottar, and his illegitimate sons were Thorgrim and Finni the Dream-Interpreter, whose mother was a foreigner, called Lekny.

245. *Hedin and Hoskuld*

Hedin and Hoskuld, sons of Thorstein Troll, went to Iceland and took possession of land south of Tungu Moor. Hedin made his home at Hedinshofdi. He married a woman called Gudrun. Their daughter Arnrid married Ketil Fjorleifarson, and their daughter Gudrun married Hrolf. Hoskuld took possession of all the lands east of Lax River, and made his home at Skord. Hoskuldswater was named after him because that's where he was drowned. Husavik, where Gardar spent one winter, is in this land-claim. Hoskuld had a son called Hroald who married Ægileif, daughter of Hrolf Helgason.

246. *Vestmann and Ulf*

Vestmann and Ulf were blood-brothers and sailed to Iceland on the same ship. They took possession of the whole of Reykjadale west of Lax River, up as far as Vestmannswater. Vestmann married a woman called Gudlaug. Ulf farmed at Skrattafell; he was married and had a son called Geirolf who was the second husband of Vigdis Konal's-daughter. Vigdis had previously been married to Thorgrim, and their son was Hall.

247. *Eyvind and Ketil*

There was a man called Thorstein Hofdi, who was a chieftain in Hordaland. His sons were Eyvind and Ketil the Hordalander. After his father died, Eyvind had a great desire to go to Iceland, and Ketil asked him to claim land for them both, in case he himself wanted to go later. Eyvind brought his ship in to Husavik and took possession of Reykjadale above Vestmannswater. He made his home at Helgastead, and that's where he was buried, in a grave mound. Nattfari, who came to Iceland with Gardar, had claimed possession of Reykjadale previously and marked his claim on trees, but Eyvind drove him out and provided him with land at Nattfaravik. When he got word from Eyvind, Ketil went to Iceland and made his home at Einarsstead.

His son was Konal, father of Einar who farmed there afterwards. Eyvind's son was Askel the Priest, who married Grenjad's daughter, and their sons were Thorstein and Killer-Skuta. Eyvind had a daughter called Fjorleif. Konal married Oddny Einar's-daughter, sister of Eyjolf Valgerdarson. Their children were Einar, who had six sons and two daughters, Thorey, whom Steinolf Masson married, and Eydis, who was married to Thorstein the Priest of Asbjarnarvik. Thord Konalsson was the father of Sokki of Breidamyri, father of Konal. Konal had a daughter called Vigdis, who was married to Thorgrim, son of Thorbjorn Skagi, and their son was Thorleif, Geirolf's stepson.

248. *Grenjad Hrappsson*

There was a man called Grenjad Hrappsson, brother of Geirleif. He took possession of Thegjandadale, Krauna Moor, Thorgerdarfell and the lower part of Laxriverdale. He married Thorgerd, daughter of Helgi Horse, and their son was Thorgeir Vamull, father of Onund, father of Hallbera, mother of Halldora, mother of Thorgerd, mother of Abbot Hall[72] and of Hallbera, wife of Hrein Styrmission.[73]

249. *Bodolf*

There was a man called Bodolf, son of Grim Grimolfsson of Agder and brother of Bodmod. He married Thorunn, daughter of Thorolf the Wise, and their son was Skeggi. The whole family went to Iceland and were shipwrecked off Tjorness, and spent the first winter at Audolfsstead. Bodolf took possession of the whole of Tjorness between Tungu River and Os. Afterwards he married Thorbjorg Island-Sun, daughter of Helgi the Lean, and their daughter was Thorgerd, wife of Asmund Ondottsson.

250. *Skeggi Bodolfsson*

Skeggi Bodolfsson took possession of Kelduhverfi up to Kelduness and made his home at Miklagard. He married Helga, daughter of Thorgeir of Fiski Brook, and their son was Thorir the Sea-Farer, who had a ship built in Sogn to be blessed by Bishop Sigurd. The beaks of this ship stand over the door at Miklagard and people tell the weather by them. Grettir composed these verses about Thorir:

> I'll not ride against warriors,
> I'll go my own way,
>   mine is a harsh fate,

---

[72]Abbot Hall was abbot of the monastery at Thver River and died in 1190.
[73]Hrein Styrmisson was abbot of the monastery at Thingeyrar and died in 1171.

I'll not face these fighters;
surely you see
I'm far from stupid;
I choose to wait
till my chances are better.

I turn my face
from Thorir's great force,
I can't say I care
to join their company;
I'll not meet these famed men,
I'll make for the forest,
I must shun fate,
shield my own head.

251. *Mani*

There was a man called Mani, who was born on the island of Omd
in Halogaland. He went to Iceland and was shipwrecked off Tjorness.
He lived at Mana River for several years, and then after Bodolf drove
him away from there, he took possession of land below Kalfborgar
River, between Fljot and Raudaskrida, making his home at Manafell.
His son Ketil married Valdis, daughter of Thorbrand who bought
the Raudaskridulands from Mani. His daughter Dalla, halfsister to
Thorgeir Galtason, married Thorvald Hjaltason.

252. *Ljot the Unwashed*

There was a man called Ljot the Unwashed, who took possession of
Kelduhverfi above Kelduness. His son was Gris, father of Galti of As,
a shrewd man and a great fighter.

253. *Onund*

Onund also took land in Kelduhverfi above Kelduness and lived at As.
He was the son of Blæing Sotason and brother of Balki of Hrutafjord.
Onund had a daughter called Thorbjorg who married Hallgils Thor-
brandsson of Raudaskrida.

254. *Thorstein*

Thorstein, son of Sigmund Gnupa-Bardarson, made his first home at
Mywater. His son was Thorgrim, father of Arnor of Reykjahlid, who'
married Thorkatla, daughter of Bodvar Hrolfsson of Gnupufell, and
their son was called Bodvar.

255. *Thorkel the Tall*

Thorkel the Tall was a young man when he came to Iceland and he made his first home at Grænawater, an inlet off Mywater. He had a son called Sigmund, who married Vigdis, daughter of Thorir of Espi-hill; this Thorir was killed in a cornfield by Glum. Thorkel had a daughter called Arndis, wife of Vigfus, Killer-Glum's brother. Thorkel had a son when he was an old man. This son was called Dag, and was the father of Thorarin, the second husband of Yngvild Sidu-Hall's-daughter, who'd been married before to Eyjolf the Lame.

256. *Geiri*

There was a Norwegian called Geiri, who was the first man to settle on the south side of Mywater, at Geirastead. His sons were Glum and Thorkel. Father and sons fought against Thorberg Cheek-Wound, killing his son Thorstein, and for this they were banished from the north. Geiri spent one winter at Geirastead near Hunawater, and then they travelled at Breidafjord and made their home at Geirastead in Kroksfjord. Glum married Ingunn, daughter of Thorolf Veleifsson, and their children were Thord, who married Gudrun Osvif's-daughter, and Thorgerd, wife of Thorarin Ingjaldsson; their son was Helgu-Steinar.

257. *Einar*

In his youth, Earl Turf-Einar had a daughter called Thordis. She was reared by Earl Rognvald who gave her in marriage to Thorgeir the Clumsy, and they had a son called Einar. He went to Orkney to see his kinsmen but they refused to accept him. Then Einar bought a share in a ship, in partnership with two brothers called Vestmann and Vemund. They went to Iceland and sailed north round Sletta and into the fjord. They put up an axe on Reistar Peak and called the fjord Oxarfjord. In the west they put up an eagle, and called that place Arnarthufa; and at a third place they raised a cross and called the place Kross Ridge after it. This is how they hallowed Oxarfjord and claimed the whole of it for themselves. Einar's children were Eyjolf, whom Galti Grimsson killed, and Ljot, mother of Hroi the Sharp, who avenged Eyjolf's death and killed Galti. The sons of Gliru-Halli, Brand and Berg, were Ljot's grandsons; they were killed at Bodvarsdale.

258. *Reist*

Reist, son of Bjarn-Isle Ketil and of Hild, sister of Ketil Thistle, father of Arnstein the Priest, took possession of land between Reistar Peak and Rauda Peak, and made his home at Leirhaven.

259. *Arngeir*

There was a man called Arngeir who took possession of the whole of Sletta between Hayararlon and Sveinungsvik. His children were Thorgils, Odd and Thurid, who married Steinolf of Thjorsriverdale. Arngeir and Thorgils set out from home to search for their sheep in a blizzard and never came back. Odd went to look for them and found them both dead. They'd been killed by a polar bear which was still at the prey when Odd came there. Odd killed it and brought it home, and the story goes that he ate the whole bear. He said he'd avenged his father by killing it, and his brother by eating it. After that Odd turned out an evil man, very hard to deal with. He was such a great shape-changer that he set out one evening from Hraunhaven, and arrived in Thjorsriverdale the following morning, to help his sister when the men of Thjorsriverdale wanted to stone her to death.

260. *Sveinung and Kolli*

Sveinung took possession of Sveinungsvik, and Kolli Kollavik, each living for the rest of his life at the place which bears his name.

261. *Ketil Thistle*

Ketil Thistle took possession of Thistilsfjord, between Hundsness and Saudaness. His son was Sigmund, father of Einar of Laugarbrekka.

262. *North Quarter: Conclusion*

Now we've written about the settlements in the North Quarter, and these were the noblest settlers: Audun Shaft, Ingimund, Ævar, Sæmund, Eirik of Goddales, Thord of Hofdi, Helgi the Lean, and Eyvind, son of Thorstein Hofdi. The farmers in this Quarter numbered about 1440 when the count was taken.[74]

263. *The East Quarter*

The settlers who took possession of land in the East Quarter will be listed now in proper order, from the Quarter boundaries at Langaness in the north to Solheimasand in the south. This Quarter is said to have been the first to be fully settled.

264. *Gunnolf Crop*

There was a man called Gunnolf Crop, son of the chieftain Thorir Hawk-Nose. He took possession of Gunnolfsvik and Gunnolfsfell, including all the land in Langaness north of Helkundu Moor, and made

---

[74]See footnote on p. 80.

his home at Fagravik. His son was Skuli Slouch, Geirlaug's father.

265. *Finni*

There was a man called Finni, who took possession of Finnafjord and Midfjord. His son was Thorarin, father of Sigurd, father of Gliru-Halli.

266. *Hrodgeir Hrappsson*

Hrodgeir Hrappsson the White took possession of land north of Digraness all the way to Midfjord, and made his home at Skeggjastead. His daughter was Ingibjorg, wife of Thorstein the White. Hrodgeir had a brother called Alrek who came to Iceland with him; he was the father of Ljotolf the Priest of Svarfadardale.

267. *Eyvind Weapon*

Eyvind Weapon and Ref the Red, sons of Thorstein Thick-Leg, fell out with King Harald and got ready to set out for Iceland from Strind in Trondheim. Each of them had his own ship. Ref was driven back, and the king had him put to death, but Eyvind reached Vopnafjord and took possession of the whole of the fjord north of Vestradale River, and lived at Inner Krossavik. He had a son called Thorbjorn.

268. *Steinbjorn Cart*

There was a man called Steinbjorn Cart, son of Ref the Red. He went to Iceland and put in at Vopnafjord. His uncle Eyvind granted him all the lands between Vopnafjord and Vestradale Rivers, and he made his home at Hof. His sons were first Thormod the Stick-Gazer, who lived at Sunnudale, second, Ref of Refsstead, and third, Egil of Egils-stead, father of Thorarin, Throst, Hallbjorn and Hallfrid who married Thorkel Geitisson.

269. *Hroald Bjola*

Eyvind Weapon had a blood-brother called Hroald Bjola, who took possession of land west of Vestradale River, including half of the valley and the whole of Selriverdale north to Digraness. He made his home at Torfastead. His son was Isrod, father of Gunnhild, wife of Oddi, son of Asolf of Hofdi.

270. *Thorstein the White*

There was a man called Olvir the White, son of Osvald Oxen-Thoris-son. He was a man of some rank and lived at Almdales. He fell out with Earl Hakon Grjotgardsson and moved over to Yrjar, where he died. But Thorstein the White, his son, went to Iceland and brought his ship in to Vopnafjord after the Age of Settlements. He bought land from Eyvind Weapon and lived for several years at Toptavellir north of Sirekstead, but then he got hold of the Hofsland by claiming repayment of a debt from Steinbjorn Cart, who had nothing to pay with except the land. Thorstein farmed there for sixty years, and he was a wise man and good adviser. He married Ingibjorg, daughter of Hrodgeir the White, and these were their children: Thorgils, Thord, Onund, Thorbjorg and Thora. Thorgils married Asvor, daughter of Thorir Gruel-Atlason, and their son was Brodd-Helgi whose first wife was Halla, daughter of Lyting, son of Arnbjorn. The son of Brodd-Helgi and Halla was Killer-Bjarni, who married Rannveig, daughter of Eirik of Goddales. Their son was Beard-Broddi, and their daughter Yngvild, wife of Thorstein Hallsson. Beard-Broddi married Gudrun, daughter of Thorarin Sæling and Halldora Einar's-daughter and their children were Thorir and Bjarni House-Long. Thorir married Steinunn, daughter of Thorgrim the Tall, and their daughter was Gudrun, wife of Flosi Kolbeinsson. The son of Gudrun and Flosi was Bjarni, father of Bjarni who married Halla Jorund's-daughter. Their children were the priests Flosi and Torfi, Einar Bride, Gudrun, wife of Thord Sturluson, another Gudrun, wife of Einar Bergthorsson, and Helga, mother of Sigrid Sighvat's-daughter.

271. *Lyting*
Thorstein Torfi and Lyting were brothers and went to Iceland. Lyting took possession of all the east part of Vopnafjord Strand, including Bodvarsdale and Fagradale, and lived at Krossavik. The Vopnafjord people are descended from him.

272. *Thorfinn*
There was a man called Thorfinn, who first lived at Skeggjastead, with Thord Straw's approval. Thorstein the Fair, who killed Einar, son of Thorir Gruel-Atlason, was his son. Thorstein's two brothers were Thorkel and Hedin, who killed Thorgils, Brodd-Helgi's father.

273. *Thorstein Torfi*
Thorstein Torfi took possession of the entire Hlid, from Osfells up to Hvann River, and made his home at Forsvoll. His son was Thorvald, father of Thorgeir, father of Hallgeir, father of Hrapp of Forsvoll.

274. *Hakon*
There was a man called Hakon, who took possession of the whole of

Jokulsdale, west of Jokuls River and above Teigar River. He made
his home at Hakonarstead. His daughter was Thorbjorg, who was
married to the sons of Brynjolf the Old, Gunnbjorn and Hallgrim.
There was an unclaimed plot of land between Thorstein Torfi's and
Hakon's. They gave it to the temple and nowadays it's called Hofsteig.

275. *Skjoldolf*

Skjoldolf Vemundarson, Berdlu-Kari's brother, took possession of
Jokulsdale east of Jokuls River above Knefilsdale River, and lived
at Skjoldolfsstead. His children were Thorstein who married Fastny
Brynjolf's-daughter, and Sigrid, Bersi Gizurarson's mother.

276. *Thord*

There was a man called Thord, son of Thorolf Straw and brother of
Helgi Toil-Head. He took possession of the Tongue lands, between
Lagarwater and Jokuls River below Rang River. His son was Thorolf
Straw who married Gudrid Brynjolf's-daughter. Their son was Thord
Spear, father of Thorodd, father of Brand, father of Steinunn, mother
of Rannveig, mother of Sæhild, Gizur's wife.

277. *Ozur Strike-Pate*

Ozur Strike-Pate took possession of land between Orms River and
Rang River. He married Gudny Brynjolf's-daughter and their son was
Asmund, Mord's father.

278. *Ketil*

Ketil and Gruel-Atli, sons of Thorir Thidrandi, went from Veradale
to Iceland and took possession of land in Fljotsdale, before Brynjolf
came to Iceland. Ketil took possession of both banks of Lagarwater
on the west side between Hengifors and Orms Rivers. Ketil went
abroad and stayed with Vethorm, son of Vemund the Old, and then
he paid money to Vethorm for Arneid, daughter of Earl Asbjorn
Skerry-Blaze, whom Holmfast Vethormsson had taken captive when
he and Grim, Vethorm's nephew, killed Earl Asbjorn. For Arneid
Asbjorn's-daughter Ketil paid double Vethorm's original price, and
after the bargain was struck Ketil made Arneid his wife. Afterwards
she found a hoard of silver buried under the roots of a tree. Then
Ketil offered to take her back to her family, but she chose to go with
him. They went to Iceland and made their home at Arneidarstead.
Their son was Thidrandi, father of Ketil of Njardvik.

279. *Gruel-Atli*

Gruel-Atli took possession of the east side of Lagarwater, between Gilja River and Vallaness, west of Oxna Brook. His sons were Thorbjorn and Thorir, who married Asvor Brynjolf's-daughter.

280. *The Sons of Thorgeir Vestarsson*

There was a well-born man called Thorgeir Vestarsson, who had three sons: one was Brynjolf the Old, the second was Ævar the Old, and the third was Herjolf. They all went to Iceland, each in his own ship. Brynjolf put in at Eskifjord, and took possession of land on the other side of the mountains, the whole of Fljotsdale above Hengifors River in the west and Gilja River in the east, all Skridudale and also the plains down to Eyvindar River, slicing off a good part of Uni Gardarson's land-claim. From this he granted land to his kinsmen and in-laws. He had ten children. Later he married Helga, who had previously been married to his brother Herjolf, and they had three children. Their son was Ozur, father of Bersi, father of Holmstein, father of Orækja, father of Holmstein, father of Helga, mother of Holmstein, father of Hallgerd, mother of Thorbjorg, wife of Loft, the Bishop's son.

281. *Ævar the Old*

Ævar the Old, Brynjolf's brother put in at Reydarfjord and travelled up to the mountains. Brynjolf granted him Skridudale, above Gilja River. He lived at Arnaldsstead and had two sons and three daughters.

282. *Asrod*

There was a man called Asrod, who married Asvor Herjolf's-daughter, Brynjolf's niece and step-daughter. As her dowry he got all the lands between Gilja River and Eyvindar River, and they lived at Ketilsstead. Their son was Thorvald Hollow-Throat, father of Thorberg, father of Hafljot, father of Thorhadd Scales. Thorvald Hollow-Throat had a daughter called Thorunn, wife of Thorbjorn Gruel-Atlason, and another called Astrid, mother of Asbjorn Shaggy-Head, father of Thorarin of Seydisfjord, father of Asbjorn, father of Kolskegg the Wise[75] and of Ingileif, mother of Hall, father of Finn the Lawspeaker.[76]

283. *Hrafnkel Hrafnsson*

There was a man called Hrafnkel Hrafnsson who came to Iceland

---

[75]For Kolskegg the Wise see Introduction p. 4.
[76]The priest Finn Hallson was Lawspeaker of the Althing 1139-1145.

towards the end of the Settlement Period. He spent the first winter
in Breiddale, but in the spring he travelled north across the mountains.
He took a rest in Skridudale and fell asleep, and then he dreamed a
man came to him and told him to get up and leave at once. He
woke up and set off, and he'd only gone a short distance when the
whole mountain came crashing down and killed a boar and a bull
belonging to him. Afterwards he claimed possession of Hrafnkelsdale
and made his home at Steinrodarstead. His sons were Asbjorn, father
of Helgi, and Thorir, father of the chieftain Hrafnkel, father of
Sveinbjorn.

284. *Uni the Dane*

Uni, son of Gardar who discovered Iceland, went to Iceland at the
suggestion of King Harald Fine-Hair with the intention of conquering
the land. The king had promised to make him his earl. Uni put in
at a place now called Una Estuary, and built a house there. He took
possession of land south of Lagarwater, claiming the entire district
north of Una Brook. When people realised what he wanted, they
grew hostile and wouldn't sell him livestock and other necessities, so he
wasn't able to stay there.

Uni moved over to South Alftafjord, but couldn't settle there either.
Then he travelled westwards with eleven companions and came that
winter to Leidolf the Champion of Skogarhverfi, who took them in.
Uni fell in love with Thorunn, Leidolf's daughter, and by spring she
was carrying a child. Then Uni tried to run away with his men, but
Leidolf rode off after them and caught up with them at Flangastead.
They fought there, because Uni wouldn't go back with Leidolf. Several
of Uni's men were killed, and he went back against his will, because
Leidolf wanted him to marry the girl, settle down there and take the
inheritance after him. A little later Uni ran away again when Leidolf
wasn't home, but as soon as Leidolf found out, he went off after him.
They met up with each other at Kalfagrafir, and Leidolf was in such
a rage, he killed Uni and all his companions.

The son of Uni and Thorunn was Hroar Tongue-Priest, who took
the whole inheritance after Leidolf and became an outstanding man.
He married Hamund's daughter, the sister of Gunnar of Hlidarend.
Their son was Hamund the Lame, a fighting man of some reputation.

Hroar's nephews were Tjorfi the Mocker and Gunnar. Tjorfi
wanted to marry Astrid Wisdom-Slope, daughter of Modolf, but her
brothers Ketil and Hrolf wouldn't let her become his wife and married
her off to Thorir Ketilsson instead. Then Tjorfi carved the images of
Astrid and Thorir on the privy wall, and every evening when he and

Hroar went to the privy he used to spit in the face of Thorir's image and kiss hers, until Hroar scraped them off the wall. Then Tjorvi carved them on the handle of his knife, and made this verse;

> Once in cruel spite
> I carved an image
> of the young bride
> with Thorir beside her;
> on my knife-handle
> I've now carved the lady,
> I used to have plenty
> of pleasure with her.

On account of this verse Hroar and his nephews were killed.

285. *Thorir the Sage*
There was a man called Thorir the Sage, who took possession of the whole of Njardvik and made his home there. His daughter was Thjodhild, wife of Ævar the Old, and their daughter was Yngvild, mother of Ketil Thidrandason of Njardvik.

286. *Veturlidi*
There was a man called Veturlidi, son of Arnbjorn Olafson Long-Neck and brother of Lyting, Thorstein Torfi and Thorbjorn of Arnarholt. Olaf Long-Neck was the son of Bjorn Whale-Side. Veturlidi took possession of Borgarfjord and made his home there.

287. *Thorir Line*
There was a man called Thorir Line, who took possession of Breidavik and made his home there. His sons were Sveinung and Gunnstein.

Now begins Kolskegg the Wise's account of the settlements.

288. *Thorstein Horse-Fly*
Thorstein Horse-Fly was the first settler of Husavik, and that's where he farmed. His son was An, from whom the people of Husavik are descended.

289. *Lodmund the Old*
There was a man called Lodmund the Old, who had a blood-brother called Bjolf. They went to Iceland from Thuluness in Vors. Lodmund was a man of unusual powers and a great sorcerer. He threw his highseat pillars overboard at sea, saying he would make his home wherever they washed ashore. The blood-brothers put in at the East-

fjords, and Lodmund took possession of Lodmundarfjord, where he
spent the first winter. Then he was told his highseat pillars were on
the south coast. He loaded all his belongings aboard his ship, and
when they hoisted sail he lay down and gave everyone strict orders
not to mention his name. After he'd been lying there for a short while
there was a loud crash, and his men could see a landslide sweeping
down on the farmstead where he had lived. Then he sat up and said:
"I lay a curse on this place that no seagoing ship shall ever put in
safely here". He sailed on southwards round Horn, hugging the coast
all the way to Hjorleifshofdi and putting in just to the west of it. He
took possession of the place where the pillars had come ashore as well
as the land between Hafurs River and Fula Brook, nowadays called
Jokuls River in Solheimasand. He made his home at Lodmundar-
hvamm and called the farm Solheimar.

When Lodmund was an old man, another sorcerer, Thrasi, was living at Skogar. It happened one morning that Thrasi saw a great flood
of water, and by means of his witchcraft he directed the flood east
to Solheimar. Lodmund's slave saw this and told him the sea was
flooding the land from the north. Lodmund had gone blind by then,
and he told his slave to get a basin and bring him a sample of what
he called sea-water. When the slave came back, Lodmund said, "This
doesn't seem like sea-water to me". He told the slave to lead him to
the flood. "Put the point of my staff into the water," he said. There
was a ferrule on the staff, and Lodmund held the staff with both
hands and bit the ferrule. Then the flood began to turn westwards
back to Skogar. In this way, each of the sorcerers kept directing the
flood away from his farm, until they met each other at a certain
ravine. So then they came to an agreement that the river should flow
where the distance to the sea was shortest. This river is now called
Jokuls River, and forms the Quarter boundary.

290. *Bjolf*
Bjolf, Lodmund's blood-brother, took possession of the whole of
Seydisfjord and farmed there for the rest of his life. He gave his
daughter Helga in marriage to An the Strong and, as her dowry,
the entire north side of Seydisfjord, as far as Vestdale River. Bjolf
had a son called Isolf who farmed there after him, and the people of
Seydisfjord are descended from him.

291. *Eyvind*
There was a man called Eyvind who came to Iceland with Brynjolf
and later moved house to Mjovafjord where he made his home. His

son was Hrafn, who sold the Mjovafjord lands to Thorkel the Clatterer, and he farmed there afterwards. The Klaka line is descended
from Thorkel.

292. *Egil the Red*
There was a man called Egil the Red, who took possession of Nordfjord and made his home out at Ness. His son was Olaf, from whom
the people of Ness are descended.

293. *Freystein the Handsome*
There was a man called Freystein the Handsome, who took possession
of Sandvik, Vidfjord and Hellisfjord, and made his home at Bardsness.
From him stem the people of Sandvik, Vidfjord and Hellisfjord.

294. *Thorir and Krum*
Thorir the Tall and Krum went to Iceland from Vors, and after they
landed Thorir took possession of Krossavik, between Gerpir and Reydarfjord. The people of Krossavik are descended from him. Krum
took possession of land in Hafraness as far as Thernuness, including
the whole coast, Skrud Isle and other sea islands and three areas of
farmland on the side opposite Thernuness. The Krymlings are descended from him.

295. *Ævar and Brynjolf*
Ævar farmed at Reydarfjord at first, before he moved inland across
the mountains, and Brynjolf farmed at Eskifjord until he set off to
settle in Fljotsdale, as was written earlier.

296. *Vemund*
There was a man called Vemund, who took possession of the whole
of Faskrudsfjord and farmed there for the rest of his life. His son was
Olmod, from whom the Olmædlings are descended.

297. *Thorhadd the Old*
Thorhadd the Old was a temple priest at Moere in Trondheim. He
had a great desire to go to Iceland, but before he set off, he dismantled
the temple and took the pillars and some earth from under the
temple with him. He put in at Stodvarfjord, and declared the whole
fjord sacred, just as his place in Moere had been, forbidding people
to take any life there except for domestic cattle. He farmed there for
the rest of his life, and the people of Stodvarfjord are descended from
him.

298. *Hjalti*

There was a man called Hjalti who took possession of the Kleiflands and all the upper part of Breiddale above Kleif. His son was Kolgrim, and many people are descended from him.

299. *Herjolf*

There was a man called Herjolf who took possession of all the lands out as far as Hvalness Slip. His son was Vapni from whom the Væpn-lings are descended.

300. *Herjolf*

Brynjolf's brother Herjolf took possession of the Heydale lands below Tinnudale River, as far as Orms River. His son was Ozur, from whom the people of Breiddale are descended.

301. *Skjoldolf*

There was a man called Skjoldolf, who took possession of the whole of Streiti, from Gnup out to the sea, and on the other side to Os and Skjoldolfsness by Fagradale River in Breiddale. His son Haleyg farmed there afterwards, and the Haleyg line stems from him.

302. *Thjodrek*

There was a man called Thjodrek, who first took possession of the whole of Breiddale, but later on fled from there for fear of Brynjolf and moved down to Berufjord, taking possession of the entire north side of the fjord, southwards as far as Bulandsness and inland up to Rauda Slip on the other side. He farmed for three years at a place called Skali. Later Bjorn the Tall bought some of his land, and from him stem the people of Berufjord.

303. *Bjorn Singe-Horn*

There was a man called Bjorn Singe-Horn, who took possession of North Alftafjord west of Rauda Slip and Svidinhornadale.

304. *Thorstein Drum-Leg*

Bodvar the White had a kinsman called Thorstein Drum-Leg, who went with him to Iceland and took possession of land between Leiru Creek and Hvalness Slip. His son was Koll the Grey, father of Thorstein, father of Thorgrim of Borgarhaven, father of Steinunn, wife of Bishop Gizur.

305. *Bodvar the White*

Bodvar the White was the son of Thorleif the Middling, son of Bodvar Snow-Rim, son of Thorleif Whale-Fringe, son of An, son of King Orn Hyrna, son of King Thorir, son of Hog-Bodvar, son of King Kaun, son of King Solgi, son of Hrolf of Berg. Bodvar and his kinsman Brand-Onund went from Vors to Iceland and put in at South Alfta-fjord. Bodvar took possession of land west of Leiru Creek, including all the valleys there, and eastwards on the other side as far as Muli. He made his home at Hof and built a large temple there. Bodvar's son Thorstein married Thordis, daughter of Ozur Hrollaugsson Keiliselg. Their son was Hall of Sida who married Joreid Thidrandi's-daughter, and many people are descended from them. Their son was Thorstein, father of Amundi, father of Gudrun, mother of Thordis, mother of Helga, mother of Gudny, mother of the Sturlusons.

306. *Brand-Onund*

Brand-Onund took possession of land north of Muli including Kambs-dale and Melrakkaness west of Hamars River. A good many people are descended from him.

307. *Thord Skeggi*

Thord Skeggi, son of Hrapp, Bjorn Buna's son, married Vilborg, daughter of Osvald and of Ulfrun, Edmund's-daughter. Thord went to Iceland, took possession of land between Jokuls River and Lons Moor in the north, and farmed at Bær for ten years or more. Then he was told his highseat pillars had been found at Leiru Creek, west of the moor, so he moved house there to the west, making his home at Skeggjastead, as written before. Then he sold the Lon lands to Ulfljot who brought the laws to Iceland. Thord's daughter was Helga, wife of Ketilbjorn the Old of Mosfell.

308. *Thorstein Leg*

Thorstein Leg, son of Bjorn Blue-Tooth, went to Iceland from the Hebrides and took possession of all the lands north of Horn and as far as Jokuls River in Lon. He farmed at Bodvarsholt for three years, then sold his land and went back to the Hebrides.

309. *Earl Rognvald's sons*

Earl Rognvald of More, the son of Eystein the Clatterer, son of Earl Ivar of the Uplands, son of Halfdan the Old, married Ragnhild, Hrolf Nose's daughter. Their son was Ivar who was killed in the Hebrides fighting on the side of King Harald Fine-Hair. Earl Rognvald's second son was Ganger-Hrolf, who conquered Normandy; the earls of Rouen and the kings of England are descended from him. The third son was Earl Thorir the Silent, who married Alof the Fecund, daughter of King Harald Fine-Hair, and their daughter was Bergljot, mother of Earl Hakon the Mighty.[77]

Earl Rognvald had three illegitimate sons: one was called Hrollaug, the second Einar, and the third Hallad who forfeited his earldom over Orkney. When Earl Rognvald heard about it, he summoned his sons asking which of them would like to go to the islands. Thorir said it was up to the earl whether or not he should go. The earl replied Thorir would be a good man and added that he was to take over his earldom after Rognvald's death.

Then Hrolf came forward and offered to go. Rognvald said he was well enough suited for this as far as his strength and courage went, but that in his opinion Hrolf's temper was too violent for him to set up as ruler.

Next Hrollaug came forward and asked the earl if he should go. Rognvald said Hrollaug would never be earl. "You've a temper which is not suited to warfare. Your paths will take you to Iceland, where you'll be highly thought of and have plenty of descendants, but your destiny doesn't lie here".

Finally Einar came up and said, "Let me go to Orkney. I can promise you something you'll like most of all and that's never to let you see me again".

The earl said, "I'm very glad you're going away, but I don't expect much of a man whose mother's descended from slaves on both sides".

Afterwards Einar went west and conquered the whole of Orkney, as is told in his saga.

But Hrollaug went to King Harald and stayed with him for a while, as he could never get on with his father after what had happened.

310. *Hrollaug*

Hrollaug went to Iceland with King Harald's approval, taking his wife and sons with him. He made landfall east at Horn where he threw his highseat pillars overboard, and they were washed ashore in Hornafjord. But he drifted westwards round the country, and suffering from the lack of water after a rough passage they put in at Leiru Creek in the Nesses, where he spent the first winter. Then he had reports of his highseat pillars and set off east to look for them. He

---

[77]Earl Hakon the Mighty was ruler of Norway c. 975-995.

spent the following winter at Ingolfsfell. From there he travelled east to Hornafjord and took possession of land between Horn and Kvia River. To begin with he farmed at Skardsbrekka in Hornafjord, and later at Breidabolstead in Fellshverfi. By that time he'd sold all his land north of Borgarhaven, but he kept the land south of Heggsgerdismull for the rest of his life. Hrollaug was a great chieftain and stayed friends with King Harald, though he never went back to Norway. King Harald sent Hrollaug a sword, a drinking horn and a gold ring weighing five ounces. The sword later belonged to Koll Sidu-Hallsson, and Kolskegg the Wise once saw the horn.

Hrollaug was the father of Ozur Keiliselg, who married Gro, daughter of Thord Illugi. Their daughter was Thordis, mother of Hall of Sida. Hrollaug had another son called Hroald, father of Ottar Whale-Clinch, father of Gudlaug, mother of Thorgerd, mother of Jarngerd, mother of Valgerd, mother of Bodvar, father of Gudny, mother of the Sturlusons. Hrollaug had a third son, Onund.

Hall of Sida married Joreid Thidrandi's-daughter. Their son was Thorstein, father of Magnus, father of Einar, father of Bishop Magnus.[78] Hall had another son called Egil, father of Thorgerd, mother of Bishop Jon the Holy. Thorvard Hallsson was the father of Thordis, mother of Jorunn, mother of the priest Hall, father of Gizur, father of Bishop Magnus.[79] Yngvild Hall's-daughter was the mother of Thorey, mother of the priest Sæmund the Learned. Thorstein Hallsson was the father of Gyrid, mother of Joreid, mother of the priest Ari the Learned. Thorgerd Hall's-daughter was the mother of Yngvild, mother of Ljot, father of Jarngerd, mother of Valgerd, mother of Bodvar, father of Gudny, mother of the Sturlusons.

311. *Ketil*

There was a man called Ketil, to whom Hrollaug sold Hornafjord Strand, between Horn in the west and Hamrar in the east. He made his home at Medalfell, and the Hornafjord people are descended from him.

312. *Audun the Red*

From Hrollaug, Audun the Red bought the area west of Hamrar as far as Vidbord. He made his home at Hofsfell where he built a large temple. The Hofsfell people are descended from him.

---

[78]Magnus Einarsson was Bishop of Skalholt 1134-48.
[79]Magnus Gizurarson was Bishop of Skalholt 1216-1237.

313. *Thorstein the Squint-Eyed*

From Hrollaug, Thorstein the Squint-Eyed bought all the lands south of Vidbord, including Myrar, as far as Heinabergs River. His son was Vestmar, from whom the Myrar people are descended.

314. *Ulf of Vors*

From Hrollaug, Ulf of Vors bought the land between Heinabergs River and Heggsgerdismull in the south, making his home at Skalafell.

315. *Thord Illugi*

Thord Illugi, son of Eyvind Ship-Hook, was shipwrecked at Breid-river Sand. Hrollaug granted him land between Jokuls and Kvia Rivers. He made his home at Fell by Breid River below Fell. His sons were Orn the Strong, who quarrelled with Thordis the earl's daughter, Hrollaug's sister, and Eyvind the Smith. His daughters were Gro, Ozur's wife, and Thordis, mother of Thorbjorg, mother of Thordis, mother of Thord Illugi who slew Killer-Skuta.

316. *Thorgerd*

There was a man called Asbjorn, son of the chieftain Heyjangur-Bjorn of Sogn, son of Helgi, son of Helgi Bjorn Buna's son. Asbjorn put out for Iceland and died at sea, but his widow Thorgerd and their sons completed the voyage and took possession of the whole of the Ingolfshofdi district between Kvia and Jokuls Rivers. She made her home at Sandfell, and afterwards Gudlaug, her son by Asbjorn, farmed there. The Sandfell people are descended from him. From another son of theirs, Thorgils, stem the Hnappafell people. Their third son was Ozur, father of Thord Frey's-Priest, from whom many people are descended.

317. *Helgi*

There was a man called Helgi, another son of Heyjangur-Bjorn. He went to Iceland and made his home at Rauda Brook. His son was Hildir, from whom the Rauda Brook people are descended.

318. *Bard*

Heyjangur-Bjorn had a third son, called Bard, who has been mentioned earlier. First he took possession of Bardardale in the north, but later he travelled by Bard's Path south through Vonar Pass and took possession of the whole of Fljotshverfi making his home at Gnupar. He came to be known as Gnupa-Bard. His sons were Thorstein, Sigmund, Egil, Gisli, Nefstein, Thorbjorn Krum, Hjor, Thorgrim, and Bjorn, father of Geiri of Lundar, father of Thorkel the Physician, father of Geiri, father of Canon Thorkel,[80] the friend of Bishop Thorlak the Holy. He founded the monastery of Thykkvaby.

319. *Eyvind Karpi*
Eyvind Karpi took possession of land between Almannawater and Geirlands River, making his home at Foss, west of Modolfs Peak. His sons were Modolf, father of Hrolf, Ketil and Astrid Wisdom-Slope; and Onund, father of Thraslaug, mother of Tyrfing and Halldor, father of Tyrfing, father of Teit.

320. *Ketil the Foolish*
There was a man called Ketil the Foolish, son of Jorunn Wisdom-Slope, Ketil Flat-Nose's daughter. Ketil went from the Hebrides to Iceland. He was a Christian. He took possession of land between Geirlands and Fjardar Rivers, above Nykomi.

Ketil made his home at Kirkby, where the Papar[81] had been living before and where no heathen was allowed to stay. Ketil was the father of Asbjorn, father of Thorstein, father of Surt, father of Sighvat the Lawspeaker,[82] father of Kolbein. Asbjorn had a daughter called Hild, mother of Thorir, father of Hild, wife of Skarphedin. Ketil the Foolish had a daughter called Thorbjorg; she became the wife of Vali, son of Lodmund the Old.

321. *Bodmod*
There was a man called Bodmod, who took possession of land between Drifandi and Fjardar River, as far as Bodmodshorn, and made his home at Bodmodstongue. His son was Oleif, after whom Oleifsborg takes its name; he farmed at Holt. His son was Vestar, father of Helgi, father of Gro who married Glædir.

322. *Eystein the Stout*
Eystein the Stout went from South More to Iceland and took possession of land east of Geirlands River, as far as the land-claim of Ketil the Foolish, making his home at Geirland. His son was Thorstein of Keldugnup.

323. *Eystein Hranason*
Eystein, son of Hrani, son of Hildir Parrak, went from Norway to

---

[80]Canon Thorkel died in 1187.
[81]See footnote on p. 15.
[82]Sighvat Surtsson was Lawspeaker of the Althing, 1076-1083.

Iceland. He bought a part of Eystein the Stout's land-claim from him and called it Medallands. He made his home at Skard. His children were Hildir and Thorljot, wife of Thorstein of Keldugnup. Hildir wanted to move house to Kirkby after Ketil died, not seeing why a heathen shouldn't farm there, but as he was coming up to the fence of the home meadow, he dropped down dead. He lies buried in Hildir's Howe.

324. *Vilbald*

There was a man called Vilbald, brother of Askel Hnokkan. He went from Ireland to Iceland in a ship he called the Kudi, and put in at Kudafljot Estuary. He took possession of the Tongue lands between Skafta and Holms Rivers, and made his home at Buland. His children were Bjolan, father of Thorstein, Olvir Mouth, and Bjollok, wife of Aslak Aur-Priest.

325. *Leidolf the Champion*

There was a man called Leidolf the Champion, who took possession of land east of Skafta River as far as Drifandi making his home at Á, east of Skafta River and West of Skal. But he had another farm, at Leidolfsstead below Leidolfsfell where at the time there were a number of settlements. Leidolf was the father of Thorunn, mother of Hroar Tongue-Priest. Hroar married Arngunn Hamund's daughter, sister of Gunnar of Hlidarend. Their children were Hamund the Lame and Ormhild. By one of his bondmaids, Hroar had a son called Vebrand. Then Hroar married Thorunn Brow, daughter of Thorgils of Hvamm in Myrdale, and they had a son called Thorfinn. To begin with, Hroar farmed at Asar, but later he took the Lomagnup lands from Eystein, son of Thorstein the Tit and of Aud Eyvind's-daughter, sister of Modolf and Brand. Thorstein had a daughter called Thraslaug, who married Thord Frey's-Priest. Onund Basket-Back, who was related to Thorstein's children, challenged Hroar to a duel at the Skaftafell Assembly and fell at Hroar's feet. Thorstein the Uplander took Thorunn Brow abroad with him. Hroar went abroad too, and killed the berserk Throst in single combat when he wanted to force Hroar's wife Sigrid to go with him even though she had refused. But Hroar and Thorstein were reconciled. The Modolfssons and their brother-in-law Thorir were present at Hroar's killing, as were Brand of Gnupar and Steinolf, his neighbour. Hamund took vengeance for the deaths of Hroar and his men.

326. *Isolf*

There was a man called Isolf, who came to Iceland late in the Settlement Period and challenged Vilbald to single combat for land, but Vilbald wouldn't fight and left Buland. Vilbald then retained the land between Holms River and Kuda River. But Isolf settled at Buland and owned the land between Skafta River and Kuda River. He had a son called Hrani of Hranastead, and a daughter Bjorg, wife of Onund, son of Eyvind Karpi. Their daughter was Thraslaug, wife of Thorarin, son of Olvir of Hofdi.

327. *Hrafn Haven-Key*

Hrafn Haven-Key was a great viking. He went to Iceland and took possession of land between Holms and Eyjar Rivers making his home at Dynwoods. He was able to foresee a volcanic eruption and moved house to Lag Isle. His son was Aslak Aur-Priest from whom the Lag Isle people are descended.

328. *The Hrolfssons*

There was a man called Hrolf the Striker, who farmed at Moldtua in North More. His sons were Vemund and Molda-Gnup, both of them great fighters and blacksmiths. Vemund sang this in his smithy:

> Eleven men
> I alone
> brought to death.
> Blow harder!

329. *Molda-Gnup*

Gnup went to Iceland because of some killings he and his brother had committed, and took possession of land between Kudafljot and Eyjar River, including the whole of Alftaver; at that time there was a large lake there, a fine place for hunting swans. Molda-Gnup sold a good many people parts of his land-claim, so the district became thickly populated. But then these lands were covered by a lava-flow, and people fled west to Hofdabrekka, where they pitched their tents at a place called Tjaldavoll.[83] But Vemund, son of Sigmund Kleykir, wouldn't let them stay there. Then they moved over to Hrossagard, where they built themselves a house. They stayed the winter there, and then fightings and killings broke out among them. In the spring Molda-Gnup and his men travelled west to Grindavik and settled down there, but they had little livestock. By this time the Gnupssons, Bjorn, Gnup,

---

[83]Literally, 'Tent Plain'.

Thorstein Hrungnir and Thord Leggjaldi, were all grown men. One night Bjorn dreamed that a cliff-giant came and offered him partnership, and that he accepted the offer. Afterwards a strange billy-goat came to join his herd of goats, and his live-stock began to multiply so fast that soon he was a wealthy man. After that he was called Hafur-Bjorn.[84] People with second sight could see that all the guardian spirits of the land accompanied Hafur-Bjorn when he attended the Althing, and Thorstein and Thord when they went out fishing. Hafur-Bjorn married Jorunn, his brother Gnup's step-daughter. Their son was Sverting who married Hungerd, daughter of Thorodd Tongue-Oddsson and Jofrid Gunnar's-daughter. Sverting and Hungerd had a daughter called Thorbjorg, mother of Sveinbjorn, father of Botolf, father of Thordis, mother of Helga, mother of Gudny, mother of the Sturlusons.

Gnup Molda-Gnupsson married Arnbjorg Radorm's-daughter, as was written earlier. Molda-Gnup had a daughter called Idunn, wife of Thjostar of Alftaness, and their son was Thormod.

330. *Eystein and Olvir*

There was a man called Eystein, son of Thorstein Rock-Man, who went to Iceland from Halogaland. He was shipwrecked and was injured by the timber. He settled Fagradale. An old woman was washed overboard and she drifted ashore at Kerlingarfjord,[85] where Hofda-river Sand is now.

Olvir Eysteinsson took possession of land east of Grims River where no one had dared to settle for fear of land-spirits, since Hjorleif was killed there. Olvir made his home at Hofdi. His son was Thorarin of Hofdi, half-brother on their mother's side to Halldor Ornolfsson whom Mord Orækja killed at Hamrar and to Arnor whom Flosi and Kolbein, sons of Thord Frey's-Priest, killed at the Skaftafell Assembly.

331. *Sigmund Kleykir*

Sigmund Kleykir, son of Ogmund Bild, took possession of land between Grims and Kerlingar Rivers which at that time flowed west of Hofdi. From Sigmund three bishops are descended: Thorlak, Pal and Brand.[86]

---

[84]Literally, 'Billy-goat Bjorn'.
[85]Literally 'Old-woman's Fjord'.
[86]Thorlak Thorhallsson 'the Holy' was Bishop of Skalholt 1178-93; his nephew and successor, Pal Jonsson, was Bishop 1195-1211; Brand Sæmundsson was Bishop of Holar, 1163-1201.

332. *Bjorn of Reynir*

There was a man called Bjorn, a very wealthy but conceited man, who went to Iceland from Valdres and took possession of land between Kerlingar and Hafurs Rivers making his home at Reynir. He had bitter quarrels with Lodmund the Old. The Holy Bishop Thorlak is descended from Bjorn of Reynir.

333. *Lodmund the Old*

Lodmund the Old took possession of Hafurs River and Fula Brook, as was written earlier. At that time the river that was called Fula Brook separated the Quarters and is now known as Jokuls River in Solheimasand.

334. *Lodmund's descendants*

Lodmund the Old of Solheimar had six sons or more. One was called Vali, father of Sigmund who married Oddlaug, daughter of Eyvind the Islander. Lodmund had another son called Sumarlidi, father of Thorstein Hollow-Mouth of Mork, father of Thora, mother of Stein, father of Thora, mother of Surt the White, Skapti's step-father. Surt was Sumarlidi's son. Skafti the Lawspeaker[87] married Thora after she had been Sumarlidi's wife. This is stated in the *Genealogies of the Olfus People*. Lodmund's third son was called Vemund, father of Thorkatla, wife of Thorstein Beetle, and their daughter was Arnkatla, mother of Hroi and Thordis, wife of Stein Brandsson. Stein and Thordis had a daughter called Thora. Lodmund's fourth son was called Ari, his fifth son Hroald, and his sixth Ofeig, who was illegitimate. Ofeig married Thraslaug, daughter of Eyvind the Islander and sister of Oddlaug. From all these a vast number of people are descended.

335. *The East Quarter: Conclusion*

Now we've written about the settlements in the East Quarter, as wise and learned men have described them. A good many important people have lived in that Quarter since, and some great sagas have been set there. These were the most important settlers in the Quarter: Thorstein the White, Brynjolf the Old, Gruel-Atli and Ketil the sons of Thidrandi, Hrafnkel the Priest, Bodvar the White, Hrollaug son of Earl Rognvald, Ozur son of Asbjorn Heyjangur-Bjornsson, from whom the Freysgydlings are descended, Ketil the Foolish and Leidolf the Champion.

---

[87]Skafti Thorodsson was Lawspeaker of the Althing 1004-1030.

336. The South Quarter

Now we come to the settlements in the South Quarter which has been the most flourishing part of the whole of Iceland, because of the quality of the land and the chieftains living there, laymen and clergy alike.

337. Thrasi

There was a man called Thrasi, son of Thorolf the Horn-Breaker, who went to Iceland from Hordaland and took possession of land between Kaldaklofs and Jokuls Rivers. He made his home at East Skogar. He was a great sorcerer and quarrelled with Lodmund the Old, as was written earlier. Thrasi had a son called Geirmund, father of Thorbjorn, father of Brand of Skogar.

338. Hrafn the Foolish

There was a man called Hrafn the Foolish, son of Valgard, son of Vemund Word-Master, son of Thorolf Creek-Nose, son of Hrærek the Ring-Scatterer, son of King Harald War-Tooth of Denmark. Hrafn went to Iceland from Trondheim and took possession of land between Kaldaklofs and Lambafells Rivers. He made his home at East Raudafell and was a man of great importance. His children were Jorund the Priest, Helgi Blue-Faggot and Freygerd.

339. Asgeir Kneif

There was a man called Asgeir Kneif, son of Oleif the White, son of Skæring Thorolfsson. Asgeir's mother was Thorhild, daughter of Thorstein the Mound-Breaker. Asgeir went to Iceland and took possession of land between Lambafells and Seljalands Rivers, making his home at a place now called Audnir. His sons were Jorund and Thorkel, father of Ogmund, father of Bishop Jon the Holy. Asgeir had a daughter called Helga, mother of Thorunn, mother of Thorlak, mother of Thorhall, father of Bishop Thorlak the Holy.

340. Thorgeir the Hordalander

Thorgeir the Hordalander, son of Bard Whey-Horn, went to Iceland from Viggja in Trondheim, and bought land from Asgeir Kneif between Lambafells and Ira Rivers, making his home at Holt. Some years later he married Asgerd, daughter of Ask the Silent, and their sons were Thorgrim the Tall and Holta-Thorir, father of Thorleif Crow and Skorar-Geir.

341. *Asgerd*

There was a famous man in Romsdale Province called Ofeig who married Asgerd, daughter of Ask the Silent. Ofeig fell out with King Harald Fine-Hair, and that's why he made preparations to sail to Iceland. Just when he was ready, King Harald sent men against him and he was put to death. But Asgerd went to Iceland with their children and her illegitimate brother, Thorolf. She took possession of land between Seljalandsmull and Markar River, including the whole of Langaness as far as Joldustein, making her home north in Kataness. Ofeig and Asgerd had these children: Thorgeir Gollnir, Thorstein Flask-Beard, Thorbjorn the Quiet and Alof Ship-Shield. Alof was the wife of Thorberg Kornamuli, and their children were Eystein and Hafthora, wife of Eid Skeggjason. Ofeig also had a daughter called Thorgerd who married Finn Otkelsson.

342. *Thorolf*

With Asgerd's approval, her brother Thorolf took possession of land west of Fljot, between the two Deildar Rivers, making his home at Thorolfsfell. There he fostered Thorgeir Gollnir, son of Asgerd, who farmed there afterwards. Thorgeir's son was Njal who was burnt to death in his house.

343. *Asbjorn and Steinfinn*

Asbjorn Reyrketilsson and Steinfinn, his brother, took possession of land above Kross River, east of Fljot. Steinfinn lived at Steinfinnsstead, and there's no one descended from him. Asbjorn dedicated his land-claim to Thor and called it Thorsmork. His son was Ketil the Wealthy, who married Thurid Gollnir's-daughter, and their children were Helgi and Asgerd.

344. *Ketil Trout*

Ketil Trout was a famous man in Namdalen Province, the son of Earl Thorkel of Namdalen and Hrafnhild, daughter of Ketil Trout of Hrafnista. The younger Ketil farmed in Namdalen at the time King Harald Fine-Hair sent Hallvard the Hard-Sailing and Sigtrygg the Swift-Sailing against Thorolf Kveld-Ulfsson, Ketil's kinsman. Then Ketil gathered forces, meaning to support Thorolf, but King Harald travelled overland across Eldueid, got ships at Namdalen, and sailed north to Sandness in Alost where he put Thorolf Kveld-Ulfsson to death. Then King Harald went back south again, following the coast, and on his way he ran into a number of men who were sailing to Thorolf's rescue. The king drove them back. A little later Ketil Trout

went north to Torgar where, in their own house, he burnt to death
the Hildiridarsons, Harek and Hrærek, whose slander had brought
about the death of Thorolf. After that Ketil decided to go to Iceland
with Ingunn, his wife, and their sons. He put in at Rang River Estuary
and spent the first winter at Hrafntoft. Ketil took possession of all the
land between Thjors and Markar Rivers where a good many important people settled with his approval. Ketil also claimed possession
of the land between Rang River and Hroars Brook, that is the whole
area below Reydarwater, and made his home at Hof. When Ketil had
brought most of his goods over to Hof, Ingunn gave birth to a boy,
and that was Hrafn, the first Lawspeaker in Iceland.[88] That's why
the place is known as Hrafntoft. Ketil Trout took over the whole
region east of East Rang River and Vatnsfell as far as the stream
that flows west of Breidabolstead above Thver River, excluding Dufthaksholt and Myri. That area he granted to a man called Dufthak,
a great sorcerer. Ketil Trout had another son called Helgi, who married Valdis Jolgeir's daughter, and their daughter was Helga, wife
of Oddbjorn the Ship-Wright, after whom Oddbjorn's Grave takes
its name. Oddbjorn and Helga had these children: Hroald, Kolbein,
Kolfinna and Asvor. Ketil Trout had a third son called Storolf, father
of Orm the Strong, Otkel and Hrafnhild, wife of Gunnar Baugsson.
The son of Hrafnhild and Gunnar was Hamund, father of Gunnar
of Hlidarend. Ketil Trout's fourth son, Vestar, married Moeid, and
their daughter was Asny, wife of Ofeig Grettir. Ofeig and Asdis had
these children: Asmund the Beardless, Asbjorn, Aldis, mother of
Valla-Brand, Asvor, mother of Helgi the Black and yet another daughter called Æsa. Ketil Trout's fifth son was Herjolf, father of Sumarlidi, father of Veturlidi the Poet. These lived at Sumarlidaby, known
as Brekkur nowadays. Veturlidi was killed by the priest Thangbrand
and Gudlaug Arason of Reykjahills for lampooning. Hrafn had a son
called Sæbjorn the Priest who married Unn Sigmund's-daughter, and
their son was Arngeir.

345. *Sighvat the Red*

There was a man called Sighvat the Red from a great family in Halogaland. He married Rannveig, daughter of Eyvind Lamb and of
Sigrid who was first married to Thorolf Kveld-Ulfsson. Rannveig was
the sister of Finn the Squint-Eyed. Sighvat desired to go to Iceland
and with Ketil Trout's approval he took possession of land from Ketil's
claim west of Markar River, including Einhyrningsmork above Deildar

---

[88]Hrafn was Lawspeaker of the Althing from about 930 to 949.

River. He made his home at Bolstead. His children were Sigmund, father of Mord Fiddle, Sigfus of Hlid, Lambi of Lambastead, Rannveig, wife of Hamund Gunnarsson, and Thorgerd, wife of Onund Bild of Floi. Sighvat had yet another son, Barek, father of Thord, father of Steini.

346. *Jorund the Priest*

Jorund the Priest, son of Hrafn the Foolish, settled west of Markar River, at a place now called Svertingsstead, and built a large temple there. There was an unclaimed piece of land east of Markar River, between Joldustein and Kross River, and Jorund carried fire around it and dedicated it to the temple. Jorund was married, and his sons by his wife were Valgard the Priest, Mord's father, and Ulf Aur-Priest, from whom the people of Oddi and the Sturlungs are descended. A good many important people in Iceland claim descent from Jorund.

347. *Thorkel Bound-Foot*

With Ketil Trout's approval Thorkel Bound-Foot took possession of land around Thrihyrning and made his home below the mountain. He was a great sorcerer. Thorkel's children were Bork Bluetooth-Beard, father of Starkad of Thrihyrning, Thorny, wife of Orm the Strong, and Dagrun, Bersi's mother.

348. *Baug*

Ketil Trout had a blood-brother called Baug who went to Iceland and spent the first winter at Baugsstead and the next with Ketil Trout. With Ketil's approval he took possession of the whole of Fljotshlid down to Breidabolstead, next to Ketil's land-claim, and made his home at Hlidarend. His sons were Gunnar of Gunnarsholt, Eyvind of Eyvindarmull and Snjallstein. Baug's daughter, Hild, was married to Orn of Vælugerdi. Snjallstein and Sigmund, son of Sighvat the Red, decided to sail abroad from Eyrar. Sigmund and Snjallstein's men came to the Sandhills ferry at the same time, each of them wanting to be the first to cross the river. Sigmund and his companions started pushing Snjallstein's men about and driving them away from the boat. Then Snjallstein came up and struck Sigmund dead on the spot. Because of this killing the Baugssons were banished from Fljotshlid, so Gunnar moved house to Gunnarholt, Eyvind went east of Eyvindarhills below Eyjafells, and Snjallstein to Snjallsteinshofdi.

Thorgerd Sigmund's-daughter was far from pleased that her father's killer should move to her district and urged her husband Onund to take vengeance for Sigmund. Onund set out with thirty men, went over to Snjallsteinshofdi and set fire to the house. Snjallstein came outside and surrendered. They took him up to the hill and killed him there. Gunnar took action, not because he was married to Orm's sister, but because he was Snjallstein's brother. Their son was Hamund who, like him, was a powerfully built and handsome looking man. Onund was sentenced to outlawry for the killing of Snjallstein. He kept a strong force of fighting men for two years. Orn of Vælugerdi, Gunnar's son-in-law, kept spying on Onund. Three years later, after Christmas, Gunnar received word from Orn and set out with thirty men. Onund was coming from the games with eleven men, on his way to see about his horses. They met at Orrustudale,[89] and Onund was killed there with three of his men, and one of Gunnar's men fell. Gunnar was wearing a blue cloak. He rode up through Holt over to Thjors River, and a short distance from the river he slipped from the saddle and fell dead of his wounds.

When the Onundssons, Sigmund Kleykir and Eilif the Wealthy, were fully grown they consulted their kinsman Mord Fiddle about what action they should take. Mord said it was a difficult matter since the dead man was already an outlaw, but they replied that of all their neighbours, they thought Orn was the worst. So Mord proposed they should make a charge against Orn carrying the penalty of full outlawry and so force him to leave the district. The Onundssons took over a charge against Orn for wrongful grazing and the outcome was that Orn could be killed by the Onundssons with impunity anywhere but at Vælugerdi and within an arrowshot of his own land. The Onundssons kept lying in wait for him, but he stayed on his guard. Eventually they got their chance when Orn was driving some cattle away from his land. Then they killed Orn, and people agreed that he'd been killed legally.

Thorleif Spark, Orn's brother, bribed Thormod Thjostarsson to make Orn's death illegal. Thormod had just arrived at Eyrar from abroad. He shot an arrow so far, it meant Orn had been killed within an arrow's shot of his land. After that Hamund Gunnarsson and Thorleif took action over Orn's killing and Mord gave the brothers Sigmund and Eilif, his support. No fine was imposed on them, but they were banished from Floi. Then Mord asked on Eilif's behalf for the hand of Thorkatla Ketilbjorn's-daughter. As her dowry she got the Hofdi lands, and that's where Eilif made his home. Mord asked for the hand of Arngunn, daughter of Thorstein Rock-Man on Sigmund's behalf, and Sigmund moved east to the district. Then Mord

---

[89]Literally 'Battle Valley.'

gave his sister Rannveig to Hamund Gunnarsson, who went back to live east in Fljotshlid, and their son was Gunnar of Hlidarend.

349. *Hildir, Hallgeir, Ljot*

Hildir, Hallgeir and their sister Ljot were of British stock. They went to Iceland and took possession of land between Fljot and Rang River, including the whole of the Eyja district right up to Thver River. Hildir made his home at Hildir's Isle; he was the father of Moeid. Hallgeir farmed at Hallgeir's Isle. His daughter was Mabil, wife of Helgi, son of Ketil Trout. Ljot made her home at Ljotarstead.

350. *Dufthak*

The brothers had a freedman called Dufthak, of Dufthaksholt. Like Storolf, Ketil Trout's son, he was a great sorcerer. Storolf lived at Hvoll, and he and Dufthak quarrelled over grazing. One evening, about sunset, someone with second sight noticed a huge bear set out from Hvoll, and a bull from Dufthaksholt. They met at Storolfsvoll and set upon one another in a fury, the bear getting the best of it. In the morning, people saw there was a hollow where they had met, and it was just as if the earth had been turned upside down. Nowadays the place is called Oldugrof. Both men were badly hurt.

351. *Orm the Unfree*

Orm the Unfree, son of Bard Bareksson and brother of Hallgrim Singe-Beam, was the first settler of the Westmanna Isles. Before that there used to be a fishing station, with hardly anyone living there permanently. His daughter was Halldora, wife of Eilif Valla-Brandsson.

352. *Eilif*

The brothers Eilif and Bjorn went from Sogn to Iceland. Eilif took possession of Lesser Oddi, as far as Reydarwater and Vikings Brook. He married Helga, daughter of Onund Bild and their son was Eilif the Young who married Oddny, daughter of Odd the Slender. Their daughter was Thurid, wife of Thorgeir of Oddi, whose daughter in turn was Helga.

353. *Bjorn*

Bjorn made his home at Svinhagi and took possession of land up along Rang River. His children were Thorstein, father of Grim Holta-Bald, and Hallveig, mother of Thorunn, mother of Gudrun, mother of Sæmund, Bishop Brand's father.

354. *Kolli*

There was a man called Kolli, son of Ottar Ball, who took possession of land between Reydarwater and Stota Brook in the west and Rang River in the east, making his home at Sandgill. His son was Egil who lay in wait for Gunnar Hamundarson at Knafahills and was killed there, along with two Norwegians and one of his farmhands called Ari. Gunnar lost his brother Hjort there.

355. *Hrolf Red-Beard*

There was a man called Hrolf Red-Beard, who took possession of all the Holmslands, between Fisk and Rang Rivers, making his home at Foss. His children were Thorstein Red-Nose who farmed there after him, Thora, mother of Thorkel Moon, Asa, mother of Thorunn, mother of Thorgeir of Ljosawater, and Helga, mother of Odd of Mjosyndi. Odd's daughter was Asborg, wife of Thorstein the Priest, father of Bjarni the Wise, father of Skeggi, father of Markus the Lawspeaker.[90]

Thorstein Red-Nose was a great sacrificer. He used to make sacrifices to the waterfall and all the left-overs had to be thrown into it. He could see clearly into the future. Thorstein had all his sheep counted and they numbered 2400; after that they all jumped over the wall of the fold. Thorstein had so many sheep because each autumn he could see which of the sheep were doomed to die, and he had those slaughtered. That's why he always had so many. The last autumn of his life, he said at the sheep-fold, "Now you can slaughter any of the sheep you like. Either I'm doomed to die or the sheep are doomed, or all of us are". The night he died, all the sheep got swept into the waterfall by a gale.

356. *Thorstein*

There was a powerful chieftain in Telemark called Ulf Gyldir. He lived at Fiflavellir, where his son Asgrim farmed after him. King Harald sent his kinsman Thororm of Thruma to claim a tribute from Asgrim, but he refused to pay. Next the king sent Thororm for Asgrim's life, and Thororm killed him. At that time Thorstein, Asgrim's son, was away on a viking expedition and Asgrim's other son, Thorgeir, was only ten years old. A little later Thorstein came back from his viking expedition and went over to Thruma, burning Thororm and his entire household to death in his own house, slaughtering the livestock, and looting everything he could lay hands on. After that he went to Iceland

---

[90]The poet Markus Skeggjason was Lawspeaker of the Althing 1084-1107.

with his brother Thorgeir and their aunt Thorunn. She took possession
of the whole of Thorunnar Ridges.

357. *Thorgeir*
From Hrafn, son of Ketil Trout, Thorgeir bought both the Strands,
Vatnadale, and the entire area between Rang River and Hroars Brook.
He was the first to farm at Oddi, and married Thurid Eilif's-daughter.

358. *Thorstein Tent-Pitcher*
With the approval of Flosi who had already settled the Rang River
Plains, Thorstein took possession of land between Vikings Brook and
the land-claim of Bjorn of Svinhagi. He made his home at East Skard.
While he was living there, a ship put in at Rang River Estuary. There
was serious illness on board, and people had refused to give any help.
Then Thorstein came along and moved them to a place now called
Tjaldastead, pitching tents for them and attending to them himself
as long as they lived, but they all died. The one who lived longest
buried a lot of money which has never been found. Because of what
happened Thorstein was nicknamed Tent-Pitcher. His sons were Gunnar and Skeggi.

359. *Flosi*
There was a man called Flosi, son of Thorbjorn of Gaular. He killed
three of King Harald Fine-Hair's bailiffs, and after that went to
Iceland. Flosi took possession of land east of Rang River, the whole
East Rang River Plains. His daughter was Asny, mother of Thurid,
whom Valla-Brand married. Valla-Brand had a son called Flosi,
father of Kolbein, father of Gudrun, wife of Sæmund the Learned.

360. *Ketil One-Hand*
There was a man called Ketil One-Hand, son of Audun Thin-Hair.
He took possession of all West Rang River Plains above Lækjarbotnar
and east of Thjors River. He made his home at Á. Ketil married
Asleif Thorgils'-daughter, and their son was Audun, father of Brynjolf,
father of Bergthor, father of Thorlak, father of Thorhall, father of
Bishop Thorlak the Holy.

361. *Ketil Aurridi*[91]
Ketil Aurridi, first cousin of Ketil One-Hand, took possession of land

---

[91]*Aurriði*, literally 'brown trout'. We leave the nickname untranslated to avoid
confusion with Ketil Trout (*Ketil Hængr*).

west of Thjors River, making his home at West Vellir. His son Helgi
Roe married Helga, daughter of Hrolf Red-Beard, and their son was
Odd the Slender, father of Asborg, whom Thorstein the Priest mar-
ried, and of Oddny, wife of Eilif the Young.

362. *Orm the Wealthy*
With Ketil One-Hand's approval, Orm the Wealthy, son of Ulf the
Sharp, took possession of land on Rang River, making his home at
Husagard where his son Askel farmed after him. But his son started
the farm at Vellir, and the Vellir people are descended from him.

363. *Thorstein Lunan*
There was a Norwegian called Thorstein Lunan, who was a great
sea-going trader. It had been prophesied that he would die in a land
as yet uninhabited. Thorstein went to Iceland in his old age with his
son Thorgils, and they took possession of the upper part of Thjors-
riverholts, making their home at Lunansholt, and that's where Thorstein was buried in a grave mound. Thorgils had a daughter called
Asleif, wife of Ketil One-Hand. Their sons were Audun, already
mentioned, and Eilif, father of Thorgeir, father of Skeggi, father of
Hjalti of Thjorsriverdale. Hjalti was the father of Jorunn, mother of
Gudrun, mother of Einar, father of Bishop Magnus.

364. *Gunnstein Berserks'-Killer*
Gunnstein Berserks'-Killer, son of Bolverk Blind-Snout, killed two berserks. One of them had killed Earl Grjotgard at Solvi inland from
Agdaness. Afterwards, on board his ship at Hefnir, Gunnstein was
hit by a Lappish arrow from the forest. Gunnstein's son was Thorgeir
who married Thorunn the Wealthy, daughter of Ketil One-Hand, and
their daughter was Thordis the Big.

365. *Radorm and Jolgeir*
Radorm and Jolgeir were brothers who came to Iceland from the
British Isles. They took possession of land between Thjors and Rang
Rivers. Radorm gained possession of land east of Rauda Brook, and
made his home at Vetleifsholt. His daughter was Arnbjorg, wife of
Sverting Hrolleifsson, and their children were Grim the Lawspeaker[92]
and Jorunn. Later, Arnbjorg became the wife of Gnup Molda-Gnups-
son, and their children were Hallstein of Hjalli, Rannveig, mother of
Skapti the Lawspeaker, and Geirny, mother of Poet-Hrafn.

---

[92]Grim Svertingsson was Lawspeaker of the Althing 1002-3.

Jolgeir got possession of land from Rauda Brook west to Steins Brook, making his home at Jolgeirsstead.

366. *Askel Hnokkan*

Askel Hnokkan, son of Dufthak, son of Dufniall, son of Kjarval, son of King Kjarval of Ireland, took possession of land between Steins Brook and Thjors River, making his home at Askelshofdi. His son was Asmund, father of Asgaut, father of Skeggi, father of Thorvald, father of Thorlaug, mother of Thorgerd, mother of Bishop Jon the Holy.

367. *Thorkel Bjalfi*

Thorkel Bjalfi, Radorm's blood-brother, got possession of all the land between Rang and Thjors Rivers, making his home at Haf. He married Thorunn of the Isles, and their daughter was Thordis, mother of Skeggi, father of Thorvald of As. It was from As that Hjalti his kinsman-in-law got horses for himself and his eleven companions to ride to the Althing when he brought Christianity to Iceland and no one else dared help him because of the power of Runolf Ulfsson who'd had Hjalti outlawed for blasphemy.

Now we've listed all those who settled in Ketil Trout's land-claim.

368. *Lopt Ormsson*

Lopt, son of Orm Frodason, came to Iceland from Gaular when still young and settled west of Thjors River, taking possession of land between Raud and Thjors Rivers up to Skufs Brook, including East Breidamyri up as far as Suluholt. He and his mother Oddny, daughter of Thorbjorn of Gaular, made their home at Gaulverjaby. Lopt kept going abroad every third summer on his own and his uncle Flosi's behalf, in order to hold sacrifices at the temple where his grandfather Thorbjorn had been in charge. Many important people claim descent from Lopt, including St. Thorlak, Pal and Brand.

369. *Thorvid*

Hild's brother, Thorvid, son of Ulfar went from Vors to Iceland, and Lopt, his kinsman, granted him land in Breidamyri. He made his home at Vorsaby. His children were Hrafn, and Hallveig, wife of Ozur the White; Hallveig and Ozur's son was Thorgrim Kampi.

370. *Thorarin*

There was a man called Thorarin, son of Thorkel of Alvidra, son of Hallbjorn the Hordaland-Champion. He put in at Thjors River Estuary and had a bull's head carved on his prow, which explains the name of the river.[93] Thorarin took possession of land on Thjors River above Skufs Brook as far as Raud River. His daughter was Heimlaug, whom Lopt married when he was sixty.

371. *Hastein*

There was a king in Sogn Province called Harald Gold-Beard. He married Solvor, daughter of Earl Hundolf and sister of Earl Atli the Slender. Their daughters were Thora, whom King Halfdan the Black of the Uplands married, and Thurid, wife of Ketil Slab-Flake. Halfdan and Thora had a son called Harald the Young, and to him Harald Gold-Beard gave his name and kingdom. King Harald was the first of them to die. Next was Thora, and lastly Harald the Younger. Then the kingdom came to King Halfdan, who put Earl Atli the Slender in charge. Later, King Halfdan married Ragnhild, daughter of Sigurd Hart, and their son was Harald Fine-Hair.

When King Harald came to power in Norway and entered into family alliance with Earl Hakon Grjotgardsson, he put his father-in-law Earl Hakon in charge of Sogn Province, and moved east to Oslofjord. But Earl Atli refused to surrender his power until he had seen King Harald. The two earls quarrelled bitterly over this and gathered forces. They met at Stafness Creek in Fjalar Province and fought a battle there. Earl Hakon was killed, and Atli was wounded. He was moved over to Atloy and died of his wounds there.

After that Hastein, his son, was in charge of the earldom until King Harald and Earl Sigurd gathered forces against him. Then Hastein fled and set off for Iceland. He married Thora Olvir's-daughter, and their sons were Olvir and Atli. Hastein threw his bench-boards overboard at sea, according to ancient custom, and they were washed ashore at Stalfjara off Stokkseyri, but Hastein made land at Hasteins Sound east of Stokkseyri, wrecking his ship. Hastein took possession of land between Raud and Olfus Rivers, making his home at Stjornusteinar where his son Olvir farmed after him. Nowadays the place is called Olvisstead. Olvir's land-claim lay west of Grims River, including Stokkseyri and Asgautsstead. But Atli got all the land between Grims and Raud Rivers, making his home at Tradarholt. Olvir died childless, and Atli inherited all his goods and lands. Atli's freedmen were Bratt of Brattsholt and Leidolf of Leidolfsstead. Atli was the father of Thord Dofni, father of Thorgils who fostered Thorgils Scar-Leg.

---

[93]Literally, 'Bull's River'.

372. *Hallstein*

There was a man called Hallstein, who was related to Hastein by marriage. To him Hastein granted the western part of Eyrarbakki. Hallstein made his home at Framness. His son was Thorstein, father of Arngrim, who was killed digging up logs, and his son was Thorbjorn of Framness.

373. *Thorir*

Thorir, son of Chieftain Asi, son of Ingjald Hroaldsson, went to Iceland and took possession of the whole of Kallnessingahrepp above Fyllar Brook, making his home at Selfoss. His son was Tyrfing, father of Thurid, mother of Tyrfing, father of the Priests Thorbjorn and Hamund of Goddales.

374. *Hrodgeir and Oddgeir*

Hrodgeir the Wise and his brother Oddgeir, to whom Finn the Wealthy and Hafnar-Orm paid money to leave their land-claim, took possession of Hraungerdingahrepp. Oddgeir made his home at Oddgeirshills. His son was Thorstein Oxen-Goad, father of Hrodgeir, father of Ogur of Kambakista. Hrodgeir's daughter was Gunnvor, wife of Kolgrim the Old, from whom the Kvistlings are descended.

375. *Onund Bild*

Onund Bild, mentioned earlier, took possession of land east of Hroars Brook, making his home at Onundarholt. A good many important people are descended from him, as has already been written.

376. *Ozur the White*

There was a man called Ozur the White, son of Thorleif of Sogn, in the Uplands. When he accompanied Sigurd Hrisi to his wedding, Ozur killed a man at a sanctuary and for this he was banished and went to Iceland. He was the original settler of the Holta lands, between Thjors River and Hrauns Brook. He was seventeen when he did the killing. Ozur married Hallveig Thorvid's-daughter, and their son was Thorgrim Kampi, father of Ozur, father of Thorbjorn, father of Thorarin, father of Grim Tofuson.

Ozur made his home at Kampaholt. His freedman, Bodvar, lived at Bodvarstoft near Vidiwood. To him Ozur granted a share in the wood on condition that Ozur should get it back if Bodvar died without issue. Orn of Vælugerdi, who was mentioned earlier, summoned Bodvar on a charge of sheep-stealing. Bodvar then handed all his possessions over to Atli Hasteinsson, who quashed the case Orn had brought. Ozur died when Thorgrim was still a child, and Hrafn Thorvidarson took charge of Thorgrim's money.

After Bodvar died, Hrafn laid a claim to Vidiwood and forbade Atli to use it, but Atli claimed it was his. Atli set out with three men to fetch some timber. Leidolf was with him. A shepherd told Hrafn about it, and he started off after them with seven men. They met at Orrustudale and fought a battle there. Two of Hrafn's farmhands were killed and he was wounded. Atli lost one of his men, and rode back home with wounds which proved fatal. Onund Bild separated them and invited Atli to his home. Thord Dofni, Atli's son, was nine years old at the time. When Thord was fifteen, Hrafn rode down one day to meet a ship at Einarshaven, wearing a blue cloak, and by the time he rode back home it was night. Thord lay in wait for him alone, at Haugaford near Tradarholt, and killed him with a spear. Hrafn's Mound stands there east of the path, and west of it are Hastein's Mound, Atli's Mound and Olvir's Mound. The killings cancelled each other out.

Thord gained a great deal of credit for this, and later he married Thorunn, daughter of Asgeir the Easterners'-Terror who killed a Norwegian crew at Grims River Estuary over a robbery he'd suffered in Norway. Thord was twenty-two when he bought a ship at Knarrar Sound and set out to claim his inheritance. He buried a great deal of money, and that's why Thorunn refused to leave, and took charge of the farm. Thorgils, Thord's son, was two years old at the time. Thord's ship was lost at sea. A year later Thorgrim Scar-Leg came to run the farm for Thorunn. He was the son of Thormod and Thurid Ketilbjorn's-daughter. Thorgrim married Thorunn, and their son was Hæring.

377. *Olaf Split-Brow*

There was a man called Olaf Split-Brow, who went from the Lofoten Islands to Iceland. He took possession of the whole of Skeid, between Thjors River, Hvit River and Sand Brook. He was a great sorcerer. Olaf made his home at Olafsvellir, and lies buried in Bruni's Mound below Vordufell. Olaf married Ashild, and their sons were Helgi the Trusty and Thorir Drift, father of Thorkel Gold-Lock, father of Orm, father of Helga, mother of Odd Hallvardsson. Olaf's third son was Vadi, Gerd's father.

After Olaf died, Thorgrim fell in love with Ashild, but Helgi objected and ambushed him at the crossroads below Ashildarmyri. Helgi told him to stop coming there. Thorgrim said that he wasn't a child. They fought, and Thorgrim was killed. Ashild asked Helgi where he'd been, and he replied with this verse:

> I was there
> when Thorgrim fell,
> food for the ravens
> when the swords rang.
> I gave to Odin
> the gallant son of Thormod;
> gave the gallows-god a sacrifice,
> gave the raven a corpse.

Ashild said the blow he'd struck would earn him his death. Helgi got a passage abroad at Einarshaven. Hæring, Thorgrim's son, was sixteen when this happened, and rode over to Hofdi with two companions to see Teit Gizurarson. Teit set off with fifteen men to stop Helgi. They met up with him and two others coming from Eyrar at Helgahill above Mork in Merkurhraun. Helgi and one of his men were killed there, and one of Teit's. These killings were considered to cancel each other out. Helgi had two sons, one called Sigurd of Land and the other Skefil of Haukadale, father of Helgi Deer who fought Sigurd, son of Ljot Ling-Back on Oxar Isle at the Althing. Helgi made this verse about it:

> My right hand's bound
> with bandages,
> wounded by the warrior;
> truthful, my words.

Skefil had another son called Hrafn, father of Grim, father of Asgeir, father of Helgi.

378. *Thrand the Fast-Sailing*

Thrand Bjarnarson the Fast-Sailing, brother of Eyvind the Easterner, who was mentioned earlier, fought against King Harald at Hafursfjord and then had to leave Norway. He came to Iceland late in the Settlement Period and took possession of land between Thjors and Lax Rivers, up to Kalf River and Sand Brook, making his home at Thrandarholt. His daughter was Helga, wife of Thormod Skapti.

379. *The Sons of Olvir*

There was a famous man in Norway called Olvir the Child-Sparer, a great viking. He wouldn't have children tossed by spear-points as was the custom of vikings at the time, and that's why he was called the Child-Sparer. His sons were Steinolf, father of Una whom Thorbjorn the Salmoner married, and Einar, father of Ofeig Grettir and Oleif the Broad, father of Thormod Skapti. Olvir the Child-Sparer had a third son, Steinmod, who was the father of Konal, father of Alfdis the Barra-Woman, wife of Olaf Feilan. Konal had a son called Steinmod, father of Halldora, wife of Eilif, Ketil One-Hand's son. The kinsmen Ofeig Grettir and Thormod Skapti went to Iceland and spent the first winter with Thorbjorn the Salmoner, their kinsman-in-law. In the spring he granted them Gnupverjahrepp. He gave the western part between Thver and Kalf Rivers to Ofeig who made his home at Ofeigsstead by Steinsholt. And to Thormod Thorbjorn gave the eastern part, and he made his home at Skaptaholt. Thormod's daughters were Thorvor, mother of Thorodd the Priest, father of Law-Skapti, and Thorve, mother of Thorstein the Priest, father of Bjarni the Wise. Ofeig was killed by Thorbjorn the Earls'-Champion of Grettisgills near Hæli. Ofeig's daughter was Aldis, mother of Valla-Brand.

380. *Thorbjorn the Salmoner*

Thorbjorn the Salmoner took possession of the whole of Thjorsriverdale and also the upper part of Gnupverjahrepp, above Kalf River. He spent the first winter at Midhouse, and stayed at three different places before making his home at Hagi, where he farmed for the rest of his life. His sons were Otkel of Thjorsriverdale, Thorkel Trandil, and Thorgils, father of Otkatla, mother of Thorkatla, mother of Thorvald, father of Dalla, Bishop Gizur's[94] mother.

381. *Thorbjorn the Earls'-Champion*

There was a man called Thorbjorn the Earls'-Champion, of Norwegian stock. He went to Iceland from Orkney, and bought land from Mar Naddoddsson in Hrunamannahrepp, the whole area below Sels Brook down to Lax River. He made his home at Holar. His sons were Solmund, father of Kari the Singed, and Thormod, father of Finna, wife of Thororm of Karlafjord. The daughter of Finna and Thororm was Alfgerd, mother of Gest, father of Valgerd, mother of Thorleif Beiskaldi.

382. *Brondolf and Mar*

Brondolf and Mar, sons of Naddodd and Jorunn, Olvir Child-Sparer's daughter, came to Iceland early in the Period of Settlements. They took possession of Hrunamannahrepp as far as the watershed. Brondolf

---

[94]Gizur Isleifsson was Bishop of Iceland 1082-1106 and Bishop of Skalholt 1106-1118.

made his home at Berghyl. His son was Thorleif, father of Brondolf, father of Thorkel Scot-Pate, father of Thorarin, father of Hall of Haukadale and Thorlak, father of Runolf, father of Bishop Thorlak. Mar made his home at Masstead. His son was Beinir, father of Kolgrima, mother of Skeggi, Hjalti's father.

383. *Thorbrand and Asbrand*

Thorbrand, son of Thorbjorn the Fearless, and his son Asbrand came to Iceland late in the Period of Settlements, and Ketilbjorn advised them to settle between Kalda Stream, and the headland that juts out towards Stakks River. They made their home at Haukadale. They thought their land wasn't big enough, as the eastern tongue was already settled, so they added to their land-claim by taking the upper part of Hrunamannahrepp, marking it off with a straight line from Muli to Ingjaldsgnup above Gyldarhagi. Asbrand's children were Vebrand and Arngerd.

384. *Eyfrod the Old*

Eyfrod the Old took possession of the eastern tongue of land, between Kalda Stream and Hvit River, making his home at Tongue. Drumb-Odd, who farmed at Drumb-Oddsstead, came to Iceland with him.

385. *Ketilbjorn the Old*

There was a famous man in Namdalen called Ketilbjorn, the son of Ketil and Æsa, daughter of Earl Hakon Grjotgardsson. He married Helga, Thord Skeggi's daughter. Ketilbjorn went to Iceland when most of the land near the sea had been settled. He had a ship called Ellidi, and put in at Ellida River Estuary, west of the moor. He spent the first winter with Thord Skeggi, his father-in-law. In the spring he travelled east across the moor looking for suitable land to settle. They built themselves a shelter for the night at a place now called Skala-brekka.[95] After they left these they came to a river they called Oxar River, where they lost their axe. They took a rest below a mountain they named Reydarmull,[96] where they left behind the trout they'd caught in the river.

Ketilbjorn took possession of the whole of Grimsness above Hoskulds Brook, as well as the entire Laugardale and all of Biskupstongue up to Stakk River making his home at Mosfell. His children by his wife

---

[95]Literally 'Shed Slope'.
[96]The first element is associated here with *reyðr*, a variety of sea-trout; but in fact the etymology is doubtful.

were Teit, Thormod, Thorleif, Ketil, Thorkatla, Oddleif, Thorgerd and Thurid. Ketilbjorn also had an illegitimate son called Skæring.

Ketilbjorn was so wealthy he told his sons to forge a cross beam of silver for the temple they built, but they wouldn't do it. Then he took the silver and hauled it up to the mountain by means of two oxen and with the help of his slave Haki and his bondmaid Bot he buried the silver, and it's never been found. Then he killed Haki at Haka Pass, and Bot at Botar Pass.

Teit married Alof, daughter of Bodvar Vikinga-Karason of Vors, and their son was Gizur the White, father of Bishop Isleif, father of Bishop Gizur. Teit had another son called Ketilbjorn, father of Koll, father of Thorkel, father of Bishop Koll of Oslo. A good many important people are descended from Ketilbjorn.

386. *Asgeir*

There was a man called Asgeir Ulfsson, to whom Ketilbjorn gave his daughter Thorgerd in marriage and as her dowry all the Hlid lands above Hagagard. Asgeir farmed at Outer Hlid. Their sons were Geir the Priest and Thorgeir, father of Bard of Mosfell.

387. *Eilif the Wealthy*

Eilif the Wealthy, son of Onund Bild, married Thorkatla Ketilbjorn's-daughter, and her dowry was Hofdi lands, where they made their home. Their son was Thorir, father of Thorarin Sæling.

388. *Grim*

There was a powerful chieftain called Vethorm, son of Vemund the Old. He fled from King Harald east to Jamtaland where he cleared the forest for a homestead. He had a son called Holmfast, and a nephew called Grim. They went on a viking expedition to the British Isles and killed Earl Asbjorn Skerry-Blaze in the Hebrides, taking his widow Alof and his daughter Arneid captive. Holmfast got Arneid as part of his share and gave her to his father who made her a bondmaid. Grim married the earl's widow Alof, Thord Vaggagdi's daughter.

Grim went to Iceland and took possession of the whole of Grimsness below Svinawater. He farmed at Ondurduness for four years, and afterwards at Burfell. His son was Thorgils who married Æsa, Gest's sister, and their sons were Thorarin of Burfell and Jorund of Midengi.

389. *Hallkel*

Hallkel, Ketilbjorn's brother by the same mother, came to Iceland

and stayed the first winter with Ketilbjorn, who offered to grant him
land. But Hallkel thought it unmanly to be given land and challenged
Grim to a duel for the land he owned. Grim fought Hallkel in single
combat below Hallkelshills, but lost his life, and Hallkel made his
home there. His sons were Otkel whom Gunnar Hamundarson killed,
and Odd of Kidjaberg, father of Hallbjorn who was killed at Hallbjarnar Cairns. Odd's other son was Hallkel, father of Hallvard,
father of Thorstein whom Einar the Shetlander killed. Hallkel Oddsson had a son called Bjarni, father of Hall, father of Orm, father
of Bard, father of Valgerd, mother of Halldora, wife of Bishop Magnus
Gizurarson.

Now we've come to Ingolf's land-claim and those listed next settled
within his territory.

390. *Thorgrim Bild*
Thorgrim Bild, brother of Onund Bild, took possession of the area
above Thver River and made his home at Bildsfell. He had a freedman called Steinrod, son of Melpatrek of Ireland, who got possession
of all the Vatnslands and made his home at Steinrodarstead. Steinrod
was a remarkably fine man. His son was Thormod, father of Kar,
father of Thormod, father of Brand, father of Thorir who married
Helga Jon's-daughter.

391. *Orm the Old*
Orm the Old was the son of Earl Eyvind, son of Earl Arnmod, son
of Earl Nereid the Old. He took possession of land east of Varma River
and over to Thver River including all Ingolfsfell, making his home at
Hvamm. His son was Darri, Orn's father. Earl Eyvind fought beside
Kjotvi the Wealthy at Hafursfjord against King Harald.

392. *Alf of Agder*
Alf of Agder fled from Agder in Norway before King Harald. He went
to Iceland and put in at the estuary which bears his name, Alf's
Estuary. He took possession of the area west of Varma River and
made his home at Gnupar. Alf had a nephew called Thorgrim Grim-
olfsson. He went to Iceland with Alf and inherited his property since
Alf had no children. Thorgrim had a son called Eyvind, father of
Thorodd the Priest and Ozur who married Bera, daughter of Egil
Skalla-Grimsson. Thorgrim's mother was Kormlod, daughter of King
Kjarval of Ireland.

393. *Thorir Autumn-Dusk*

Thorir Autumn-Dusk took possession of Sel Creek and Krysuvik, and his son Hegg lived at Vog. Thorir had another son, called Bodmod, father of Thorarin, father of Sugandi, father of Thorvald, father of Thorhild, mother of Sigurd Thorgrimsson. The sons of Molda-Gnup farmed at Grindavik, as was written earlier.

394. *Steinunn the Old*

Steinunn the Old, Ingolf's kinswoman, went to Iceland and stayed with him the first winter. He offered to give her the whole of Rosm-hvalaness, west of Hvassahraun, but she paid for it with a spotted coat and called it an exchange. She thought this would make it more difficult to break the agreement.

395. *Eyvind*

There was a man called Eyvind, who was related to Steinunn and had been fostered by her. To him she granted land between Kviguvoga Cliffs and Hvassahraun. His son was Egil, father of Thorarin, father of Sigmund, father of Thorarna, mother of Thorbjorn of Krysuvik.

396. *Asbjorn*

Asbjorn Ozurarson, Ingolf's nephew, took possession of land between Hraunholts Brook and Hvassahraun including the whole of Alftaness, making his home at Skulastead. His son was Egil, father of Ozur, father of Thorarin, father of Olaf, father of Sveinbjorn, father of Asmund, father of Sveinbjorn, father of Styrkar.

397. *South Quarter: Conclusion*

Now we've surveyed the settlements in Iceland, according to what we've been told about them. These were the outstanding settlers in the South Quarter: Hrafn the Foolish, Ketil Trout, Sighvat the Red, Hastein Atlason, Ketilbjorn the Old, Ingolf, Orlyg the Old, Helgi Bjolan, Kolgrim the Old, Bjorn the Gold-Bearer, and Onund Broad-Beard.

398. *Leading Chieftains*

According to the learned, Iceland was fully settled over a period of sixty years, and has never been more widely settled since. At the end of this period a good many of the settlers and their sons were still living. After the land had been lived in for sixty years these were the greatest chieftains in Iceland: in the South Quarter, Mord Fiddle, Jorund the Priest, Geir the Priest, Thorstein Ingolfsson, and Tongue-

Odd; in the West Quarter, Egil Skalla-Grimsson, Thorgrim Kjallaks-son and Thord Gellir; in the North Quarter, Midfjord-Skeggi, Thorstein Ingimundarson, the men of Goddales, the Hjaltasons, Eyjolf Valgerdarson and Askel the Priest; in the East Quarter, Thorstein the White, Hrafnkel the Priest, Thorstein, father of Sidu-Hall, and Thord Frey's-Priest. Hrafn, Ketil Trout's son, was the Lawspeaker at the time.

399. *Christian settlers*

According to well-informed people some of the settlers of Iceland were baptized, mostly those who came from the British Isles. These are specially mentioned: Helgi the Lean, Orlyg the Old, Helgi Bjolan, Jorund the Christian, Aud the Deep-Minded, Ketil the Foolish, and a number of others who came from the west. Some of them kept up their faith till they died, but in most families this didn't last, for the sons of some built temples and made sacrifices, and Iceland was completely pagan for about 120 years.

Index of Chapters

Index

Names of Settlers (*Numbers refer to chapters*)

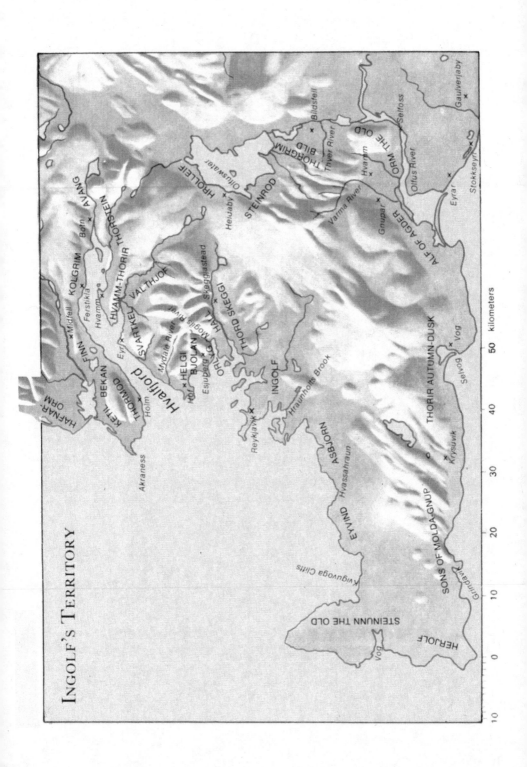

INGOLF'S TERRITORY

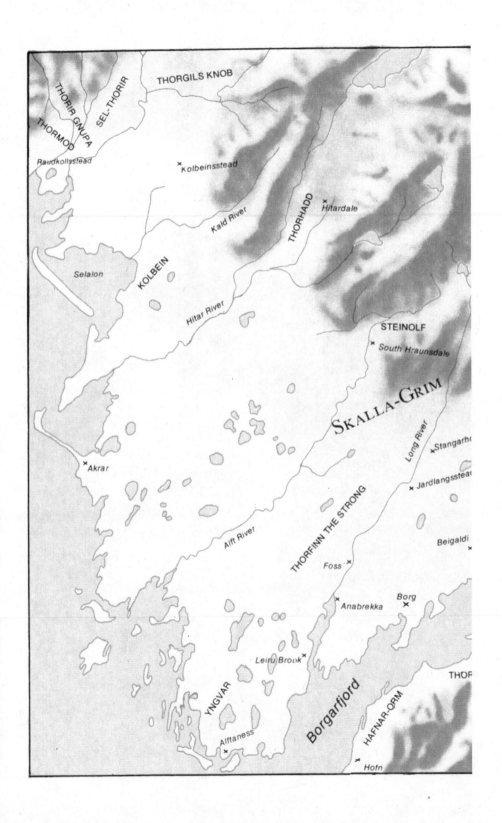

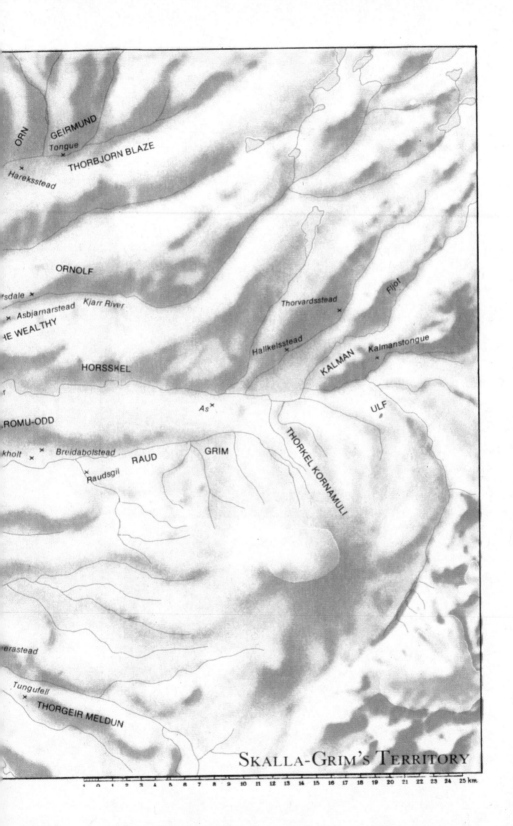

ORN GEIRMUND
Tongue
THORBJORN BLAZE
× Hareksstead

ORNOLF
'sdale ×
× Asbjarnarstead   Kjarr River
HE WEALTHY
Thorvardsstead ×
Fljot
Hallkelsstead ×
KALMAN   Kalmanstongue
HORSSKEL
r
ULF
As × ×
ROMU-ODD
THORKEL KORNAMULI
kholt ×   Breidabolstead   RAUD   GRIM
× Raudsgil

erastead

Tungufell
× THORGEIR MELDUN

S\scriptsize KALLA-G\scriptsize RIM'S T\scriptsize ERRITORY

1 0 1 2 3 4 5 6 7 8 9 10 11 12 13 14 15 16 17 18 19 20 21 22 23 24 25 km.

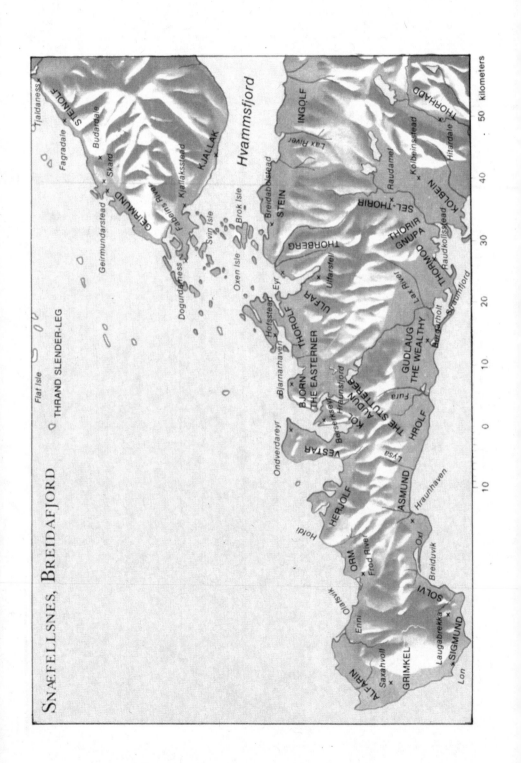

SNÆFELLSNES, BREIDAFJORD

Flat Isle

THRAND SLENDER-LEG

Hvammsfjord

STEINOLF
Tjaldaness
Fagradale
Budardale
Skard
Geirmundarstead
GEIRMUND
Fabeins River
Kjallaksstead
KJALLAK
Dogurdaness
Svin Isle
Oxen Isle
Brok Isle
Breidabolstead
STEIN
Eyr
Hofsstead
Bjarnarhaven
THOROLF
ULFAR
Ulfarstell
THORBERG
INGOLF
Lax River
Raudamel
Kolbeinsstead
THORHADD
Hitardale
SEL-THORIR
THORIR GNUPA
Raudkollsstead
Bergtholt
KOLBEIN
THOROLF
Ondverdareyr
VESTAR
Berserkseyr
Hraunsfjord
KOLL
Fura
BJORN THE EASTERNER
AUDUN THE STUTTERER
GUDLAUG THE WEALTHY
Hraunsfjord
Swanfjord
HROLF
Lysa
Holdi
HERJOLF
Hraunhaven
ASMUND
Frod River
ORM
Oxl
Breiduvik
SOLVI
Olafsvik
Enni
Saxahvoll
GRIMKEL
ALFARIN
Laugabrekka
SIGMUND
Lon

50 40 30 20 10 0 10 kilometers

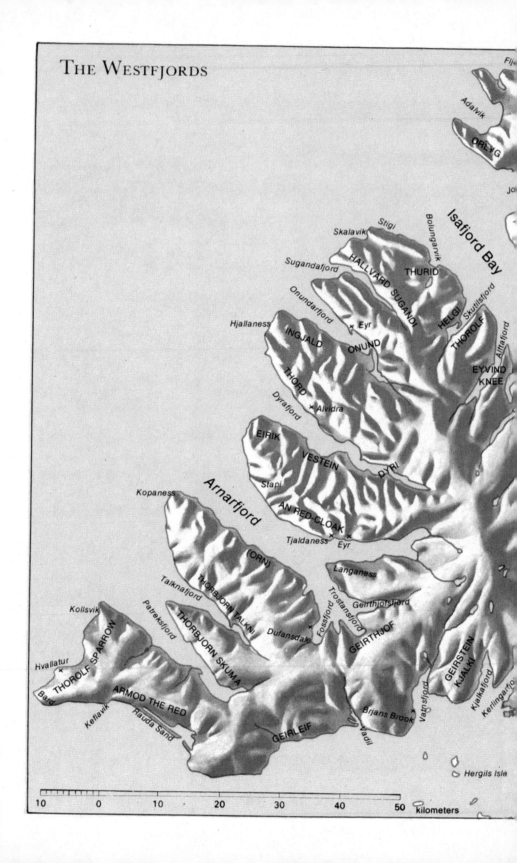

THE WESTFJORDS

Fj[...]

Adalvik

ORLYG

Jo[...]

Isafjord Bay

Stigi

Skalavik

Bolungarvik

Sugandafjord

HALLVARD SUGANDI

THURID

Onundarfjord

HELGI

Skutilsfjord

Hjallaness

INGJALD

Eyr

THOROLF

Alftafjord

ONUND

ONUND

EYVIND
KNEE

THORD

Dyrafjord

Alvidra

EIRIK

VESTEIN

DYRI

Arnarfjord

Stapi

Kopaness

AN RED-CLOAK

Tjaldaness

Eyr

(ORN)

Langaness

Talknafjord

THORBJORN TALKNI

Trostansfjord

Geirthjofsfjord

Kollsvik

Patreksfjord

THORBJORN SKUMA

Fossfjord

GEIRTHJOF

GEIRSTEIN
KJALKI

Hvallatur

THOROLF SPARROW

Dufansdale

Vatnsfjord

Kjalkafjord

Barg

ARMOD THE RED

Brjans Brook

Kerlingarfjo[...]

Keflavik

Rauda Sand

GEIRLEIF

Vadil

Hergils Isle

```
10      0      10     20     30     40     50  kilometers
```

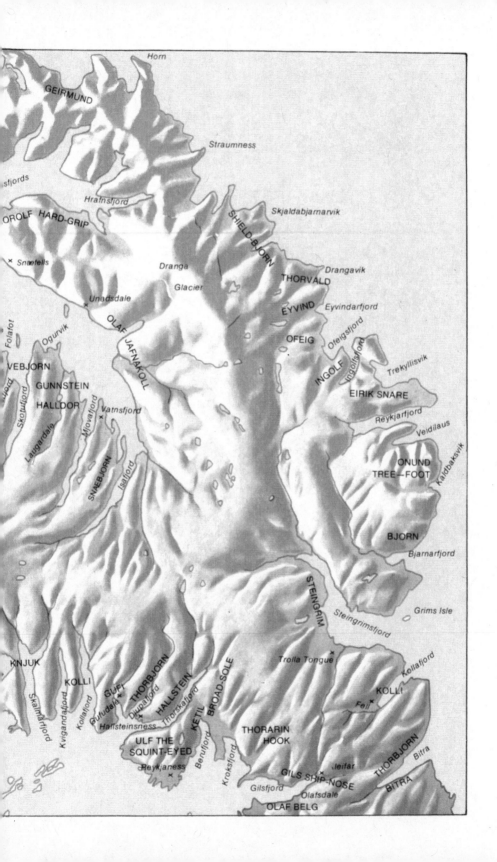

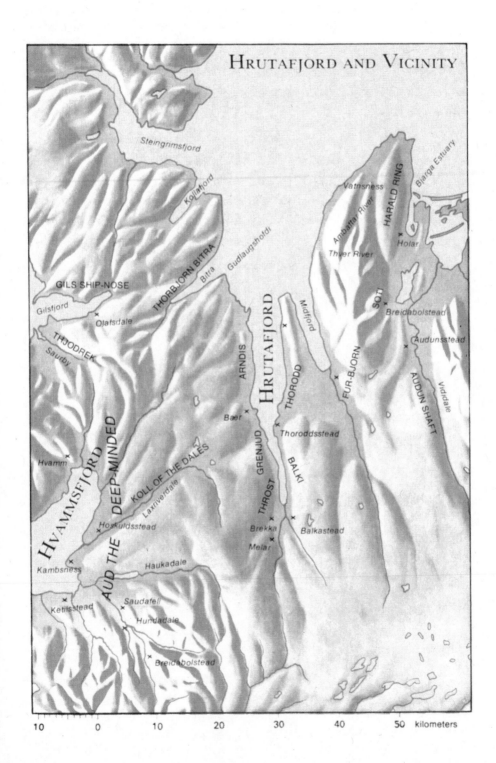

HRUTAFJORD AND VICINITY

Steingrimsfjord

Kollafjord

THORBJORN BITRA

Bitra

Gudlaugsholdi

GILS SHIP-NOSE

Gilsfjord

Olafsdale

THJODREK

Saurby

HVAMMSFJORD

DEEP-MINDED

Hvamm

KOLL OF THE DALES

Laxrivardale

Hoskuldsstead

AUD THE

Kambsness

Haukadale

Ketilsstead

Saudafell

Hundadale

Breidabolstead

ARNDIS

Baer

GRENJUD

THROST

Brekka

Melar

HRUTAFJORD

Madfjord

THORODD

BALKI

Thoroddsstead

Balkastead

Vatnsness

HARALD RING

Ambattar River

SOTI

Thver River

Holar

FUR-BJORN

Breidabolstead

Audunsstead

AUDUN SHAFT

Bjarga Estuary

Vididale

10   0   10   20   30   40   50   kilometers

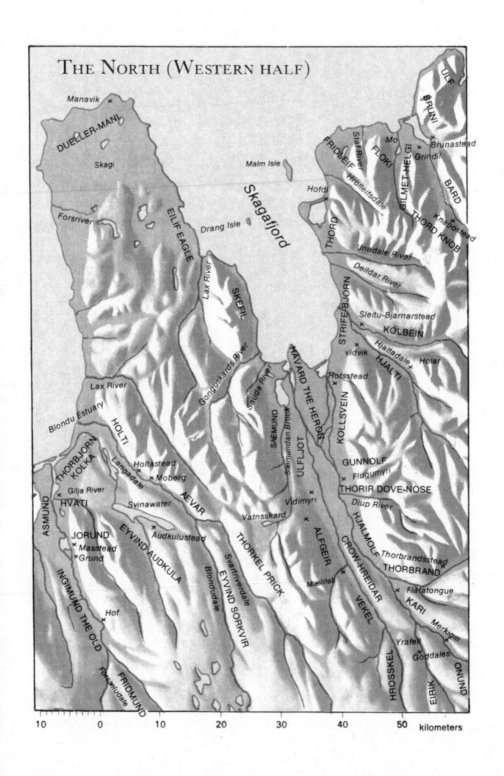

The North (Western half)

Manavik ×

DUELLER-MANI

Skagi

Forsriver

EILF EAGLE

Malm Isle

Skagafjord

Drang Isle

Lax River

SKEFIL

Gonguskards River

Lax River

Blondu Estuary

HOLTI

THORBJORN
KOLKA

Langadale

Holtastead

× Moberg

Gilja River

HVATI

Svinawater

JORUND

AEVAR

× Massstead
× Grund

EYVIND AUDKULA

Audkulustead

ASMUND

INGIMUND THE OLD

Hof

FRIDMUND

Forsaeludale

Svartrivardale

Blondudale

EYVIND SORKVIR

THORKEL PRICK

Vatnsskard

SAEMUND

Soemundan Brook

ULFLJOT

Vidimyri

ALFGEIR

Maelifell

Snuda River

HAVARD THE HEROR

KOLLSVEIN

GUNNOLF

× Flugumyri

THORIR DOVE-NOSE

Diup River

HJALMOLF

CROW-HREIDAR

Thorbrandsstead

THORBRAND

VEKEL

HROSSKEL

EIRIK

Flatatongue ×

KARI

Merkigil

Yrafell

Goddales

ONUND

STRIFE-BJORN

Sleitu-Bjarnarstead

KÖLBEIN

vidvik ×

Hjaltadale

HJALTI

Holar

× Hotsstead

Unadale River

Deildar River

THORD

FRIDLEIF

Stal River

Hrolleifsdale

FLOKI

Mo

Hofdi

GILMET-HELGI

THORD KNOB

Knafhostead

BRUNI

ULF

× Brunastead

Grindil

BARD

| 10 | | 0 | | 10 | | 20 | | 30 | | 40 | | 50 | | kilometers |

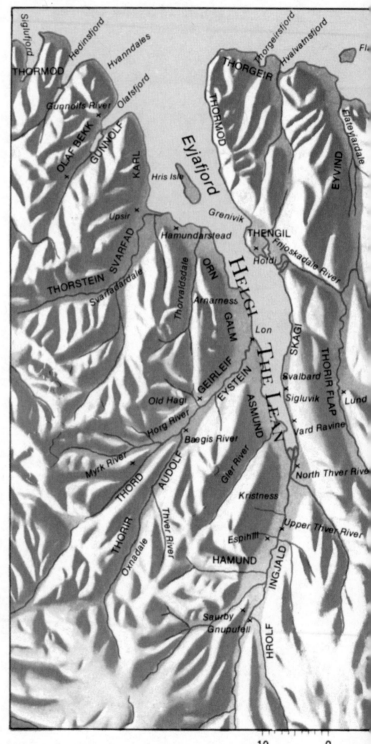

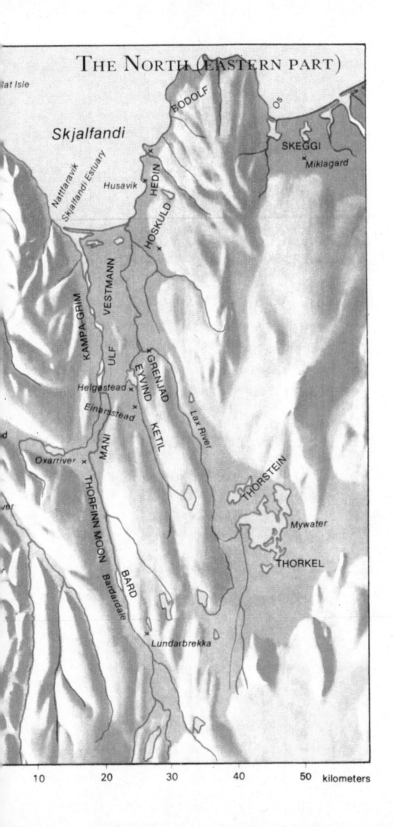

THE NORTH (EASTERN PART)

lat Isle

Skjalfandi

BODOLF

OS

SKEGGI

× Miklagard

Natttaravik

Skjalfandi Estuary

Husavik

HEDIN ×

HOSKULD ×

VESTMANN

KAMPA-GRIM

ULF

GRENJAD ×

EYVIND

Helgastead ×

Einarsstead

KETIL

Lax River

MANI

Oxarriver ×

THORSTEIN

THORFINN MOON

Mywater

BARD

Bardardale

THORKEL

Lundarbrekka ×

| 10 | 20 | 30 | 40 | 50 | kilometers |

The North-East

THE EASTFJORDS (NORTHERN HALF)

Vopnafjor

HROALD BJOLA
Torfastead
LYTING
Outer Krossavik
Inner Krossavik
STEINBJORN
Seiriverdale
Vestradale River
Hoi
Vopnafjord River
THORSTEIN THE WHITE
EYVIND
THORSTEIN TORFI
Fotsvoll
Hofteig
Rang River
Jokulsdale
Skjoldolfsstead
OZUR
Lagarwater
HAKON
SKJOLDOLF
Knefilsdale River
KETIL
Arnheidarstead
Hakonarstead
GRUEL-ATLI
HRAFNKEL
BRYNJOLF THE OLD
Arn
Skridudale

10   0

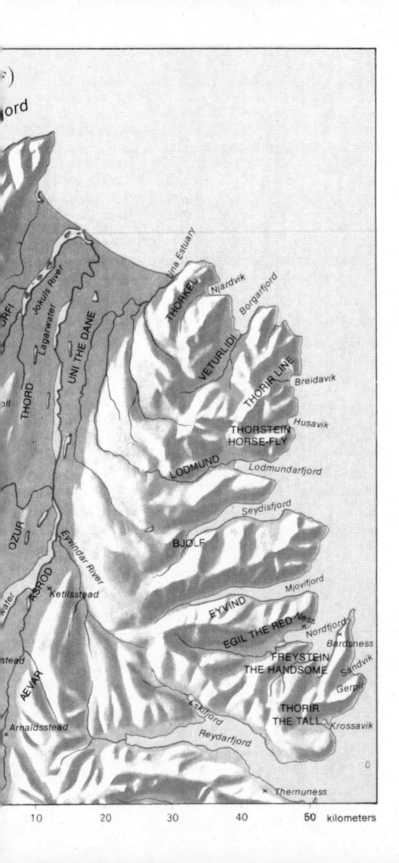

ord

THORKEL

Una Estuary

Njardvik

Borgarfjord

VETURLIDI

THORIR LINE

Breidavik

THORSTEIN
HORSE-FLY

Husavik

LODMUND

Lodmundarfjord

Seydisfjord

BJOLF

Mjovifjord

EYVIND

EGIL THE RED

Ness

Nordfjord

Bardsness

FREYSTEIN
THE HANDSOME

Sandvik

Gerpir

THORIR
THE TALL

Krossavik

ORFI

Jokuls River

Lagarwater

UNI THE DANE

THORD

oll

OZUR

Eyvindar River

ASROD

Ketilsstead

AEVAR

Arnaldsstead

water

stead

Lskifjord

Reydarfjord

Thernuness

0

10   20   30   40   50   kilometers

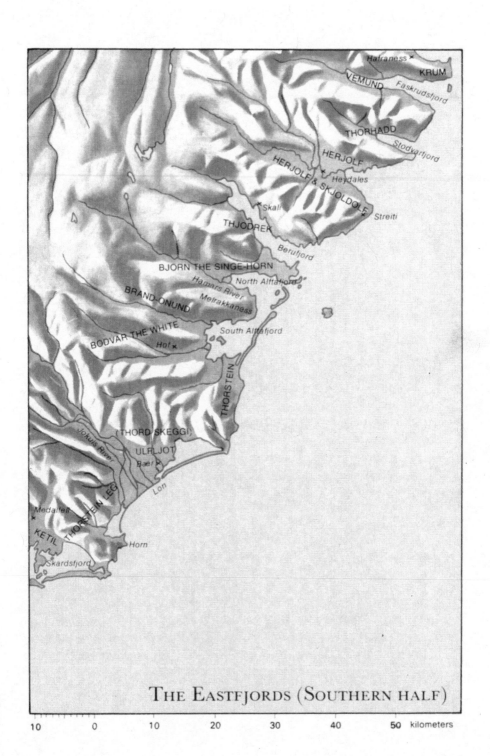

THE EASTFJORDS (SOUTHERN HALF)

Hafraness

KRUM

VEMUND   Faskrudsfjord

THORHADD

HERJOLF   Stodvarfjord

HERJOLF & SKJOLDOLF

Heydales

Skali   Streiti

THJODREK

Berufjord

BJORN THE SINGE-HORN

Hamars River   North Alftafjord

BRAND-ONUND   Metrakkaness

BODVAR THE WHITE   South Alftafjord

Hof

THORSTEIN

(THORD SKEGGI)

ULFLJOT

Baer

Jokuls River

Lon

THORSTEIN LEG

Medalfell

KETIL

Horn

Skardsfjord

10   0   10   20   30   40   50   kilometers

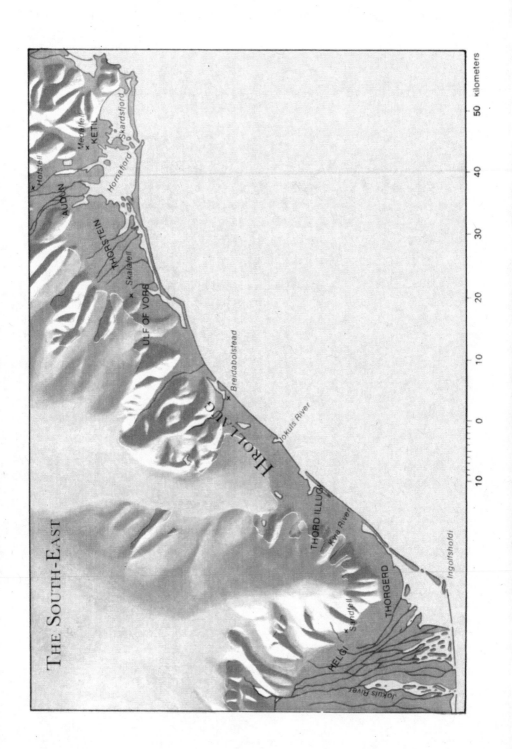

THE SOUTH-EAST

Hofsfell
AUDUN
Mcdalfell
KETIL
Skardsfjord
Hornafjord
THORSTEIN
Skalafell
ULF OF VORR
Breidabolstead
HROLLAUG
Jokuls River
THORD ILLUGI
Kna River
Sandgil
HELGI
THORGERD
Ingolfsholdi
Jokuls River

10   0   10   20   30   40   50   kilometers

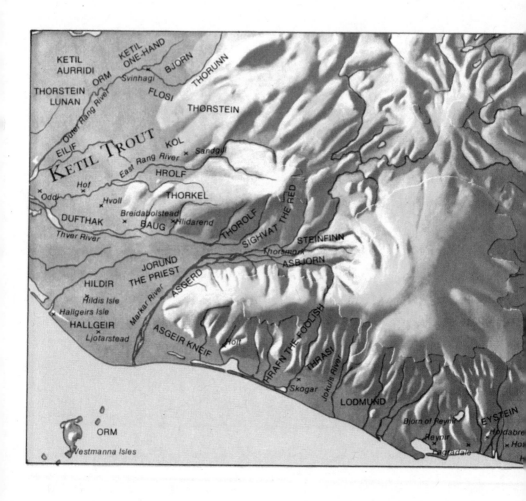

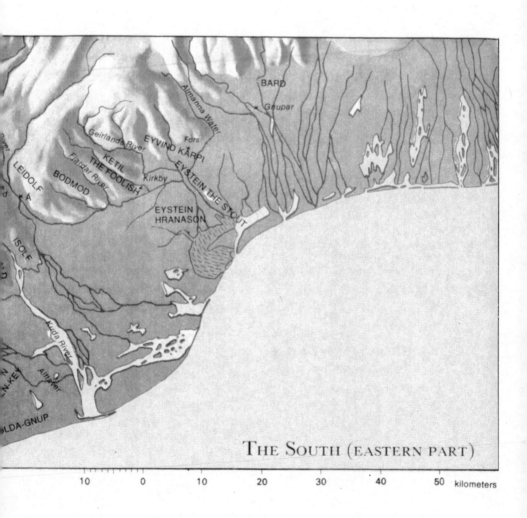

THE SOUTH (EASTERN PART)

BARD
Gnupar

Almanna Water
Fors
Geirland River
EYVIND KÅRPI
KETIL
THE FOOLISH
Flardal River
BODMOD
Kirkby
EYSTEIN THE STOUT
EYSTEIN
HRANASON
LEIDOLF
ISOLF
Kuda River
Allt River
N-KEY
LDA-GNUP

10   0   10   20   30   40   50   kilometers

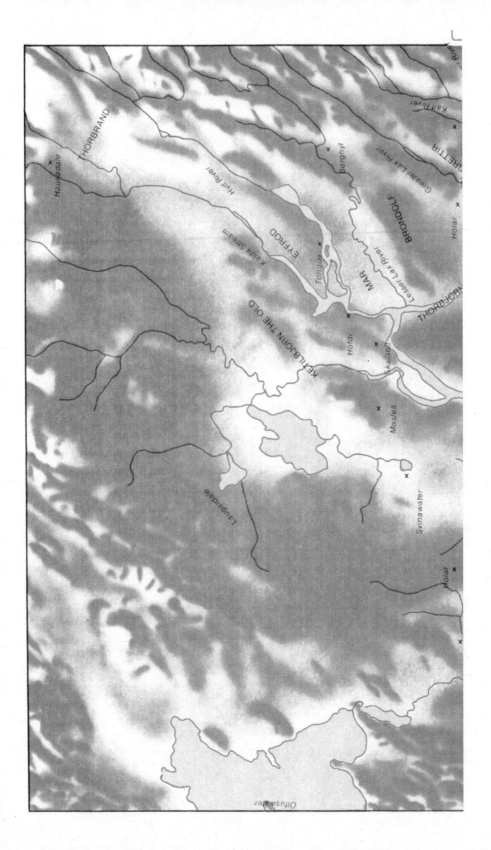

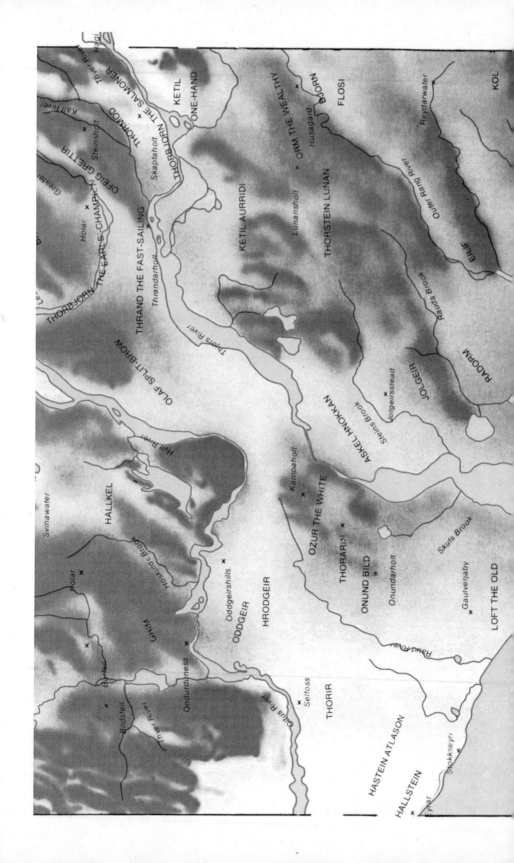

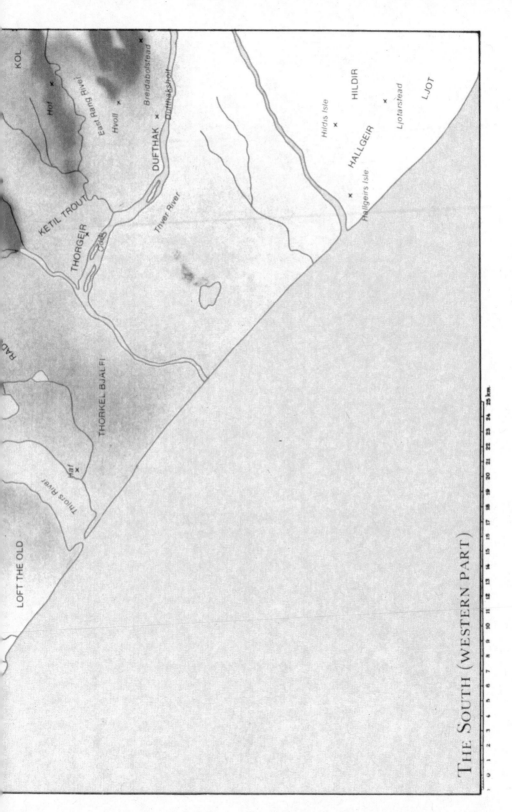

THE SOUTH (WESTERN PART)

KOL

Hof

East Rang River

Hvoll ×

Breidabolstead ×

Dufthaksholt

DUFTHAK

Tnver River

KETIL TROUT

THORGEIR

Gods

THORKEL BJALFI

Hof ×

Thiors River

RAD

LOFT THE OLD

Hildis Isle ×

HILDIR

HALLGEIR

Ljotarstead ×

LJOT

Hallgeirs Isle ×

0 1 2 3 4 5 6 7 8 9 10 11 12 13 14 15 16 17 18 19 20 21 22 23 24 25 km